The Light Switch

Plugging into your core power to transform how you lead

Heidi K. S. Frye

IMPETUS
PRESS

Grand Rapids, Michigan USA

Published by:
Impetus Press
4519 Cascade Road #4
Grand Rapids, Michigan 49546
info@impetuspress.com
616.464.4100

Cover Design: Madison E. Frye
Author Photo: Rachelle Rae Photography
Editing: Leya Booth
Interior and Ebook Formatting: Steven W. Booth, GeniusBookServices.com

ISBN: 979-8-9854905-2-7

211219

Acknowledgments

To Gretchen Devault, musician/music supervisor, entrepreneur, marketeer extraordinaire, coaching partner, and friend, without whom this book would not have been written. Thank you for the nudge, the push, the ear, the feedback and, most of all, the encouragement. I am forever grateful.

To the many wonderful clients who have trusted me with their core light. You've inspired me with your intention, hard work, courage to dive in, and forever friendship. Cheers to you… *with a mug of Yogi Tea in hand!*

To my kids, Madison E. Frye and Matthew P.S. Frye. The trajectory of this book shifted with your Christmas gift. I am forever grateful. It meant the world to know you supported me in this endeavor. Thank you for your constant belief and support. I love you lots (to infinity and beyond!) and am so proud of the people you've become. Thank you for sharing your spectacular light with me. An extra thank you to Madison for helping wrap up artistic and technology loose ends (the cover, diagrams, etc.).

To my amazing family. I can't imagine who I'd be without you. Thank you for always being there. I love all of you so much. *Mom, you are the best.* You instilled the belief in me that *I could do anything.* Thank you for your unwavering support. Linda & Lisa, the best sisters a girl could ask for. Brothers-in-law, sisters-in-law, cousins, nephews, you name it… I am blessed. *Dad, I miss you so much.* Thank you for the many life lessons, and for inspiring me throughout this writing. Happy Heavenly Birthday, Dad (and date-twin).

To Robert and the Johnston family. Robert, your subtle prodding had a huge impact… thank you. I so appreciate the continued connection with the family.

To Jonathan Harris & Christine Ware, mentors, development colleagues, dear friends, and owners of Change2 Limited, UK. I cannot imagine the last fifteen years without our special in-person visits, the boisterous and hearty Facetime/Zoom conversations and, of course, our deep friendship. *Thank you.* I'm so grateful for you, and that fateful workshop in Chicago!

To my many friends who supported me along the way in countless aspects. Your friendship is cherished and invaluable.

To Therese Marie Smith, a woman of many talents (from business to singing in a band!). Thank you for the many years of intertwining friendship, deep conversations, and the connections which make this book possible... Robert, Leya, M.Jay, and YOU, a fellow author.

To Shelly Winney and the team, thank you for the spark, the presence, and the grounding. Namaste!

To Leya & Steven Booth at Genius Book Services, thank you for taking such good care of me during the editing and book design process!

To Valerie Atkins, training guru, mentor, friend, and owner of Wells Street Marketing. Thank you for all the early training gigs, the many lessons, the inspiration, and *showing me how it is done.*

Thank you to the countless thought-leadership heroes in the world of leadership, development, self-help/improvement, and spirituality. Your insights, messages, and teachings conveyed through your books, interviews, and Master Classes have been invaluable and inspirational. Special thanks to Eckhart Tolle; Richard Rohr, O.F.M.; Daniel Goleman, Ph.D.; Brene' Brown, Ph.D., MSW; Esther Perel, M.A., MLFT; and Shefali Tsabary, Ph.D. In addition, special thanks to Oprah Winfrey, CEO of Harpo Studios, and Vishen Lakhiani, CEO of Mindvalley, for countless hours of some of my favorite interviews and content.

To my children, Madison E. Frye and Matthew P.S. Frye

Seeing your inner light shine is one of my greatest joys

Contents

The Light Switch

Section I:

Infinity Light of Leadership

The Inspiration

I excitedly opened the box, removed the top layer of packaging, and stared down at the light fixture I had just received. I hesitated. I had ordered an interesting asymmetrical light fixture, and here I was, staring down at something that at first glance felt uninspiring.

Feeling a bit deceived, I reviewed the online picture. Compared it to my delivery. Well, it was quite unique, regardless, so I determined I would need to hang it to see the full effect. My daughter was planning to stop by later, and I was sure I could cajole her into helping me.

Together we hung the fixture, she awkwardly contorting to carefully support the piece due to its fragility, while I connected and twisted wires as quickly as I could. When it was done, we stood back and admired our handiwork and the installation. It looked great! It did not inspire the same giddiness as when I first saw it online, but it was nevertheless intricate and interesting.

Days later, as I was sitting in the room where we had installed the light fixture, I looked up and studied it with interest. Something was different. Attached to the ceiling by various thin cables, the fixture had settled in. As a result, a new shape had emerged. I was delighted. It was magnificent again!

With inspired focus and curiosity, I reflected on the light. On one hand, looking from underneath, I saw three distinct symmetrical clusters. But observing it from the side, its three-dimensional asymmetrical flowing shape was beautiful, complicated, and unique, with no beginning and no ending. And then, with a flash of insight, I realized *the infinity light* perfectly captured my view of leadership. This was so exciting as I had been drawing models attempting the same. Woohoo!

Leadership Wholeness

Looking at my Infinity light fixture, I was overwhelmed by how beautifully it captured my perspective of Whole-Leadership. The totality of the design and how the individual aspects were each represented, uniquely separate yet one, fascinated me. Intrigued and consumed by the parallels to leadership, I couldn't wait to share my observation.

I reached out to my longtime UK-based colleagues to tell them of my discovery. Because of our shared passion for leadership and experiential learning, I knew they'd be interested in discussing the model. They did not disappoint. Our discussion led to in-depth conversations about leadership, whole-ness, and fluidity.

As leadership development program designers and facilitators, we settled on three main overarching themes: 1. Knowing and managing yourself, 2. Managing, executing, and working with teams, and 3. Visioning and strategic perspective, including additional miscellaneous topics that could not be isolated into one area. Basic core foundational themes like awareness, feedback, communication, and perspective, threaded through all three themes concurrently, created an extensive foundational network of interlocking parts and underlying complexities.

All said and done, despite our attempts to prioritize and edit the list, the foregone conclusion was simple: all components are necessary for great leadership. Missing any one component short-circuits flow. It was unanimous, *whole-ness* is essential in great leadership.

If you are curious and want to see this simplistically complex "infinity light fixture" leadership model inspiration, go to **www.UPwordsInc. com/infinity**.

WHOLE-NESS

When I was young, my parents bought an 80-acre farm which became our weekend getaway. As city farmers, we had very unique show-and-tell stories between raising animals (horses, cows, goats, cats, dogs, chickens, geese, pigs, rabbits, raccoons, and Angora goats), the biology of life, the rhythm of nature, and the antics of life on a farm.

Even through death, we learned about life. Although we took great care of our animals, treating them very humanely (and lovingly!), many of them did eventually end up on our dinner table. The chickens being the most relatable because we saw the process from beginning to end. My mother plucked the outside, and my aunt gutted the inside. Plucking was so boring, but I found the innards quite en-*gross*-ing. Fascinated, I decided to take the innards to my classroom show-and-tell. As my mother predicted, after a few days in containers, my precious possessions were super stinky, but I didn't care. I could not contain my excitement. Showing and telling the various organs and systems while conveying another amazing complexity of nature was a rush… all while they groaned, made faces, and pinched their noses shut.

Fast forward to college. My major was pre-med until I realized I didn't love the endless reading and memorizing. I changed my major to business, but never lost my love and appreciation for biology, health, and nutrition, and the awesome, complex, and amazing human body.

Why am I telling you this? I must confess something. I have an odd habit of seeing leadership metaphors everywhere in everyday life. I can't help myself. The human body is yet another excellent metaphor for leadership. Each system is a part of the whole, independent while dependent, complex and interrelated. When healthy and running smoothly, it is deceptively simple and easy to take for granted. I've been thinking, *where is the leader best represented in this whole-body metaphor?* The brain? The heart? The guts? Maybe the Whole-Leader is a combination of all three?!

While working with leaders, I take a mental inventory of the organization, the culture, and the players. And the leadership maladies. The common go-to quick fix for surface, behavioral ailments is the application of a *knowledge bandage*. The assumption being that once the bandage is applied, you "know" it won't happen again. Despite outside education, training, and workshops, without addressing internal core issues or providing the organization with ongoing attention, these are often only temporary solutions. At some point, the bandage falls off, and old behaviors resume, *unless a leader is treated whole-istically*, or develops from the inside out (working on the innards is always more interesting anyway). Whether working with corporations or nonprofits, teams or individuals, the overarching goal is fostering long-term healing.

LAYERS

Our amazing body systems are cellularly interrelated and inextricably linked. Without fully understanding the dependencies and intricacies, we know on a gut level (pun intended) systems, like the circulatory and lymphatic systems or the role of immune response and hormones in metabolism, must work well together to be healthy and whole. The same holds true for leadership.

The mind and body were once believed to be dualistic, separate entities. Research confirms our system is non-dualistically linked and wholly interdependent, hence the inherent need for a holistic, or whole-istic, view for complete health and wellness. Hippocrates added the third component to the mind-body concept, witnessing, acknowledging, and documenting the unexplainable healing power of the spirit, beliefs, and faith, as well as the detrimental, harmful, and toxic effects of the same. The power of the non-physical spirit connection and the will to live, for example, occurs when one spouse unexpectedly dies on the anniversary of the deceased spouse's passing.

Growing research acknowledges there is a seemingly non-physical consciousness operating on a physical, cellular level. There is no other explanation for what happened to my friend. Born with a life-threatening kidney disease, it was kept in check for years. Unexpectedly and suddenly, the disease became active, which forced her to shut down her business, have a kidney removed, and go on daily dialysis. Registered on the kidney transplant list, her very compassionate, loving, soulmate husband helped her in every way he could. He was tested as a potential donor, but he was not a match. He went on the KPD (Kidney Paired Donation) list to no avail. He took on full responsibility for the family while she focused on her healing. One day, in the midst of her health crisis, he experienced identical symptoms to hers. They hoped and half-expected them to be sympathy pains. As it turned out, to the shock of everyone, he had an identical tumor growing in an identical location on his kidney. The doctors were unable to explain this bizarre incident. They subsequently had to remove his kidney. When they tell the story, she quips, "He practically loved me to death."

Mindset is powerful. Research has proven this over and over again. Sales managers know for a fact that sales is a complicated *mind game*. Despite time and talent, sales success or failure is closely dependent on the rep's attitude and mindset.

Bottom line, the body is complex and interrelated. *We* are complex and interrelated. We are one whole being. The most efficient, effective, and healthy version of us is when our systems are strong, vigorous, and working together. Similarly, in leadership, when all of the (interrelated) business systems are strong and working together in unison, the organization thrives. Any one weak link or disconnected layer prevents the organization from reaching its fullest potential, which is why healthy leadership, healthy leaders, and healthy organizations are *whole* ones.

MOVING FORWARD

I hope you crave leadership whole-ness, and are ready for the hard work it entails. There are a number of experiential exercises throughout the book, including real life examples, stories, leadership models, and a variety of concepts. What is required from you is time, effort, and personal vulnerability. I highly recommend you begin this journey with a fresh new journal. A journal you love, with your favorite line size, color, cover material, and even binding. Although simplistic, this is a first step in figuring out who you are, what inspires you, and is itself a lesson in intentionality.

P.S. I used my original favorite journal for many important conversations with myself, and it was an integral part of many career strategy sessions, including creating UPwords Inc.

Exercise Caveat: Personally, I do not like stopping in the middle of my reading to do an exercise, which usually means *I don't do the exercises.* Which means I am at risk for losing the essence of the particular book. This is one such book. In addition to being listed at the end of each chapter, the exercises are also repeated toward the end of the book, in the Whole-Self Workout section.

If you are like me, keep reading, and complete the exercises at the end. Hopefully you will be pondering the exercise questions while reading, and able to complete the exercises quickly when you reach The Whole-ness Workout chapter.

For others, having aha moments along the way is the preference and the way to go. Many clients prefer this. If this is you, pause during your reading to complete the exercises. The approximated time to complete each exercise is noted. Jump back into the reading when you are finished.

Whole-You

Tuning into our biweekly virtual meeting, I detected intense sadness on my client's face, the same look as of a child finding out Santa Claus isn't real.

As a super smart, successful, business services professional who was challenged by the hamster wheel-ness and lack of respect within his firm, he had definitely shifted during our work together, but had not yet had what I refer to as *the big aha*. He was very good at doing what he was supposed to do, according to others. His natural driver personality resulted in a lifetime of high achievement accolades, and awards. All of this lifted his ego, but he was drained by the constant push. Having dutifully gotten married, and now gifted with three beautiful children, he was committed to his complicated life on the treadmill. Although our work together was business related and professional, he couldn't help but bring his *whole* life into the coaching conversation. His current state of mind reflected a bit of *is this all there is* crisis, especially when reflecting on his long work hours, business building efforts, ongoing people issues, and scarce family time. Ultimately and optimally, you operate at home, work, and play from your Whole-Self. It is very appropriate you bring your Whole-Self into the coaching conversation.

Initially we tackled surface-y, low-hanging-fruit type of work issues which provided immediate relief. Each time, however, underlying words like *alignment, honor, responsibility, supposed to, should, worthy,* and *authenticity* popped up. We were both amused by the frequency. He discovered that his life reflected his paradigm of what he *thought* his life should look like. In that respect, he was definitely on track. What was not on track was the *life* he *wanted*. On some level, he knew something was *off*, or *wrong*, or *missing*, hence the discontent. Although we did not immediately name the problem, I suspected the source of his issues would be revealed as we explored his foundational layer.

He was surprised how pervasive the *authenticity* subject was, and soon realized it to be at the core of everything, including how out of alignment he felt, which was overwhelming. During our time together, the blame and finger-pointing aimed at his partners shifted to self-ownership and self-realization, as well as the need for organizational culture work. His evolving awareness was that he was not living, working, family-ing, operating from, or *being* from his Authentic/CORE-Self.

Through focus and hard work, he went from drowning to head barely above water to treading water to swimming across the pool—his words, not mine. The no-longer-drowning analogy mimicked what was happening in his practice. With a revitalized sense-of-self, his confidence perked up as he accomplished more in a shorter amount of time, stabilized his team, and experienced client interactions as positive, energized, and productive. On the personal side, he also resolved his marital issues, committed to a better work-life balance, and renewed his relationship with his children. He was operating more authentically—feeling the impact at his core. Excited by the shift, he anticipated a similar positive domino effect on the operational and strategic parts of his business.

Back to our virtual meeting. The reason he had looked so dejected was because a very bright light had turned on. He had gained incredible insight, literally overnight, and in his words, "I can't un-know this." His ego had let go. He was breathing again. He had a newfound clarity about everything. Which was good. *Really good.* But then, why the long face? His sadness was due to his newfound clarity. With new insight, as if having X-ray vision, he saw others in a way he hadn't before. He saw their whole person. How their egos triggered bad behavior, their need for control, their harsh words… everything. He said it was like pulling back the curtain and finding out the Wizard of Oz was merely a man.

MORTALS

Between this "big aha" session and his next, he recalibrated. Accepting the newly realized mortal status of his workplace heroes, he entered the conversation with recharged energy. Suddenly, everything was on hyper-speed. With uncharacteristic action and sense of urgency, he introduced development work into the firm, knowing the culture would be positively impacted. Realizing it would be a tough sell, he was up for the challenge, hopeful and armed with research and data supporting the financial benefits of employee engagement, culture work, and leadership development. It is not uncommon for technically proficient, smart, successful leaders and professionals, who are quite comfortable with (and revered for) their achieved levels of expertise, to resist delving into the unknown. It is especially risky for the ego.

Our society, especially Western culture, is incredibly mind-oriented and accomplishment-oriented. Starting at a young age, parents encourage and celebrate child development, based on physical and intellectual achievements. It is quite normal to hear seemingly benign comments like "… she is speaking in full sentences," "… he knows his alphabet," "… he won the trivia contest," "… she has straight A's," and "… he got a trophy." Parents derive personal satisfaction in their young protégé's accomplishments, and the children themselves begin to understand what motivates and captures Mom and Dad's attention. Performance. *Doing.* "If I am the best at X, Mom and Dad will be very proud of me." And so the conditioning begins—the heavy dominance on mind-centered achievement and cerebral prowess, which is everything. *It sends a subtle message, doesn't it?*

As leaders, it is especially important to recognize the *whole person* in others and in ourselves. Human nature craves comfort, which is why it is incredibly normal to experience resistance when opening up, being vulnerable, exposing ourselves to the unknown, or *navel-gazing* as one client calls it. Let yourself off the hook for feeling those feelings. However, hold yourself accountable for stretching and getting out of your comfort zone. Be intentional in your development. How you lead is at stake—providing a well-rounded experience to those in your charge. Don't accept anything less than being the best version of you.

Finally, please understand, I'm not suggesting you become everything to everyone, and I'm certainly not suggesting you learn every aspect of every task, or have expertise in all areas. You do not need to be a superhero leader. Be patient with yourself as you explore this mindset. Just be the real you.

YOUR VERY IMPORTANT LAYERS

I've had hundreds of emotional affairs. Well... *kind of.* My client interactions are satisfyingly deep and rich, and when an engagement concludes, whether individual or team, I experience withdrawal. I'm so grateful to be doing this intensely personal and fulfilling work—caring for a client's well-being while championing their growth. Pushing boundaries, asking provocative questions, calling out behavior, reflecting the mirror, and sharing perspectives has been a career highlight.

Thank you to all of my clients. I am honored by your vulnerability, trust, and hard work. Because of the intensity and depth of our work together, we are forever bonded.

I will do almost anything to help my client have an aha moment. My job is to figure out how to get through to the client. In the egg-sperm analogy, I am the sperm, and the client the egg. Each client is unique and individual and, often, various methods and tools are necessary to get through to them. When one method fails, I try another, and then another, attempting to enter from new and various perspectives and vantage points. *Whatever it takes.* I've been labeled *unconventional.* Yes, with an expansive bag of tricks, I draw on numerous models, assessments, analogies, pictures, metaphors, stories, examples, observations, experiential and somatic exercises, as well as my own intuitive inner guidance.

Standing in the middle of the supermarket looking at a joke book, I had a flash of insight. At nine years of age, I knew my life's purpose was to make people smile. I didn't know the particulars at the time, but it stayed with me and has been an underlying driving force ever since. Now, given my line of work, I get it. Clients are happy and smile more as they work on themselves, step into their authentic power, and operate from their Whole-Selves. *Joyful alignment.*

THE WEDDING CAKE

The intangibility of development work—internalizing *experiential training* and *three-dimensional development*—is ᴠ grasp, which is why even family members ask, "What do you ..actly?" While facilitating a leadership retreat and responding to a spontaneous organic question regarding our time together, I created an on-the-spot 4-layered cake model to communicate the big picture. I finally had a quick way to describe my profession. A variation of this model is the best and simplest way to describe the need for, and process of, Whole-Self development.

The original 4-layered cake model:

While the intention has always been for clients to work on all 4 layers, over and over again, we consistently find that the top priority is to work on the bottom Self Layer. Higher-level leaders (mistakenly) feel this is entry-level work, and grow impatient working at the bottom. Quite the contrary. Working at this layer requires advanced openness. Letting go of and reformatting your concept of self to align with your core is a critical foundational layer.

Over time, my concept of the four layers merged into three, better representing the fluidity of leadership.

The Whole-Self Wedding Cake model:

Although work is focused on the three leadership systems separately, it often ends up being synchronous. I love a good analogy, so here is my perspective of what happens when leaders embark on self-development.

You are at a wedding. You head over to the sumptuous wedding cake to admire the edible art. Your focus and admiration is, of course, drawn to the top layer. The beautifully decorated top layer is adorned with eye-catching jewelry, and is the one most photographed, and most remembered. It is even saved for the first anniversary. You *oooh* and *ahhh*, praising its beauty. *Did you notice the bottom layer?* I bet not. The poor, often overlooked, forgettable bottom layer probably did not grab your attention. Because it was basic. It did its job. It was supportive and foundational. Period.

When well-executed, the bottom layer looks simple and easy—the effort in its creation, underestimated. If the wedding cake's bottom layer isn't large enough or well-made or fully baked, the foundation necessary to support the cake is compromised. The bottom layer is larger and stronger for a reason. Although not flashy, the strength of the bottom layer supports the weight of the top layers—the layers everyone sees and admires (wink wink). What is missed by the naked eye is the science, time, energy, knowledge, and process involved in baking the cake, as well as the focus and intention to get it right. The bottom layer has a heavy responsibility to make a great impression as the slices are shared with family and friends during the celebration.

I know this to be true because my father was an excellent baker/ entrepreneur. He owned and operated three bakeries in his baking career, creating numerous wedding cakes and delicious treats. I remember one particular wedding cake he made for the daughter of a respected and prominent member of his men's club. It was a twelve-layer cake with fountains and such. This was way before Cake Boss, and yes, in our eyes, he was the OG Cake Boss. He shared his vision for the final creation, practiced the setup, tested weight limits and support systems, produced mock components, planned the execution schedule, and even tweaked recipes a bit to get the best consistency and, thus, the best results. This was obviously not a *make it in one night* endeavor. Just like leadership. It took time to get it right. Vision. Execution. Process and practice.

Having grown up helping him in the business, I witnessed the time, energy, knowledge, and process necessary to get it right. *Just like leadership.* In my experience working with high-level leaders as well as high potentials, just as in the scenario above, the most intriguing layer is the top layer. Everyone wants to focus on their top layer. It is the one everyone sees, and is surrounded by hype and glamour. It's the layer vulnerable to critique and judgment. The top layer is the final presentation, the big payoff, the crowning jewel. It is not surprising that the leader's crowning jewel in the Whole-Self model, the Strategic Self, gets the attention. In my experience, the more senior the leader, whether in tenure or rank, the more likely he/ she wants to play at the seductive Strategic Self Layer and ignore the other stuff.

I hope you're not offended by what I'm about to say. With all due respect, if you have not done your work developing your bottom foundational layer, a.k.a. your core, true, Authentic Self Layer, only developing at the Strategic Self Layer is more about your ego. *It just is.* *(More on ego later.)*

Development at the underestimated and overlooked, woo-woo, touchy-feely, seemingly not cool, soft and intangible Authentic/CORE-Self Layer is, quite frankly, *where it's at*. This all-important layer is more than just a strong foundation. Consider this. During the creation and formation of this layer, each decision impacts *the whole* going forward. The recipe. The flavor. The aroma. The texture. The airiness. The taste. The essence of the cake, like the essence of your leadership, is influenced by your simple choices at this layer. You could surmise that the remaining higher up and more distinguished layers—operations and strategy—take their cue from this layer. It is as if the Authentic/CORE-Self Layer is transmitting its energy, its aroma, and its essence to the layers above—influencing the rest of the cake. I strongly urge you to consider your important bottom layer. Your leadership depends on it.

Today of all days, while working with an exceptional long-time CEO client, she mentioned how her best leadership emanates from within, and how it took years for her to figure this out. How getting in touch with herself at the core has allowed her to be the best version of herself, and as a result, the best leader she can be—authentically, operationally, and strategically. She is excited to now truly be above the trees (more about this in the Forest chapter). Without realizing it, it had been an underlying goal for her. Without realizing it or naming it, her growth, intention, and focus has always been on her Authentic/CORE-Self Layer.

If Whole-Self Leadership is your goal, begin your development at the Authentic/CORE-Self Layer. Dollar for dollar, this is the smartest investment you'll ever make, and where you'll find the highest ROI. Investing time, energy, emotional, and financial resources on the Authentic/CORE-Self Layer has the same impact as investing in the stock market as a 25 year old vs. a 50 year old, paying itself forward exponentially in a way you could never have anticipated.

Personally, I find *organizational misalignment* incredibly discouraging. Hopeful and optimistic the organization is healthy and able to pull off its lofty strategic goals, I often begin with one-on-one discovery interviews, hoping the leaders invested in themselves at 25 versus 50. While excited about the leadership vision, I nearly always soon realize the organizational infrastructure does not fully support its execution. Despite great strategic plans, initiatives often fail because of the lack of *follow-ship*. Or the team commitment was misread. Or the strategy does not benefit the entire organization, resulting in dissension. Or influencers stay silent for fear of the repercussions of true and open dialogue. Or, a very common occurrence, employees drag their feet, waiting for the leader to lose interest in the *flavor of the week*. All of these missteps appear at the operational and strategic levels because the authenticity-related root causes have not been addressed.

Sometimes it is a basic *trust issue*. Sometimes it is a personality trait that loses followers. Sometimes it is due to communication issues. Sometimes it comes from lack of personal integrity. And sometimes it is the level of commitment (underlying issues of not feeling appreciated, fairly paid, or heard, for example). I'm often privy to a spectacular view of an organization's people. *I wish you could see what I see.* If you did, you would work on, and support, the development of the Authentic/CORE-Self Layer, in yourself and in others.

Literally and metaphorically, without a strong, foundational Authentic/CORE-Self Layer, the rest of the cake is unstable. Many high-level leaders have the intention of authenticity, healthy communication, and whatever else it takes to run a healthy organization. However, intention isn't enough. *People problems* will be your signal that there are underlying areas you could strengthen through foundational soft skills like awareness, clarity, depth, and capability.

If you are like most leaders, you will experience much resistance working on this layer in lieu of the more exciting top layers. That is fine. If you are truly locked into working on your top strategic layer right away, do it in conjunction with the other layers. Not *instead of*, but in addition to. At some point, you'll realize the top two layers take their cue from the Authentic/CORE-Self, and fine tuning this layer allows you to successfully and more easily flow into the others. I urge you to hang in there. At some point, you'll feel a shift, one, thankfully, you cannot unlearn. This is deep work which will be with you always.

As my client beautifully articulated, "Just work on yourself, and the rest will take care of itself."

THE ORGANIZATION AS A WHOLE

The mind-body-spirit analogy is incredibly intriguing as it relates to wholeness at the organizational level beginning with contributing *individual-self leader wholeness*. A mind-body-spirit overview provides a framework for long-term organizational focus and healthiness.

1. The *Mind* is the ruling head within the organization, governing the strategic mindset, setting standards and expectations for how the body (of the organization) will function—like an electrical circuit. Business planning, visioning, seeing the whole. Mapping out the identity. Responsibility for overarching messaging and tough decisions in the whole's best interest—setting the tone. Developing execution plans, communication standards, and goal setting. Overall direction, transparency, and culture is powered by the *Mind* system.

2. The *Body* represents the inner workings of the organization—its physicality. The inner workings includes tactics, systems, networks, and relationships. The people. The doing parts. Management, motivation, performance, and feedback. Emotional Intelligence. How we treat people—how we treat our organizational bodies. Communication. Accountability. Perspective. Healthy interactions. Efficiency, execution, performance, communication, and accountability are all powered by the *Body* system.

3. The essence of the organization, *the pulse*, is symbolized by the *Spirit*, also known as Ethos, the lifeblood, heartbeat, soul, and culture. This system contains and describes the indescribable, that for which the organization stands—*its spirit*. This is where we discover our individual selves within the whole. How we operate. Our personality, the motivations, and the drive. Assessments, blind spots, Core Self. Belief systems. Paradigms and other barriers to being our best selves. Collectively and individually. Confidence, communication (again), openness, vulnerability, courage, and more (self) accountability. Individual excellence is powered by the *Spirit* system.

Ideally, these systems should/would be represented in leadership concurrently. It is impossible for these structures to be distinctly separate, operating in a vacuum. Healthy whole organizations operate from these three perspectives in unison—each department, each microsystem, each individual—simplistic in theory yet complex in execution. For the purposes of this discussion they will be addressed separately.

THE WHY

If you need motivation, here is a glimpse into the future… imagine a world with healthy-at-the-core individuals.

People have broadened perspectives. They consider others while taking care of, and thinking about, themselves. There is balance. Rather than unstated competitiveness and a *they are out to get me* mentality, people desire that everyone thrives. In this state of caring for the whole, individual talents and accomplishments blossom, and are recognized and celebrated by all.

Because people are healthy at their core, their old beliefs—the ones keeping them stuck—are eliminated or minimal. People flourish. Gone are the survival instincts of stepping on one another. They have become evolved.

Not threatened by others who are not like us, we bask in our own individuality. We understand, accept, and celebrate the uniqueness of others. We no longer see the special talents of others as threatening. We are tolerant and applaud the contributions of every person. Unique personalities, cultures, and gender make no difference. Even the most unmotivated become motivated. All contribute. There are those who think differently, who offer new perspectives, and those with special gifts and talents who contribute in ways we cannot. Collectively we are better. But this can only be realized and appreciated if we are whole.

Whole people are happy. Excited to be alive and personally fulfilled, their theme is "thriving" (vs. surviving). Since they have such a strong sense-of-self and personal foundation, confidence exudes. This spills over into kindness and graciousness toward others—more trusting, accepting, and connecting than ever. Interactions are fun. Our impact is multiplied when working together. As a society, we become unstoppable. Everything feels fresh, and the world shines anew.

This feels a bit "rainbows and unicorns" on such a grand scale, so let's break it down and consider this ambitious scenario on a smaller scale. Maybe within an organization. Your organization. Let's take it down further to a common denominator and start with your team. Let's say *you*, a healthy-at-your-core leader who has a strong foundation and sense-of-self applies these principles to those who report to you. What would that look like?

Qualifier: You are probably already a kick-ass leader with mad skills in one area or another. I'm not taking anything away from you or making any assumptions. I'm just saying it is likely, and you already know this, that there is an area in which you could improve. This particular "opportunity for growth" might even get in your way sometimes. It could be the reason you are reading this book, *correct*? To take yourself to this next level, picture this hypothetical *you* interacting with your team.

- Team meetings go from dead air, posturing, and side glances to engaging, dynamic, real interactions.

- Conflicts, for the most part, are a thing of the past. Individuals understand and appreciate, and dare I say, *celebrate*, their varied perspectives. There is a sense of camaraderie and win-win.

- Those leaders weighed down by problem-oriented direct reports experience a shift. As team members grow in confidence and empowerment, they exercise solution-oriented thinking. As a direct outcome of Whole-Leadership, the endless list of problems reduces to a focused and collaborative problem-solving initiative.

- There is an uptick in the happy-factor due to transformed management/leadership practices. All organizations benefit from "top talent," and with recharged authenticity, self-awareness, and self-management. Yours is no different, thriving financially and operationally.

- Whole-Self Leadership Equation: Dynamic Interactions + New Perspectives + Solution-Oriented Thinking + Top Talent = Best Place to Work! (Impacting health and wellness, as well as the bottom line.)

Wholeness is work. However, the potential rewards are well worth it. Aren't you tired and exhausted from the repercussions of non-wholeness? Would the people you lead benefit from your Whole-Leadership—expanding and cascading out to the entire organization? Is there a possibility you might feel a bit more energized, engaged, and happy if you did the work and experienced the benefits of your true and Whole-Self as a Whole-Leader?

THE INFINITE LEADERSHIP SUPER MODEL

While the Whole-Self wedding cake model served a purpose, I needed a better explanation/model to organize the complexities of leadership. In my perfect world, merging my various multi-layered and complex models into one, easy-to-understand super model was the ideal. Despite numerous failed attempts to visually capture my thoughts, many old drawings and discarded scraps of paper proved how complex this leadership model is. Convoluted yet simplistic. And then, literally, the light turned on—my hanging infinity light fixture perfectly captured my vision of the ultimate leadership model. And the *Infinite Leadership Super Model* was born.

As far as infinity lights go, mine is fittingly simplistic. Viewed from below, the three symmetrical components are easily and immediately identifiable, representing the three layered wedding cake model. Upon closer inspection, however, the more intricate view is revealed—the optical illusion of infinity created by one never-ending core light tube, winding and twisting, creating a unique 3D shape. The fixture is so complex in its simplicity. I love symbolism and hidden meaning. As an added bonus, I was thrilled to learn this particular shape symbolizes eternity, empowerment, and everlasting positivity.

THE ILLUSION

Merging these two views: the *simple*, easy to see, three-sectioned, symmetrical piece with the *complex*, connected, infinitely flowing, unending art piece was a 3D model representing my view of leadership, and it was exhilarating.

Operationalizing the Infinity Model will profoundly affect you and your organization. Imagine a culture where people are excited and engaged. The energy is palpable. People are fulfilled, relationships are meaningful, and the work is rewarding; purpose, accomplishment, and momentum being the key descriptors.

If truly creating a healthy-at-the-core organization and transforming leaders is your goal, intentionally developing the three systems simultaneously is a must. *Remember, the three systems as separate entities is an illusion, created by one core light changing shape and twisting throughout.* Just as this fixture lights up the room, flowing wholeness leadership lights up and energizes the organization.

NUANCED YOU

I am not suggesting you become a super-leader who is perfect and unfailing. This leader does not exist. I *am* suggesting you further develop and focus on wholeness, which means working on the subtleties of your ever-evolving leadership skills.

I know you're already a strong and capable leader. *How else could you lead as effectively as you do?* I am merely suggesting you nuance your leadership skills. It is the same approach I take with new clients—I expect and look for: 1. Connection, 2. Commitment (to doing the work), 3. Time Capacity (to do the work), and 4. Capability (to have the aha moments while doing the work). Capability is the most difficult to manufacture. Merely based on the fact that you are reading this book and some inductive reasoning, I know you are a talented leader and, hopefully, *ready to nuance YOU.*

Development is a journey, not a destination, and to some extent, a re-discovery (I'll explain more about this in a later chapter). I dare you, challenge you, and implore you to continue your leadership development with the Whole-Self Workout—strengthening your core and becoming the Whole-Leader I know you to be.

EXERCISE: LEADERSHIP SUPER MODEL—
Total Time: 5 minutes

Rank the three leadership systems (authentic, operational, strategic) in order of your capability. What is at the bottom? Note this in your Leadership Journal to reference it later.

The Authentic/Core-Self

"We don't see things as they are, we see them as we are."
—Anais Nin

Who we perceive ourselves to be colors our view. What we take in about who we are—our perceptions, bias, and filters, in addition to the attitude and judgment of others—alters our sense-of-self. This distorted picture, this False Self, conceals our True Self and is the new lens through which we see the world, and ourselves. This distorted picture becomes a protective shell, supplying us with an identity, creating our self-structure. Our ever-growing reliance on this outer covering creates distance from our core and our true nature, and a disconnection from our Authentic and True Self. This is the proliferation of the False Self.

The False Self has many opportunities to grow in our modern day world. As we take in and accept a variety of input (as well as others' well-meaning opinions and judgment of that input), we replace whole-some core values with incomplete external standards, such as accomplishment, money, and beauty. We give these external standards power, and thus, learn to measure ourselves falsely, forgetting our inner core goodness. We accept ourselves as less than. Not enough. As a result, *our wholeness and sense of being is replaced with a need to do more, in an effort to be more.* And so it begins—the weakening of the True and Authentic sense-of-self.

EXERCISE: THE AUTHENTIC/CORE-SELF—
Total Time: 30 minutes

What are the characteristics of your Core Self?
What are the characteristics of your False Self?

The Operational Self

Of the three leadership layers outlined in the Whole-Leader model, the Operational Self Layer is probably the most familiar. It is where you spend most of your time and energy. Focusing on this layer is second nature and your comfort zone. Examining this layer developmentally, the dominant operational topics include:

Trust
Feedback
Teamwork
Engagement
Management
Accountability
Team Dynamics
Communication
Conflict Resolution
Performance
Mentoring
Systems
Goals

For perspective, I ask that you review this short list twice. The first time, approach it through the lens of *healthy* leaders (those who report to you and those to whom you report). The second time, review the list through the lens of *unhealthy* leaders.

I trust you instinctively know that each of these operational efforts, without great detail or explanation, is easier when leaders are healthy vs. unhealthy. A strong Authentic/CORE-Self Layer provides a healthy foundation, which merges and flows into healthiness at the operational layer.

OPERATIONAL SYNERGY

The collective energy of the many people who spend their days (lives) working together, synergistically, toward common goals is the heartbeat of the organization. Strong teams are built by healthy leaders who honor team members—celebrating contributions and accomplishments, providing real feedback, and instinctively leveraging Whole-Leadership.

Trust is a key component in operational synergy. Teams learn to trust each other, their leader(s), and themselves by investing in robust interactions, perspectives, and communications. Awareness of, and openness to, ego, bias, and filters is a crucial entry point for healthy management, leadership, and team development.

Synthesizing the healthy and developed Authentic/CORE-Self and Operational Self Layers creates a natural (positive) impact on the organizational culture, paving a way toward wholeness, and the ultimate *personal power transformation*.

THE ENTRY POINT

One client was particularly frustrated at the Authentic/CORE-Self Layer. No matter the questions I posed or the self-reflection exercises he completed, he wasn't much further along in his self-discovery journey as when he started. It seemed futile. "Doing his work" (working on himself) was the last thing this business owner wanted to do, but it was forced upon him as a last resort as he was experiencing ongoing low morale and huge turnover issues in his business. As he put it, "I'm obviously the common denominator." Despite his desire for a quick fix, his vague responses, resistance to diving in, and lack of vulnerability, all delayed his progress. He definitely (obviously) needed to work on this bottom layer to unlock the source of his issues, but he was stuck and frustrated.

As an alternate strategy, I changed my approach. I shifted my focus to the team, while he hung out in the background, observing and absorbing. Immediately apparent, his players did not match his high standards. As a result, I believed this mismatch was in part responsible for his unmet expectations. I evaluated the team using a battery of assessments, translating my observations into data, which he loved. As an incredibly visual leader who wanted concise output, he needed what I have since marketed as *The Dossier*™, a one page per player visual reference guide highlighting their assessment results. This team consistently uses this piece during team meetings, retreats, and account management conversations to advance their goals and their development efforts, helping them have candid conversations.

Once he saw the data and heard the explanation behind it, he quickly corrected the misalignment. Grateful for the relief, thinking he was all good, he took his foot off of his own development journey as we trained the team based on the various assessments they had taken. I am a big believer in training capability in conjunction with individual and team assessments—*learning who you are is only one piece of the puzzle*. It's almost more important that you know *how* who you are impacts others—how you communicate, how you are perceived, your motivation, understanding others' styles, and the misunderstandings that naturally arise when interacting with different people. What happened without him noticing, since he too had taken the assessments and was in the room during the workshops, was that while learning about the others, he accidentally learned about himself.

As a side note, he and I have become very close friends over the years. During a recent get together, he referenced the work we did. "I couldn't have figured out who I was without the assessments. Operationalizing that part of the process opened the door to my self-discovery." He referred to The Dossier™ as a "constellation of assessments," because it did illuminate his metaphorical sky. And yes, viewing the assessments as a constellation revealed each individual's unique shape, including his own.

The assessments were an entry point into his Authentic/CORE-Self. The tangibility of the assessments revealed his form. Through the lens of the assessments, he saw himself in relationship with others. Then, and only then, did he begin to understand authenticity was not about lying or deceiving, it was about being, showing, and honoring SELF—the True and Authentic Self. This was when his resistance began to melt away.

During this process, he learned (and confirmed) he was part of the problem. In an effort to keep people happy while trying to get his point across, and kind of, *sort of* hold them accountable, he did backflips.

While walking on eggshells. His resulting inauthenticity—not honoring himself—created distance. And mistrust. The eroding trust caused people to *not* feel connected or safe, and as a result, they left the organization. His intention, albeit noble, was misguided. He was trying to keep people happy, but his impact was distrust and disconnection.

Figuring himself out using the assessments prompted him to develop insight at his Authentic/CORE-Self Layer. As a result he became more vulnerable and open and, consequently, unstuck. He took his team and his business to new heights. It turns out that the success of his team and his business was directly tied to the healthiness of his Authentic/CORE-Self. All of his knowledge, his learned management prowess, the infrastructure, and the operational plan had been useless without developing this strong foundation. With this huge awareness, he worked on both the Authentic and Operational Layers simultaneously, leveraging the operational situations as experiential learning moments.

He now approaches others based on their own individual style—knowing their language, triggers, and perspective—versus using his own as the default. He delivers real, authentic feedback courageously, without negative consequences. He has learned to be kind vs. nice (more on this later). He understands the nature of their problem behaviors and discusses them proactively, nipping them in the bud. I think his favorite win is sharing *the plan*. Previously met with confusion and resistance, he now delivers the plan in a way that they get it, and enjoys watching it shift their energy. His hard work has paid off. The organization recently celebrated a record year, with employee turnover at an all-time low.

Over time he operationalized The Dossier™ and integrated self-awareness into the business—genius! He and the team grew so strong in their knowledge and use of the assessments, I worked myself out of a job, which was always the goal.

As is the case in real-life leadership, all of the layers interact simultaneously, benefitting the whole. They cannot truly be separated. They are one. The stronger the Authentic Layer, the better the operational and strategic integration, and vice versa. Whatever the starting point, merging these layers is the path to wholeness. In wholeness, my client expanded and leveraged awareness and healthiness, which widened his peripheral view, which allowed him to see the organization in a new way. He shifted from reactive to proactive. When the team stabilized operationally, he set his sights on the next layer. His Strategic Self had always been his strongest and most dominant layer, and for the first time while working with a team, his lofty strategic goals materialized effortlessly.

The Strategic Self

I am honored to have worked with a particular favorite client for a decade now, as a partner in her leadership transformation. In the early days, thinking she had successfully tackled and completed her heavy-duty problems (her stated reason for engaging with an executive coach), I let her know she had graduated. I thought she'd be thrilled by the news, but instead, as she became very present and silenced her ego, she stared at me blankly and blurted out, "I'm not done. I want to continue to grow. Let's create a maintenance plan. I want to be intentional about keeping the important topic of leadership at the forefront of my mind." She knew instinctively she had more work to do. In retrospect, I now see her pushback was in fact indicative of her growth. She was ready to advance beyond her Authentic/CORE-Self.

Well, her instincts paid off. Since that time, not only has she grown, her view over the forest (a metaphor explained at the end of this section) is remarkable. She has transformed into a Whole-Leader, and I'm thrilled to have witnessed each new awareness, shift, and milestone. During her former frantic juggling act, she held her breath, hoping to keep the balls from dropping. Since that time, her juggling act has transformed into an easy game of catch, resulting from her strategic initiatives, re-orgs, talent structuring, succession planning, and artful delegation. Again, none of this would have, could have happened without her growth and newly expanded view of leadership.

Speaking of leadership, what percentage of time do you spend on leadership vs. management? Be thoughtful to arrive at an accurate percentage. Where did you land? 50%:50%? 80%:20%? 25%:75%? Whatever your final leadership percentage, take that number and multiply it by 40 hours. This number represents the number of hours you believe you are focused on leadership weekly. Are you surprised? This number is high, isn't it? I am betting you do not actually spend this amount of time actually *engaged strategically*. Rarely, if ever, is this number achieved. The many responses for what gets in the way range from "I feel guilty if I'm not working at my desk" to "I don't have the time" to "I know it is important, but other things take priority." P.S. *Thinking strategically* is still "work."

The client mentioned above is now at a point in her career and in her Whole-Leader development that her authenticity is on autopilot. Initially, struggling to assign one or two hours a week for this luxury, she allowed other commitments to swallow up the time. Back then, she literally said, "Spending time *thinking* feels very decadent, like eating bonbons." Once she shifted, her priorities changed. What had once been a decadent treat is now a fundamental part of her day. While easily carving out time for strategic endeavors, namely thinking, creativity, and idea generation, she leans in. As a result, her scheduled, proactive, strategic thinking time, providing important space and energy for creativity, is now fiercely protected. Referencing those she leads, "They spend a lot of time in the weeds. They miss solutions and the perspective I have because I make space to see it." Her early game of checkers has become a strategic game of chess, proactively seeing the moves, opportunities, gaps, and leverage points that others do not.

By working on her important foundational Authentic/CORE-Self *bottom layer* as a starting point, she strengthened, grew, and merged in her Operational and Strategic Self Layers. Knowing herself at the core helped her get out of her own way. She wiped away outdated beliefs, limitations, and paradigms. She opened up, *and dared*, to be her True Self, growing in aptitude and connection.

She has changed her tune. Indulgence is now a necessity. To be the best leader she could be, a proactive backpack clean out was necessary (a topic we'll discuss more later), after which, she cleaned up her Operational Layers. She masterfully and proactively analyzed, anticipated, and aligned the organizational positions, her relationships, and the critical players. The luxurious strategic space she now enjoys and leverages is the result of dedicated hard work on herself and her team. By developing proactively, understanding the soft dynamics at play, and how to skillfully handle situations, the big issues fell away. By preventing most crises from materializing, she had time and space for the strategic, fun stuff.

A common client reaction to our working on mitigating strategies for potential situations is, "You know, we spent all that time for nothing. It was a non-issue. He/she took it in stride." Let me tell you something. It was not for nothing. This is not a coincidence. You did this. Your work as a Whole-Leader pays itself forward tenfold.

Inflow

There is a staggering amount of information flowing through us on a daily basis. Based on 2018 estimates, every human is exposed to a whopping 34 gigabytes of information daily. *Daily!* Similarly, it is estimated we are exposed to 40,000-100,000 ads daily, which research shows is conservative. All that to say, we are bombarded by, and take in, an incredible amount of information.

An addition to outside information, we are also inundated by inside information. Namely, LIFE. Our responsibilities as leaders, achieving our KPIs (Key Performance Indicators), taking care of our teams, strategic thinking, goal performance, self-development, etc., is only the beginning. Keeping track of lists and to-do's, juggling multiple conversations while tending to family obligations, hours of multitasking, and an endless stream of emotions—worry, doubt, fear, anger to name a few—demonstrates our capacity for intake is incredible.

The big question is, "Based on these staggering intake numbers, how much flows through us, and how much is retained?" Our brains are sent approximately 11 million bits of information per second for processing, and yet we only process .0005% of that information. Given the sheer intake and our limited capacity, it is a wonder we have not lost our minds.

You do not consciously comprehend the majority of the information flowing through you. It requires focus. Even now, while reading this page, information is flowing through you—you are not hanging onto it. It's kind of like learning a person's name at a party. Unless you consciously retain it, it flows right through you. Personally, I am working outside on my computer. It is a beautiful sunny day and I am focused. However, if I shift the direction of my focus, I now notice life that was not in my awareness a moment ago, flowing *through me*. I tune in, my senses are suddenly alive. I hear the melodic chirpings of the insects making their presence known. I smell newly cut grass. I see leaves falling from the tree. I notice the whimsical nature of the coneflowers. I feel the soft breeze, gently flipping the pages of my book. I absorb the sunshine on my face. I sense the fresh crisp air.

As you go through life and take in information, it is important you are intentional about the flow and its direction, not complicating matters with hyper-focus, interruption, or suspension. Your thought selection, or *thought path*, has powerful ramifications.

The trick to sanity and well-being is being in the moment (present) vs. judging and narrating the moment (not present). "The insects are making their sounds—how do they do that? Oh geez, I can smell the neighbors newly cut grass... mine really needs to be cut soon—maybe later today if I can find the energy. Those leaves are so brilliant and colorful, and they'll need to be raked soon. There is so much to do. I love those flowers. The breeze feels nice but it's probably going to cause my stack of papers to fly away. Hmmm... the warm sun reminds me... did I use sunscreen this morning?"

The incessant narration and analysis is an indication you've taken a wrong turn on your thought path. With this awareness, stop processing if you are able, and instead let it flow. *This is presence.* The trendy version of presence is termed mindfulness, but for the sake of our conversation, I would rather you stay in the groove of "presence" and whatever meaning that holds for you. Developing a presence muscle will benefit you more than relying on a full mind.

STUCK

When present, our intake flows through us and around us. There is no active processing. No judgment. No absorption or action. Just clean and fresh flowing throughput.

Deep down, we know we are rarely present. What we might not know is our lack of presence limits flow. When flow is blocked, we get stuck. A visual of this occurrence, which works well for my clients, is imagining the body as an empty mesh form, made out of the material used for window screens. Life easily flows through and around this *mesh body form* when truly present.

Now imagine breezing through your day, clean and fresh, with life flowing through your mesh body. Suddenly, something specific catches your attention and for a few suspended seconds you hyper-focus, maybe arousing a particular emotion. Seemingly minor, flowing ceases. Imagine, at that moment, a leaf, caught and stuck on your mesh, causes a blockage and prevents flow in that particular area. Over time, more leaves pile up in the blocked area, creating a barrier. This seemingly minor pile up creates resistance, in addition to a few unwanted occurrences. 1. you are no longer present, 2. unless you are intentional about processing it and letting it go, the leaf will prevent future items from flowing, and 3. this particular leaf/ subject matter, if left unattended, will change who you are at your core.

Clients are initially hesitant about this metaphor, not fully understanding what potentially causes them to be stuck and out of balance. Perhaps an out of alignment observation—a perception that felt off: an overheard conversation, a triggered emotion, resistance, pain, not saying what you wanted to say, staying silent when you wanted to make an important contribution to the conversation—any ego-induced interaction qualifies.

Any *greater than* or *less than* perspective can cause a stuck moment.

Do you recall the childhood rhyme "sticks and stones may break my bones, but names will never hurt me"? Turns out, names can and do hurt. The examples described above are out-of-alignment hurts, pains, judgments, perceptions, and wounds, which are metaphorical sticks and stones, and leaves on your mesh body form—preventing life to flow through you.

A real life example. Let's say you are having a great day at the office, getting a lot accomplished and truly in flow. As you head toward the restroom, you overhear whispering. It catches your attention. Your senses are completely engaged, and you've determined the voices are coming from the water cooler. You hear a comment about your project, "That project is doomed to fail." You seize up. With a pit in your stomach and a sharp intake of breath, you know there is a new leaf stuck on your mesh form.

Now you have a choice, and your decision determines how long that leaf stays stuck. The longer you wait, the more it becomes a part of you, altering your essence. A few available options are that you can let it go, deal with it, or reframe it.

1. *Letting it go* allows life to continue flowing right through you. You process this immediately as something that does not matter. "They don't know what they are talking about... oh well."
2. *Dealing with it* might mean joining the conversation to provide additional info, removing the impediment. "Haha, you have no idea how far along we are... that's okay, our group can't wait to see you at the finish line!"
3. *Reframing it* dissolves it by shifting the focus of the outcome: "I know we are on track to deliver this, and it will be fun to see their surprise when we finish."

THE EGO'S PERSPECTIVE

The ego loves hanging onto debris. It will direct you, "Do not let go of this. Keep it as a souvenir of how you've been wronged. You should be mad." This is how it starts. First one leaf, then another, a stick, and then a couple more leaves. All of this blockage over what you overheard. What if you hadn't heard it? You would be ignorant to their comments, and you wouldn't have any blockage. These sorts of situations are triggers, and steal your attention. Without intention or awareness, you might have feelings of self-doubt, lack-of-support, feeling misunderstood, and/or not being heard. It might also create sub-level unhealthy self-talk, creating doubt about your own value. The more stuck "leaves" you choose to hang onto (and to some degree, yes, it is a choice), the more you lose flow, disconnect from your True Self, and "not present" you are.

Hopefully by now you understand how costly it is to be "covered in leaves." Those out of alignment moments have disallowed flow, and your mental and emotional leaves cover you up, hiding your essence. Your core, true essence is unable to shine through. This is the *great cover up*—hiding the real, true, authentic you.

When the issue is fresh, it is much easier to go against your ego. Get present, with awareness, clear off your leaves, and get back in touch with

YOU. Kids do it all the time. When my children were very young, I marveled at how easily they bounced back from hurts and pains, physically and emotionally. They would carry on as if nothing had happened. No life-altering wounds, no retreat into our shells hurt, no lashing out hurtfulness, no long term baggage.

Children are cleaner, more spirited, and pure, keeping their whole sense of worthiness intact. We would benefit from accessing our childlike innocence again. This beautiful wholesomeness erodes as children grow up and the ego forms. They learn to listen to their judgmental self-talk. They learn to accept comparisons and critiques. As they mature, they too learn to collect leaves.

Self-Worth

I had a *stop dead in my tracks* career moment. I was working 60-80 hours a week in a newish, very demanding, corporate enterprise sales job. With two children under five, I was running myself ragged, performing cartwheels and backflips hoping to make everyone happy, at home and at work. I was a *make it happen* goal-oriented person who put myself on hold in the process. Walking to my desk—I remember it like it was yesterday—I had a very clear flash of insight. I was exhausted proving myself. *Why in the world am I running around like a crazy person so they can determine if I am good or not? Again?*

Allowing others to determine my value and worthiness, based on my successful performance of arbitrary goals and targets, assigned to me by them, was suddenly crazy and unacceptable. The goals weren't crazy or unacceptable, per se. The expectation to successfully meet these goals and targets wasn't crazy or unacceptable either. ME, basing my self-worth, value, and sense-of-self on their assigned goals and targets? Now that was crazy and unacceptable.

LESSONS IN THE NEIGHBORHOOD

Speaking in generalities, valuing who we are intrinsically, at our Core Self level, is not taught in Western cultures. We do not learn to value our inner selves, or that our mere existence is enough. Societally, we actually learn to tie our self-worth to outside messages—top layer values, like performance, looks, and the opinions of others.

During his famous TV series, *Mister Rogers' Neighborhood*, the iconic Mr. Rogers taught children the most important lesson they would ever learn: to value themselves for their mere existence. And with that lesson of self-love, they were able to love others. His teachings were simple and sweet. He taught them to cherish their uniqueness. He taught them they were special—inside. No outside performance necessary. Grounded and authentic, Mr. Rogers provided a great service to children's souls… if only they would remember these lessons of self-worth as adults.

HANDING OVER OUR POWER

When we forget our intrinsic self-worth, we look for meaning and validation elsewhere. Often allowing another person's opinion of what's important to shape our self-beliefs and sense of worthiness. All of our insecurities, self-doubts, and hesitancies are based on another's judgment of us. How have the beliefs of others shaped you? What arbitrary, innocently intended comments contributed to your sense-of-self? Was it your parents' belief of "when you're finished with your work, then and only then, are you allowed to play" that caused work/life imbalance or lack of joy? Or maybe your favorite teacher who demonstrated significant attention or pride when you achieved an "A," letting you know straight A's, a.k.a. performance, was the ticket to praise and admiration? Did playground bullying send the message you were not cool because you were too smart? How about basing your appreciation of your looks and attractiveness on a girlfriend or boyfriend's interest, or lack thereof? Maybe it was where you stack-ranked on the Hall of Fame? Or watching where others stack-ranked on the Hall of Shame, creating fear about future performance? Did comments about what was normal stir up feelings of not fitting in? Did a peer's conflict orientation, personality traits, or unhealthiness cause you to feel like you were less than? How about a neighbor's raised eyebrow or scornful view?

I'm guessing the list above triggered a memory. Perhaps you remember the origination of a particular stuck leaf. Did it stir up some righteous indignation or wanting to blame others? Whatever just popped up for you, despite your desire to blame the perpetrator, please know it will do you no good. Blaming them will not help you in the end. And it is certainly not the answer to clearing yourself. Beliefs or comments directed at you did not shape you on their own. I'm sorry to tell you this, but only *you* have the power to give them power over you. While it's easier to assign lifelong blame to someone who might have hurt, judged, or shaped you, *you* took it in and allowed those comments/leaves to influence you. YOU, not them. I'm not suggesting the other person is off the hook for poor behavior. I am not suggesting you blame yourself either. I'm merely suggesting self-ownership. *You have a choice.* You are in control.

Whatever decisions you make about what you take in, know this. Judgment and the opinions of others can only impact you if your own sense of worthiness is under-developed. Nobody has the power to alter your sense of worthiness without your consent. Your true inner core sense of worthiness is grounded and knowing. The quality of the connection to your inner self acts as an indicator of your sense of worthiness. I know, without a doubt, that at your core you are *pure goodness.*

EXERCISE: SELF-WORTH—
Total Time: 10 minutes

Quickly jot down what came up for you while reading the "handing over your power" questions. (*How have the beliefs of others shaped you? What arbitrary, innocently intended comments contributed to your sense-of-self? Was it your parents' belief of "when you're finished with your work, then and only then, are you allowed to play" that caused work/life imbalance or lack of joy? Or maybe when your favorite teacher demonstrated significant attention or pride when you achieved an "A," letting you know straight A's, a.k.a. performance, was the ticket to praise and admiration? Did playground bullying send the message you were not cool because you were too smart? How about basing your appreciation of your looks and attractiveness on a girlfriend or boyfriend's interest, or lack thereof? Maybe it was where you stack-ranked on the Hall of Fame? Or watching where others stack-ranked on the Hall of Shame, creating fear about future performance? Did comments about what was normal stir up feelings of not fitting in? Did a peer's conflict orientation, personality traits, or unhealthiness cause you to feel like you were less than? How about a neighbor's raised eyebrow or scornful view?*)

Can you identify any core messages that shaped you?

Inspiration vs. Motivation

As you begin this work, start with this simple challenge. Attempt to shift your actions from motivated to inspired. It is very subtle, and you will love the impact. It's important to note, in general, most of this work is subtle, and results in a big payoff.

Early in my career, the word "motivated" was an apt descriptor for every person on my sales team. We charged after big corporate goals with intensity, fervor, and determination. As responsible team players, we all felt the duty to perform and contribute to the whole, each accomplishment indicating we were winners.

This was all perfectly timed. All of this motivation happened while our ego structures were forming. Since what happened *then* shaped who I am *now*, in the end, it's all good. In hindsight, however, I've had a sobering realization. The targets, contests, and prizes were based on numbers set by managers, corporate leaders, shareholders, peer pressure, and my own ego. Those numbers had great power over me. Although I made my own decisions—accepting the job, driving performance, working hard/playing hard, and even having fun in the process—I relied on motivation originating from the outside. Then the motivation triggered something inside, which caused action. Ideally it should have been emanating from the inside, driving me from within my core. I reflect on those days and wonder, "Whose measuring stick was I using to evaluate *me*?" I can hear my mother's words, "Oh Heidi, you're so hard on yourself." In hindsight, my underlying motivation was about perfection, fear, and worthiness. Quite simply, I was busy proving I was good enough… for others. *This was motivation.*

Today, my actions are happily based on inspiration. What do I want to accomplish? What inspires me? Where do I derive energy? What feels right? What do I know to be true? Even something as mundane as household chores is a practice in inspiration. When I set an intention to do something specific like hang pictures, rather than forcing action based on the ranking and order of my list (a.k.a. self-motivation), I patiently wait for the internal flame of inspiration to ignite. Recently, while in the middle of a completely different project, I suddenly felt moved to hang those pictures. It required time and attention to get the grouping straight and aligned, and because I was excited, driven, and propelled in the moment, it was easy, and the outcome was excellent. *This is inspired action.*

There is a sort of slow-motion luxury and lackadaisical space reserved for inspiration that involves patience and faith to create action that is not forced. Because I am not bound to my list, I get to follow my intuition. I enjoy the spontaneity. With my inner sense guiding me, uninspired to-do's fall away, and are replaced by tasks that spark interest in the moment. The list isn't actually a list, but a pool of options from which I can choose.

This might not be practical in the day-to-day pressure cooker, but I strongly urge you to try it. Tap into your intuition. Allow your inner voice to drive you. Listen to your inner knowing-ness. Learn how it feels and learn to trust your inspiration. Who knows. You might enjoy the shift.

EXERCISE: INSPIRATION—
Total Time: Open

Set an intention to get a particular activity/task completed within a certain period of time (especially one you are excited to finish, but not excited to do), and then let it go. When it pops into your mind and you feel it is time to do it, a.k.a. inspired, do it. Record how you felt during the activity/task.

Core Development

Core: The central or most important part of something.
The part of something that is central to its existence or character.
—Oxford Languages

Although I am not a fan of starting out with a definition, I had to make an exception when I saw this one. It is so perfectly stated, "something that is central to its existence or character." Yes, in my view, a person's core is absolutely central to their existence and/or character, while providing critical space for growth.

Early in my coaching career, I noticed what I thought was a client trend, which in hindsight had more to do with my own core development. Professionally, I didn't ever "socialize" with clients in real life. And yet, over and over again, I felt an intense connection with them, which stemmed from *being*. Being with them in the moment and experiencing them at their core. On a truer, deeper level, we bonded.

One client in particular taught me the extent of this lesson by testing (stretching?) my boundaries in a way I could not have imagined. Arms folded, a scowl on his face, and tucked into the furthest corner of the couch, he brusquely informed me, "You're not going to change me, you know. There is no reason for me to be here. This is not going to work." He was unflappable and nothing I said could deter him. Despite my cartwheels and acrobatics (which is a "no no" in coaching—the coach should never work harder than the client), I was getting nowhere. A final shameless and transparent attempt to solve his current problem and gain trust furthered his annoyance. With him resolved in his stubbornness, I chased his belligerence around in circles. Finally, I let go and followed my instincts. I gave him an ultimatum and a homework assignment. I fully expected I would have to terminate the contract at our next session, anticipating he would not have completed his work. To my complete surprise, when he arrived, he was practically skipping. With a strange, uncharacteristic giddiness, he bragged about the outcome of his assignment to initiate a candid conversation with his manager. "… it was great, we even went to lunch. We weren't hugging it out necessarily, but at least we're on the same page. Okay, I'm ready to get to work." [Note to managers: Do not underestimate the power of clear, well-intentioned feedback. It is the kindest gift you can give a struggling team member.]

Because he was/is a very intelligent and independent-minded engineering leader, he still didn't totally trust me. He challenged me again, "You're not going to change me, you know." I agreed and repeated my opening statement. "You're right, I can't change you. You are who you are. I can only help you be a better version of you. I can help you with new tricks and tools to grow your capability, new awarenesses, and aha's, and ultimately your alignment. However, you are correct, I'm not going to change who you are at your core, per se." This time, he heard me. The conversation with his manager had cracked his shell ever so slightly, which allowed something from our exchange to seep in. Once he realized he wouldn't be judged, he softened ever so slightly, and allowed himself to grow.

Not only was he not judged, we actually celebrated those overused qualities that were getting in his way. They were awesome qualities, but the only tools in his toolbox. They were overused, and not helpful in every situation. He needed new tools. As he grew his skillset, his inner core shined. The best of him, the part that did not defend or argue, the part of him that was smart, capable, and clear-sighted—his essence and real spirit—emerged.

On the last day of our coaching engagement, he gave me an inscribed copy of his favorite book. The gesture spoke volumes about the incredible hard work he had done to develop his core, and the resulting connection we discovered remains intact today, a decade later.

I'm happy to say that this deep connection is a common occurrence. No matter how out of alignment, once a client digs in and taps into their true essence, connecting authentically is the outcome. Not because they've changed per se, but because they returned to their center and are healthy again. I've seen this over and over. Everyone has core goodness in them. And when they dare to operate from this place, they find the holy grail: deep connection in union with others while being authentically themselves.

Every engagement I have with a client begins with an assumption of *core goodness*. There is no reason to judge, shame, blame, withhold, or distrust. This allows us to get to work quickly, clearing out the backpack, reestablishing self-worth, and finding/revealing the core goodness within (more on this in later chapters).

FINDING YOUR CORE

As mentioned, each client has goodness and worthiness within. I am given the gift of fulfillment each time a client finds their inner-core goodness. For some, there is minimal build-up, and glimpses of their core shine through quickly. For others it takes heavy excavation, and sometimes a backhoe, a result of built-up barriers and being out of alignment for so long.

We are a very defined species, us humans. We have the gift of a rational mind. And an ego. We give great power to our families, our surroundings, our friends, our careers, and society to influence our self-perception. This creates distance from our core.

When I ask client leaders, "Who are you, without your titles and roles?" I am almost always met with silence. This might be your reaction as well. If you can strip away and isolate the unsolicited judgment and advice you've been given, look inside. Who are you underneath all of those layers? Are you able to separate yourself from those opinions?

The opinion that matters is yours. *Who are you?*

EXERCISE: CORE A—
Total Time: 15-30 minutes

Please use your Leadership Journal to answer the question: "Who are you at your core?" Do not use titles, roles, and/or responsibilities to describe yourself. Be honest. Even if you land on a description that is unflattering, please keep going. It might mean you have not dug deep enough, which you'll have an opportunity to do later.

UNDERNEATH

Sometimes our outer layers can get very thick and crusty, making it difficult to see the inner gooey goodness. Who you are, and how you respond when nobody is watching—when you are pure and raw and real—defines you.

Let's consider the CORE from another perspective, one not so squishy. When principled, you are of character. You know what you stand for, you understand your boundaries, and you are grounded in your actions. As a leader, knowing yourself at the core is essential. This knowingness shapes your response to pressure, doing the right thing (even when difficult), making tough decisions, and affecting how you treat others, and how you treat yourself. Basically, your core is how you operate as a person—*your personal* S.O.P. (Standard Operating Procedure).

Our S.O.P., whether positive or negative, is often shaped in our formative years. Those early years help define who we are in our most innocent state, which is the nature of our core selves. Revisiting pivotal moments from our past gives us opportunities to witness, remember, tap into, and rediscover our true being.

I was picking up my then four year-old daughter from daycare, and the lead daycare provider beelined over to me, gleeful, "You should be so proud of your daughter today!" Of course, my mind went straight to thinking she must have won a contest or something. *Maybe she demonstrated intellectual superiority or physical aptitude? Maybe she dominated in some other cerebral or developmental challenge?* None of the above. Apparently the kindergarteners had arrived for afternoon daycare, and a now in charge five-year-old rounded up the preschool girls to let them know that, because she had deemed a particular little girl not acceptable, they were to approach the ostracized girl one by one and shame her by saying, "I am not your friend." The little pre-fives lined up and proceeded as instructed— the ultimate groupthink. As it was conveyed to me, my daughter was at the tail end of the line. When she arrived in front of the targeted child, she said, "I will be your friend," and then she turned and faced the mean girl and company to say, "This isn't very nice and I'm not going to do it."

Looking back, I am so grateful to have had the opportunity to hear about my kid doing something truly great. Seemingly insignificant, this story is a part of her legacy and a beautiful memory to help her understand her true nature, so she can remember what strength and courage she had, and has, inside of her. It is also a nice reminder for me, the parent, about an important lesson in her development. In hindsight, this one story outshines any academic success or developmental triumph. This is who she is at her core, and it still defines her as an adult—her sense of compassion and fairness, and her desire to be in relation with pure souls, is everything, and explains her deep love for children and dogs.

EXERCISE: CORE B—
Total Time: 30-60 minutes

Again, using your Leadership Journal, further dig into the question posed earlier, "Who are you at your core?" Your follow-up question is, "What does my personal S.O.P. look like?" Record your thoughts.

WHO ARE YOU?

I received a call from a CEO friend who was establishing a local organization for leaders of all ages. He is incredibly passionate about reaching and shaping "leaders in their prime," and is especially invested in the Eagle Scouts, having walked the walk and talked the talk with his own boys when they were young. His first goal was to set up a curriculum for the high schoolers. He asked that I participate in shaping these young hearts and minds. "Before we dive into leadership, they really should know themselves. That's where I thought you could help," he said. Two comments. One, what a smart leader to have this awareness. And two, *Yes!* As if he had opened a faucet, my thoughts flooded out, "Great! Who they think they are probably isn't even who they really are at their core, right? They have been influenced by the outside—the right and wrong based on their parents' beliefs, school-provided labels, what friends think, the wisdom handed down from elders, what their egos tell them is important, their internal voices, and so on. Who are they, really?" He chuckled, "You need to be involved."

Do you know who you are at your core? You might not. It is quite easy to lose your True Self in the many roles you play. Child. Student. Friend. Adult. Parent. Spouse. Even Leader. To name a few. Sometimes, often, we get so immersed in a given role, we lose touch with who we really are. A classic example is the stay-at-home mom who is so identified in her role that she struggles to regain her identity once the kids leave the nest.

We take on, accept, and wear labels provided by others. Dork. Jock. Helper. Goody Two-shoes. Bad Boy. Einstein. Druggie. Drama Queen. Soccer Mom. Boy Scout. Our preconceived notions of these roles and their corresponding behaviors actually encourage us to perform in an expected way, which is sometimes oddly comfortable. It makes it easier to fit in, fulfilling the expectations of others when we conform to a role. So immersed in our given roles/false identities, we forget to take off the mask, or that we're even wearing one. Classic personas include Intellectual, Martyr, Femme Fatale, Macho Man, Intellectual, Tiger Mom, Class Clown, World Traveler, Hard-ass. Our occupational titles can also be roles we fill, identification, and labels we wear on a daily basis. When you strip away your roles, responsibilities, labels, and titles, *who are you?*

When I challenge leaders to be their real selves, my invitation is often met with resistance, followed by an exasperated dismissal, "Of course I know myself." Yes, you obviously know yourself... to some degree. You know yourself at the surface—roles, labels, and titles. And even deeper, you probably know your strengths and weaknesses. But do you truly know yourself underneath?

To challenge your thinking: Are you the same YOU whether you are talking to a team member, your spouse, your neighbor, the board, or a child? Probably not, right? You are most likely a different YOU in each scenario. Each of these situations requires you to wear a different mask, and I submit you've gotten so good at slipping the mask on and off, you do not even realize you're doing it. Or maybe you realize it, but think it normal. Occasionally, while taking an assessment, a client will ask, "Should I take this as my work-self or my home-self?" *This is an immediate red flag.*

You might be thinking, "What's the big deal? Of course I speak to my child differently than the Board Chair." *But why?* I'm not talking about the content and size of your words. What about your stance, your tone, and your attitude? Is there a hint of dominance, superiority, or authority when you speak to your child? Conversely, is there a sense of looking up to, lowered sense of status, or maybe nervousness disguised as respect when talking to the Chairperson? Whenever you make yourself greater than or less than, you are playing a role.

This bears repeating:

> *Any time you make yourself greater than or less than,*
> *you are not your true, authentic self.*

Pause for a moment, this is big. This means that whenever we use the greater than/less than measuring stick in our interactions…

- » The more we engage in role-playing, the less real we are.

- » The less real we are, the more fake we are.

- » The more fake we are, the less connected we are to our Core Self.

- » The less connected we are to our Core Self, the more out of alignment we are with our True Self.

- » The more out of alignment we are with our True Self, the less real and fulfilling our relationships, our work, and our life.

- » Out of alignment is the opposite of authenticity.

I have years of client experience as proof.

CORE SELF

I have been coaching business leaders for 15+ years. Regardless of gender, age, experience, role, title, status, self vs. manager nominated, patterns emerge. Clients walk into the coaching engagement with a certain sense about them. For the purpose of our conversation, it generally ranges from low-grade dissatisfaction to overflowing unhappiness. On some level, there is this awareness (often subconsciously) which drives and motivates growth, learning, repair, or expansion. And when the coaching engagement concludes, clients are happy and glowing, with a deep sense-of-self. The degree of transformation depends on the person but, always, there is a palpable shift. This is alignment.

Initially I had to create a model to better understand the pattern I was noticing. What was initially purposeful for me now helps clients relax, breathe, and know there is a payoff on the other side, once they do the work.

The CORE-Self model includes BEFORE and AFTER diagrams. Both diagrams have three concentric circles, like a target.

- The inner circle represents the CORE Self

- The middle circle represents the PRIVATE Self

- The outer circle represents the PUBLIC Self

As I label the circles, each time, as the leader absorbs the meaning behind the model, I see the lightbulb turn on, and hear an audible sigh. It resonates with them. And then they notice the outer circles are distinctly larger in the *before* than in the *after*; however, the center circles are actually the same size in both. Remember we all have core goodness within, and *there it is*, constant and intact. But the before inner circle seems so much smaller when surrounded and covered up by the outside stuff.

The distance between the inner/Core Self circle and the outer Public Self and Private Self circles is noteworthy. It is the radius, if you will. The greater the distance between the inner circle and the outer circles, the greater the gap from the true, authentic, inner core. The greater the gap, the greater the unhappiness. This means that the further a person is from their true Core Self on a regular basis, the unhappier they are. The correlation is real.

Suddenly, the feeling of being misunderstood, disoriented, or not comfortable in your own skin makes sense, and the first step of awareness is awakened.

Core Self model – Before and After

I was contracted to work with a manager/leader who struggled in her leadership role. The challenges were immediately apparent as our initial interaction was quite awkward. I found her to be *incongruent*. Once trust was established, with caution and high regard for her as a person, I called out her behavior. I had a suspicion she was faking herself into being someone she was not. Dumbfounded, this model helped her realize, in some ways, she had been out of alignment (and faking) for over 20 years. Head spinning, she left my office. Two weeks later, she returned, gleeful. "In the last two weeks, I tightened my circles, and am so much more me!" Over the next six months, she reported that all of her relationships, professional and personal, had improved substantially. *She radiated.*

THE CORE CIRCLE

Do you remember I said that I know everyone has core goodness within? This is why the CORE circles are the same size in the before and after diagrams. Everyone is pure at their core. The question is how "covered up" is it? The surrounding inflammation comes from what we allow in—input from well-meaning friends, family members, teachers, society, media of all kinds, and ourselves, creating the gap from our true, Core Self.

Knowing everyone has core goodness within them has had a huge payoff for me, personally. I experience (and enjoy) a new depth in all of my relationships, trusting and caring for the other person right away, without the need for them to earn trust or prove anything. Adopting this perspective has been a game changer. What I didn't see coming was the reciprocal trust that is extended back. When authentically YOU, in union with another, the other person is incentivized to open up and be authentic in return. And then the wonder of deep connection occurs.

Understanding the model is not as important as understanding and knowing that core goodness resides within everyone, including you. Learn to dig beneath your private and public personas, removing your masks, to find out who you are at your core is the work, even if difficult at first. Ultimately, my role is helping clients reconnect to their inner goodness to be the best versions of themselves!

SIDE NOTE: The distortion of the private self occurs when a person is less real in the privacy of their own home and with family and friends. The distortion of the public self occurs when a person is less real at work or out in the world. Both of these distortions block and cover up the Core Self from being seen, as was the case with the client mentioned above. In 10+ years of using this model, I have only experienced one client whose private self extended beyond their public self—she was more real at work than at home—drowning in her roles, without a strong support system or partner. Years later, I ran into her and we laughed at the seismic shift this realization created, and her resulting return to happiness.

EXERCISE: CORE C—
Total time: 10 minutes

Use your Leadership Journal to record your response to the following questions: How thick is each wall of your Core-Self model? Which circle is the furthest from your core? What are the primary reasons for the distance between your Core and outer circles?

MIND THE GAP

You might have heard the famous UK term "mind the gap," a phrase inspired by the broadcast message heard in London's underground tube stations. Years ago, when I learned this was a real thing, I found and ordered postcards for my bulletin board. It perfectly addresses the Core-model gap. The gap, the radius I mentioned earlier, is the distance between the core and the outer private and public circles. When a person is not really who they appear to be, the gap is the space between the real you and the fake you. Mind your gap!

What causes a gap?

- Telling someone "it doesn't matter" when it does, or that "it's fine" when it's not

- Giving a direct report a good review, when you know it is not deserved, because you dislike conflict and are afraid to tell the truth

- Couples who show well at parties and other social events—having fun, teasing each other, telling great stories—only to go home and retreat separately into silence

- Playing the role of '50s wife—cooking, cleaning, and keeping the peace after a long hard day of being a modern-day makin'-it-happen woman on the go decision-maker and financial contributor

- Showing up as Mike Brady, the iconic father figure role from the '70s sitcom, *The Brady Bunch*—even though it is not the real you (NOTE: this one is not too bad, especially if you are attempting a healthier relationship with your child—motivation hopefully will become true inspiration)

- Only ever showing up to your child as the parent—sadly they do not know you at your core, and are missing the best version of you

- Only ever showing up to your direct reports as your paradigm of the boss—they, too, will miss knowing who you are at your core

- Not celebrating your team, even you know/feel they deserve it, because you just don't have enough time

- Playing Switzerland on an issue you feel strongly about, because you don't want to offend anyone

- Having an outburst, a.k.a. *throwing an adult tantrum*

- Saying nothing when you are not invited to an I-should-be-there critical meeting (assuming your boss doesn't want you there)—maybe he/she does not see your contributions

- Placation (which is different than compromise)

- Saying YES when you feel NO

After using this model for many years, many leaders have minimized their gap. Their outside circles align with their core in a new way, and they live more authentically. Often, as a result, because they have really done the work, something special and unique happens. Something extraordinary. Because they have shifted, their inner goodness actually grows (!) and gets bigger. Their Core Self expands. They become more fully themselves as they shine and radiate their essence into the world, which is incredibly exciting and beautiful.

As you work on yourself and/or with others, understanding this model will have a very positive side effect, encouraging your relationships to grow. You will extend more grace toward others, knowing that at their core there is goodness. Likewise, you will be granted reciprocity, continuing the positive momentum you created through your own alignment and awareness. It is all goodness.

The Development Tree Metaphor

Nature is a favorite reference for metaphors and analogies. This particular metaphor is a great one I use during coaching.

Clients enter the coaching session discussing their leaves. The leaves represent their individual situations causing them problems.

There are hundreds and thousands of leaves on a tree. We will never get to discuss all of them. As a matter of fact, as we remove leaves, new ones are growing.

The given situations, or leaves, are critical discussion points in the context of leadership, but not in lieu of leadership. In our precious time together, only discussing leaves is counterproductive. I would rather we grow long-term capability and insight by focusing on the root system and the trunk. This is where every new growth emanates. If we do a good job at the root and trunk foundational levels, every new leaf will be healthy. No intervention required!

Metaphorically speaking, we work on the quality of the soil. We water and feed the tree. We even check to see if the weedwhacker is damaging the tree bark, or if growth is impeded by other weeds and root systems. If your development-tree root system is strong and healthy, over time you'll learn to easily handle your own leaves, grounded and confident. From my perspective, self-coaching and self-management is our end goal, so you can handle your own newly sprouted leaves

Strengthen Your Core, and Ground

It's understandable that clients prefer answers regarding specific situations versus thinking things out for themselves. While in the middle of a personal or professional crisis, survival instincts rule, and the focus is to get out of discomfort or panic as quickly as possible. But these situations are merely leaves, not the main focus of your development work. Strengthening your core is.

By strengthening your core, your current and future leaves will be handled with intentionality, capability, and awareness. There is little benefit in only discussing the situational leaves without including "development" opportunities. The main goal is development and growing capability. Use the real life situations to dig deep and strengthen your core at the root and trunk systems. As a result, your future leaves will sprout from your strong core, and consequently will be healthy.

Your favorite fitness guru probably touts a version of the same:

> *"Strengthening your core leads to*
> *better overall balance and alignment."*

CORE STRENGTH

If the following mantra were mastered, I would be out of business... which, in the grand scheme of things, would be a wonderful consequence. "Honor self while respecting others" is one of a handful of building block concepts presented in this book, that are linked, and I daresay, tangled. Once separated, straightened out, absorbed, and then reassembled, you'll understand why "honor self while respecting others" is a starting point as well as a basic foundational premise in developing core strength. If you approach each situation from this perspective, *checking your balance*, your core and self-worth will expand.

GROUNDING

Another important development exercise is grounding. It's better understood in person, using a volunteer, but I hope to translate it to you by retelling what happened at an in-person event.

In a room with 40 female leaders, discussing how prone women are to self-doubt, I suggested they combat this tendency by grounding. This mental exercise requires a high degree of concentration and visualization, and is a favorite exercise of mine for demonstrating the power of the mind.

I asked for a volunteer. "Who often feels off-kilter, and would like to learn how to ground?" A 30-something woman joined me at the front of the room. She faced the audience as I turned toward her profile. I asked her to imagine roots coming out of the bottom of her feet, holding her in place—deep roots grounding her into the center of the earth, with hands appearing from the sky, stabilizing her shoulders. I said, "Like a strongly rooted tree, be one with the earth. While still maintaining flexibility, feel yourself firmly rooted in place." While prompting her with these cues, I was gently pushing her forward from behind her right shoulder. She swayed forward over and over again, losing her balance. I repeated more powerfully, "Root yourself. Focus. You are a strong tree. Your roots give you stability. Your roots go deep. They keep you grounded and confident." Suddenly, as if something inside her snapped to attention, she did not fall forward as I pushed behind her shoulder. She was strong and unshakeable. Not rigid but s-t-r-o-n-g. The audience literally gasped. Up until that point, I think they felt sorry for her. It seemed futile. But in that instant they witnessed her inner strength, deeply rooted and deeply grounded. Her face and body said it all, "I've got this." Without exchanging a word, I nodded and she went back to her seat. The transformation was amazing.

Both men and women can enjoy the benefits of a grounding exercise. This exercise mimics that of body language expert Amy Cuddy's "Wonder Woman/Superman" pose. Her noteworthy research demonstrates the effects of standing in this pose for 2 minutes. Testosterone levels increase and cortisol levels decrease. *It only takes 2 minutes.* This was a favorite for my daughter and her sorority sisters while in college when preparing for interviews and presentations.

EXERCISE: GROUNDING—
Total time: 3-5 minutes

Stand with your feet shoulder-width apart and your hands on your waist/hips. Set your timer for 2 minutes and breathe deeply. Imagine your feet rooting, and the roots growing deeply into the ground, planting you into the core of the earth. Imagine a string pulling up from the top of your head, causing you to elongate, stabilize, and feel supported. Imagine yourself grounding the entire time. You might even feel expansive once you're practiced in this exercise. When you are finished, take a few deep breaths, realign, and take a moment to assess how you feel. Maybe a combination of refreshed, centered, and powerful? Hopefully your Leadership Journal is handy to record your experience.

P.S. I literally ground every morning—described in greater detail in a later chapter.

The Emotional Elevator

Have you ever witnessed the sudden shift of emotions in a tantruming child? Ranging from high and happy to low and out of control in a split second? Adults moving through life can be similarly sparked emotionally. Maybe less volatile than a child's tantrum, an adult's outburst is still equally substantial and disconcerting. Whether negatively "triggered" or positively "exhilarated," our emotions drive us, and can result in emotional imbalance.

THE COACHING ENGAGEMENT

Meeting new coaching clients begins with presence, staying open and energetically sensing their vibe, gauging their energetic starting point and momentum. For me, this resembles the upward and downward spiraling of the popular 1940s children's toy, *the Slinky*. I typically begin our engagement with a visual explanation using my hands to illustrate. Often, the new client is in a downward spiraling state of mind. I notice their heads nodding, affirming their downward spiral, sometimes accompanied by glassy eyes. Describing my intention as a coach, I slip my hand into the spiraling momentum, their momentum, to catch and stop the downward spiral. Given their downward descent, the first goal is to help them neutralize. I explain we will work on a few easy, quick fixes and techniques that will provide immediate relief and early success, giving them stability so they can rest and catch their breath. Not a plateau, but a place where they can steady themselves and build strength. Once stable, we engage in deeper work, eventually instigating upward movement and positive, uplifting momentum.

The Slinky is a great metaphor since, in this state, emotions are difficult to handle, movement/behavior is inconsistent and unpredictable, and behavior, like the toy, is a little out of control. This visually resonates well with the client and is a precursor to the *giving away your power* conversation.

THE EMOTIONAL SCALE

I stumbled on a scale that aided my own emotional self-development years ago, the Abraham-Hicks version of the Emotional Scale. I've since adapted it to help clients see and visualize their own in-the-moment emotions, providing the necessary awareness for development.

Easy to understand and use, the scale of 20 Emotions ranges from Joy, Freedom, Appreciation, and Love at the top (20) to Fear, Grief, and Powerlessness at the bottom (1). Clients pinpoint where they spend most of their time to establish their baseline. This allows the client to be intentional about rising up on the scale, and is an excellent exercise in awareness.

The greatest challenge for naturally goal-oriented leaders is that once they decide to move up the scale, they expect it to happen in one fell swoop. But you know it doesn't happen that way, right? The original adaptation of the Emotional Scale was a ladder, and like climbing a ladder, it is unrealistic you would go from the bottom rung to the top rung in one giant step, bypassing 18 rungs. It's just not possible. Clients believe these emotions to be mercurial, easily accessed and switched in the moment just because they want a positive, happy thought. Yes, positive outlook is the beginning of change, but it is only one piece of the puzzle. This scale measures your predominant emotional state, mindset, or frame of mind. Energy.

Clients intellectually learn that they (indirectly) "chose" their position on the Emotional Scale. However, as visually representative as the scale is, clients were only able to access it as a stagnant model, a snapshot of a moment in time, rather than referencing it as a concept to be used in the day to day.

The Emotional Scale as a ladder is definitely a step up, pun intended, but not the end all. While working with an ambitious, results-oriented, high level leader, who was heading into a career defining conversation, it was important to access this key concept in the moment. Conversations involving career are deeply personal and emotional, and easily trigger imbalance. To make it a more functional model to be accessed in the moment, the concept of the ladder morphed into an elevator. And it worked.

THE EMOTIONAL ELEVATOR

20. Joy/Appreciation/Empowerment/Freedom

19. Love

18. Passion

17. Enthusiasm/Eagerness/Happiness

16. Positive Expectation/Belief

15. Optimism/Hopefulness

14. Contentment

13. Boredom

12. Pessimism

11. Frustration/Irritation/Impatience

10. Overwhelm-ment (feeling overwhelmed)

9. Disappointment

8. Doubt

7. Worry

6. Blame

5. Discouragement

4. Anger

3. Revenge/Hatred/Rage/Jealousy

2. Insecurity/Guilt/Unworthiness

1. Fear/Grief/Desperation/Despair/Powerlessness

WHAT FLOOR, Please?

You open your email just prior to your career defining meeting with your up-line. A little irritated with the sender, you drop from your normal position of hopefulness, #15, down to #11, impatience. Your smile not quite as bright, is now accompanied by a slight edginess. While waiting for your meeting to begin, you read a second email, an angry email, criticizing the work of someone on your team. With a sudden jolt to your system, you cannot see straight, and want to take care of this before you head into your meeting. Without thinking, you drop to their level, matching their emotional state, sending you to level #4, anger. You write a response, fingers banging furiously on the keyboard. The more you think about it, the angrier you get. You are fuming. In haste, you pick up the phone to call them directly and land in voicemail. They've gone to lunch and have not given you a second thought.

Let's imagine this scenario using the *20-floor Emotional Elevator*, with the 20th floor at the top and the 1st floor at the bottom. You dropped from the 15th floor to the 11th floor. And then, while tapping into your descending emotions, you get on the elevator and drop down to their floor to deal with them directly. You repeatedly press the 1st floor button, as if it will help you get there faster. Outraged, you exit the elevator. Your goal is to talk to them and literally give them a piece of your mind. You hear the elevator doors close behind you. The elevator has left. There you are, fuming on the 1st floor. Then you find out they went to lunch and are no longer there. You are stuck. Can you see what has happened? By actively getting on the elevator and pressing the button for the 1st floor, you took yourself down, *literally*.

The vibe on the 1st floor is significantly darker. There aren't any windows. People are scowling. And there is a weird unhealthy energy. The longer you stay, the more palatable the rhythm and culture of the 1st floor becomes, and the more difficult it is to leave. It starts to feel normal. So you stay for a while. Can you imagine having a successful career conversation while on this floor? Whether by choice, habit, or reflex, this is a severe price to pay for getting off on the wrong floor.

With the imagery of the Emotional Elevator in mind, my client accessed this concept during their career conversation, understanding the need to be fully conscious. As a reminder to stay high up and not get off on the wrong floor, the slogan became, "Do not get off on the wrong floor," which then transitioned into "Stay on your own floor," and finally turned into "You deserve to be on the top floors."

GIVING AWAY POWER

With newfound self-control, my client had a present moment awareness. Seemingly outside-of-self interactions with others were not the actual cause of imbalance. *Imbalance is an inside job.* This was a major realization. Your happiness is yours. To keep, to give away, to control, to own. It is your choice. Anything less is you giving away your power. Let everyone else off the hook. They are not responsible for your happiness, joy, balance, or any other positive state of mind. It is on you. YOU get to be in this state of mind whenever you want. It is the ultimate freedom and personal power.

Diligently notice and practice balance, and you will soon stay in this powerful place whenever you choose. I hope it becomes your default mode. When you are no longer relying on others for balance, joy, or happiness, you'll find you actually enjoy others more. They are not the source of your happiness or sadness. You are free to be on the floor of your choosing. This is ultimate *self-accountability.*

Don't laugh, but I'm about to quote a scene from the movie *Pretty Woman.* In the opening scenes, after Vivian inquires why a guy who is afraid of heights would rent the top floor, Edward says, "It's the best. I looked all around for penthouses on the first floor, but I can't find one." As a follow-up, in the final scene, Edward says to Vivian, "Had to be the top floor, right?" She responds, laughing, "It's the best."

To help you reach the metaphorical elevator top floor buttons, you'll have to tackle a few inner-work items first, which will be laid out in Section 2. In the meantime, please work on your fear of heights and on balance, and the courage to hang out on the top (best) floors of your Emotional Elevator.

EXERCISE: EMOTIONAL ELEVATOR—
Total time: 10 minutes

What is your Emotional Elevator baseline? Please be honest. There is no right or wrong answer, it is what it is. Your response will not be judged. It is important to have an outside-looking-in perspective of you. Record your answer in your Leadership Journal along with a short paragraph about your rationale.

Ego

We are egoic creatures, with a necessary ego structure, created in the first 25-30 years of life. As we build this basic ego construct, it is important we not give our ego too much power. The resulting "big cover-up," the loss of your core essence, is when your ego overrides your authenticity and sense of knowing (often without your knowledge or permission). The ego begins a crusade to create restlessness and fear within. As one of my heroes, Eckhart Tolle, wrote in A New Earth, the ego creates stories to "convince you that you cannot be at peace now or cannot be fully yourself now" and "maybe at some point in the future I can be at peace—if this, that, or the other happens, or I obtain this or become that." Or it says: "I can never be at peace because of something that has happened to me in the past."

The ego operates from a binary perspective, loving the yes/no, right/wrong, good/bad, on/off, and white/black view.. This is a common issue. The tendency is to apply the same binary view to the mantra mentioned in the last chapter: "Honoring self while respecting others." If only considering either end of the spectrum, "respecting the other person so much, it causes you to lose your voice" or "honoring yourself so much, you lose your consideration of the other person," your ego has the power. Does your ego drive you to lose your voice and become silent, or forget the other person and tax relationships with your bold voice?

A stereotype of "a person with an ego" is an outgoing, over the top, assertive person. On a scale of 1-10 on the mantra spectrum, this person is imbalanced toward "honoring themselves" at 8-10. Would you be surprised to know the ego is equally engaged when a person is respecting others, registering at 1-3? How in the world can a silent, quiet person be ego-based? It's counterintuitive to think a shy, quiet person has an ego, but we all have an ego. The question is more about how ego-based we are. In an earlier chapter, we talked about role playing, looking through a lens of superiority/inferiority, and consequently being out of alignment. If consistently silent, the quiet person is also trapped in their ego. Perhaps silence (and loss of voice) is based on not believing an idea is good enough, or the other person knows more, or not wanting to cause conflict, or the idea does not matter. Regardless, the ego has the power.

GETTING AROUND THE EGO

A CEO group asked me to give an (interesting) three-hour talk on executive coaching. Although challenging, I managed to design a program leveraging examples, live demonstrations, and experiential learning exercises. The executives gathered in a circle, shoulder-to-shoulder, and for the purpose of the exercise were free to move their heads and shoulders. When asked the question, Who can you see? One by one, each answered a version of "everyone." Seeming logical, this was in fact not the correct answer.

When asked the question "who can you see" their view did not take themselves into consideration, the only person not visible to them. The correct answer, and missing perspective, was realized by one of the leaders who had a flash of insight. *He considered the whole view.* Although a seemingly simple exercise, the big metaphoric message was that we do not fully see ourselves.

Our confident egos instruct and guide us based on this flawed perception. We do not, cannot, see the 360° view of ourselves. Since the ultimate goal of coaching is self-development, the coaching circle exercise demonstrated the need for clients to energetically see themselves from various vantage points. The goal for each of us is to learn to leave our bodies energetically while standing in our physical body, thus offering new perspectives and seeing ourselves anew. Coaching helps clients deal with this reality, not their perception of reality.

A little trick I play on the client's ego to distract it during the coaching session is to drop something in the middle of the metaphorical coaching circle, which acts as a new lens to diffract the view. As a result, self-perception shifts with this new focus. The ego has been circumvented. In other words, the client is re-routed. They sidestep their ego and look at themselves more objectively. The *something* might be just about anything—a business model, an assessment, an analogy, a theory, etc.

This is a really cool pivot point in the coaching process. When the client learns about this new perspective, it temporarily lets their ego off the hook and they perk up. Looking through this new lens, they get present, *which is a state of being where the ego cannot exist.* Despite my holding them accountable for their behavior, in light of this new information and perspective, they are leaning in with interest. The ego is egotistically (LOL!) very interested in itself, and wants to know more. Interest is piqued. Fully engaged. The ego is looking at a new shiny object—about itself! By introducing new information, via a model/theory/assessments/educational material, the ego is thrown off guard, and its gatekeeper is bypassed, opening access briefly to new awareness and perspectives to the Core Self by way of presence.

When the ego is driving, the view is narrow and limited, like the side blinders worn by horses during a race. Opening up awareness and learning about who we are through new perspectives, models, and assessments, is as if we are literally and figuratively taking off our blinders. Our peripheral vision opens up and expands. Clients' views of themselves grow from a 30 degree view to a 45 degree view to 90 degrees and beyond. Greater understanding of one's triggers, tendencies, interaction patterns, and internal trip wires expands the self-view, which promotes self-management and the capability to get out of one's own way.

DOING THE WORK

A podcast featuring author and therapist Dr. Shefali Tsabary was discussing how much money could be saved if people walked into therapy acknowledging, "I know I am the problem." In this excellent talk, she goes on to say that the ultimate job of a therapist is to help the person see their role in the issue. Again, the patient needs to get out of their own way, which is a nice way to say *pry your ego's grip off the steering wheel,* and allow your Core Self to drive.

Renowned therapist Esther Perel, another brilliant favorite featured podcaster, similarly shares her recipe for healing. She instructs patients to use a tube of lipstick to write "I am enough" on their household mirrors, and repeat this mantra numerous times throughout the day (until it is believed). "I am enough" is a great starting point. From there, you can expand into other personal affirmations, like "I am worthy" and "I am whole."

As the list of supporters for inner work is endless, I round out mine with shame and vulnerability researcher, and best-selling author, Brene' Brown. After reading *Daring Greatly*, I remember thinking *this is the best leadership book I've ever read*. And yet, it is not a leadership book. Essentially, it is a book about the ego. She dares people to show up for themselves, as themselves. Take off the mask. Be vulnerable, open, real, and authentic. The coach in me was smitten with her research. The woman in me, dealing with and daring greatly in life, was equally enamored.

EXERCISE: EGO—*Total Time: 45 minutes*

- On what end of the *Honor Self vs. Respect Others scale* are you? Journal a quick paragraph about where you are with an example if possible

- List 5 positive *defining ego structures* you formed prior to age 20

- What does your *ego mask* look like? Or, who are you when you are wearing the ego-mask?

- Write "I am enough" on your bathroom mirror (or a sticky note in your car, message on your calendar, etc.), and whenever you see the message, take 5-10 seconds (*surely you have 5-10 seconds!*) to let it sink in

Feeling Naked

Earlier in my career, while working in sales for a corporate America Fortune 500 company, I ran after and accomplished what felt like lofty goals. I lived large, traveled, went to big meetings, stayed in great hotels, interacted with fellow winner colleagues, had fun, won contests, and received plaques, monetary rewards, and trips—all proof of my value. I was 28 when I earned my first six-figure income, which was at a time when earning six figures was a huge feat. I was beginning to believe my own greatness and infallibility. Then I started my own business…

I experienced a huge encounter with my ego when I first started my business, UPwords Inc. Being on my own was a time of truth telling. During those early years of working for big corporate entities, I had effectively worn their well-known names like expensive mink stoles, each providing warmth, protection, and an identity. My ego had convinced me I was great for getting through the rigorous interview process, being hired, and then achieving the aggressive targets set out for me. My ego whispered sweet nothings to me like, "You are in this exclusive club. You are worthy. You are enough. Prove they made a great choice." And prove it I did.

Over and over again, I rose to the challenge. My value and self-worth was based on their standards and my accomplishment of their goals. Because I was not balanced in my Authentic/CORE-Self, my worth, value, and sense-of-self fluctuated based on my performance.

It took courage and self-growth to build my business, and I experienced a new sense of freedom. I was exhilarated and excited. Yet, oddly, it also triggered a strange sense of loss. A void. Nobody gave me goals. I could do whatever I wanted, yet it was unsettling to not be measured and stack-ranked. How would I know how I was doing? I had not thought to de-program messages like "Your worth is measured by your income—make more than the previous year to be considered any good," "Hit your numbers to prove your worth," and "Congratulations, you are in an elite club, you are lucky to be working for the best of the best." Messages intended to motivate me/us into action and thus performance in retrospect, very deeply and subconsciously, also triggered fear and shame.

Which is why, when I started UPwords Inc., I was totally unprepared for my reaction to *just being me*. This stripped down version of myself, attending public events and interacting with those from other Fortune 500 companies, which I was no longer a part of, triggered insecurity. I felt less than. There was no longer a mink stole protecting me, keeping me warm and cozy, giving me an identity. *Just me*. Naked.

THE EGO IS IN CHARGE

The ego does not like to be naked. When it is in charge, it encourages us to feel unsettled. When unsettled and imbalanced, not on solid footing, the ego persuades us to take action and cover up. We drape ourselves in protective beliefs, identity, and self-talk. Thus, my mink stole moment.

When the ego is in charge, we inadvertently forget about our Authentic Self. We give up supporting and standing up for ourselves. Self-talk shifts from *honoring our truth* about who we know ourselves to be to "it isn't a big deal" and "it doesn't matter." Giving up our voice, we allow ourselves to be less than, giving away our power. The ego uses a variety of coercion tactics like fear, shame, titles, high-level degrees, authority, money, and beauty to intimidate us into submission. Or the reverse. It uses these same tools to build a platform on which we can stand. As my friend used to say, "He thought he was so much taller standing on his wallet."

Regardless, whether a *greater than* or *less than* moment, not having our own backs and protecting ourselves when open, exposed, and naked is a form of self-betrayal. I challenge you. If you heard a friend being wronged or disregarded, wouldn't you righteously, adamantly, and passionately urge them to advocate for themselves? To stand up for what they know to be true? Yet, when in similar situations, we allow fear, shame, panic, guilt, and other ego emotions to rule us.

In my experience, everyone desires best outcomes. *Obviously*. Even assertive leaders do not intentionally cause a scene. Yet it happens.

Coaching leaders to best express, honor, and operate from their true core intentions, while encouraging them to communicate respectfully for best impact, is a goal. Growing out of a passive-aggressive all-or-nothing *binary mindset* into a grounded and centered honor-and-respect perspective is a first step.

OWNING MY NAKEDNESS

Like any entrepreneur in start-up phase, I was running 100 mph. Despite lack of time, my desire for skill advancement won out as I enrolled in a rigorous 18-month advanced coaching program. Although my coaching practice partners, a successful, savvy businesswoman from Detroit and a wise, thought-provoking, retired CEO from Texas, were not local, I had the opportunity to meet them during our Coaching Intensive retreat in Jackson Hole, WY at the nine-month mark. After settling into our rooms, we met in person for a fabulous dinner, not missing a beat and transitioning easily from phone to in-person conversation. Thoroughly satiated from delicious food and meaningful conversation, ready to head back to the hotel, we were wrapping up our evening. The woman excused herself to use the restroom, while he and I lingered at the table. This is when he made the bold statement that forever changed me. Deeply affected and stopped in my tracks, his comment challenged my sense-of-self and personal power, upending who I thought myself to be. In this single moment, I was stripped naked. And suddenly I knew I had to do the work to which he was referring. It was the only way forward. My life's course had been drastically redirected.

You're probably thinking, *What did he say specifically?* I promise, I'll get to it, but not just yet. It's not important at this point. What *is* important is how his comment prompted an incredible path of self-discovery. It was two years before I truly understood the wisdom behind his words. And many more years before I appreciated how deeply I had been impacted.

After much work, I now happily and consistently operate from my CORE. I am authentically and unapologetically the stripped down version of me, comfortably standing in my truth, naked and vulnerable.

Binary Mindset

A male friend was explaining how simplistically men view sex. While this was not exactly new news, I had not heard it framed this way before. I certainly did not anticipate how basic the thinking was, especially given my complicated female perspective. In addition, although I knew he was being especially provocative to evoke a response, I couldn't help but be surprised. *And looking back, I'm surprised I was surprised.* Basically, he said men see, meet, and rate women in a binary way. Two simple options. Yes or no. *Would I* or *wouldn't I?* All that to say this silly conversation stayed with me for quite a while, and opened up my thinking about this binary view.

My only memorable exposure to anything binary was a not so beloved college computer class. Binary thinking was the only way to get through the course. There were only two options, "0s" or "1s" and no middle ground. No gray area. Only black or white. On or Off. Yes or No. Good or Bad. Right or Wrong. Pure extremes.

While this concept was taking up space in my brain, I noticed the same (extremist) thinking in a few clients who were quite challenged by people and/or communication issues. They were only able to consistently access two perspectives. Their reactions, communication, and behavior reflected rigid perspectives and narrow views. *They were stuck in a binary way.*

This was a beautiful shift in my own awareness. As I observed clients in the context of this binary awareness, this merged into what I now call the "binary mindset." This new tool helped me see and unravel clients' underlying issues—those with stubborn, closed-minded, and fixed perceptions finally shifted from "stuck" to "neutral" by merely exposing their binary mindset. In neutral, they were more open. This made space for possibilities they hadn't considered in a binary mindset. Rather than only 0- *Say nothing* or 1- *Risk conflict* responses, their view and capability expanded.

Then a second correlation revealed itself. Binary communication was directly related to conflict (risk) tolerance. Those with a low risk tolerance stayed out of the conflict zone, operating in an "off" communication mode. As a result, they reported being overlooked/overshadowed and not heard. Conversely, those with a higher risk tolerance jumped in, and operated in the "on" communication mode. They reported feeling blamed for disagreements, and judged harshly for their strong opinions. In addition, those in the "off" mode reported fear, withdrawal, and the shutdown of ideas when in the presence of those in the "on" mode. Binary thinking was also present in clients labeled passive-aggressive—staying silent (off) until they couldn't take it anymore (on). In all of the binary mindset communication issues, the extent of the damage was completely dependent on personality, intensity, fuse length, topic, and healthiness/ego attachment. Although leaders do not intend to "leave dead bodies in their wake," it happens, especially given a binary communication style and a limited toolbox.

If you do not believe yourself to be restricted by this communication style, *that is great*. But I know you know someone who is. Quite prevalent in the leadership ranks, leaders are typically heralded for their quick and decisive action, and as a result strengthen their binary mindset which becomes their default mode.

Leaders are quite comfortable thinking, and acting, in terms of 0s and 1s. The quiet/nice/introverted leader is challenged to hold people accountable. The opposite, bossy/dictatorial/overbearing leader, leans on formal authority and intimidation to get things done. In the coaching arena, in the first example, the leader is ambitious and climbing the corporate ladder (which is often a surprise to onlookers), and works to be more assertive. In the second example, the leader, while formidable, subconsciously feels people withdraw, learns to balance, and works toward toning it down while staying strong.

BINARY LEADERS

If not conscious, leaders overuse these two primary muscles. In keeping with the binary mindset, when only accessing these two major muscles "honoring self" and "respecting others," when flexed, feel passive or aggressive.

Passive behavior has an underlying mindset of "If I don't say anything I'll avoid the conflict." Motivating self-talk might sound like a) I've been told I come on too strong, so I'll be soft, b) In an effort to be "nice" I will hold back and not speak my mind, c) I am a leader who does not believe in or use conflict.

Aggressive behavior has an "I'm getting results" underlying mindset. Self-talk motivating behavior might sound like a) This is my go-to strategy to get things done, b) They didn't hear me the last time so I'll make sure they hear me this time! c) I'm not aggressive, I'm just misunderstood.

SHIFTING FROM BINARY TO WHOLENESS

Healthy and whole communication is balanced, not binary. Robust and dynamic, *yes*. Binary, *no*. Shifting out of a binary mindset happens when there is consciousness, openness, and present awareness. And if encouraged to grow, this move toward wholeness transforms into strategic business outcomes.

Whole-Leadership requires expanded consciousness,
which leads to an expanded mindset,
which leads to an expanded scale,
which leads to an expanded belief, view, and capability,
which leads to expanded muscles and operational healthiness,
which leads to increased trust and hope,
which leads to engagement,
which leads to strategic outcomes!

Presence

Scenario 1:

You are driving home from work and thinking about the day's events. *Oh geez, what a scene in the conference room between my two leadership team members—yikes, they were acting like children. Speaking of children, I better call the dentist to get their cleanings set up over vacation. Oh... vacation. Mmmm... I would love to visit Rome someday. Well, hanging out on the beach in Fiji would be okay too...* An endless stream of thoughts and to-do lists. Suddenly you realize you are home and pulling into the driveway. A sudden wave of dread. *How did I get here? I don't even remember driving home.* As you enter the house, you are pulled in every direction by family members. Reacting to their needs—proud of yourself for your ability to multitask— listening to what happened at the science fair while cooking dinner and compiling the menu for your holiday dinner. Before you know it, the evening is gone, you are exhausted, and you drop into bed without having had a moment to yourself. Sound familiar?

Scenario 2:

You are driving home from work and thinking about the day's events. After two minutes of processing the conference room debacle, you consciously shift. You leave your work at work (in the past), while holding off anticipating what's in store for you at home (the future). You take a few deep breaths. You decompress by becoming present. You feel your fingers on the steering wheel, noticing how they wrap around the leather. You settle into your seat, comforted by the familiarity of your beloved car—so grateful "she" has been so reliable this winter, starting up every morning, and tracking effortlessly through the snow. You drive. You notice every stop light, and feel the flow of traffic (not labeling or judging anything or anyone). You focus on your breathing. As you drive the remaining few miles you are relaxed and calm—your mind is empty, peaceful, and spacious. You pull into your driveway. Before you shut off the engine, you take an intentional two minutes to pull out your notepad and write down your goals for the evening: dinner, dentist appointments for the kids, send out cards, create menu for the holiday dinner, work on inbox clean-up, and watch the finale of your favorite TV show. You head into the house feeling grounded, centered, and in control. Immediately your family members pummel you with questions and stories from the day... *When is dinner? You know what happened at school today? Can I go over to Bobby's? What are we doing for the holiday? What did you say we're having for dinner?* You stay grounded, take a deep breath, and chuckle at their enthusiasm. You turn to each of them one by one, using your index finger to check off the boxes in the air as you answer their questions in one long stream of consciousness. Playfully you razz them for the assault, give them each a hug, and head into your goals for the evening.

By now, given these two scenarios, I'm hoping you better understand the difference between being present (Scenario 2) and not present (Scenario 1). Did you feel the scattered, non-present energy of Scenario 1? And the calm presence of Scenario 2? If so, excellent! You know, and feel, what presence is at your core. Maybe your presence muscles need a workout, and that is fine. *You're heading in the right direction.*

My definition of presence:

> *Presence is being completely in the moment.*
> *All the while grounded and centered so you are*
> *able to handle whatever comes your way. Operating from your core.*
> *Balanced.*
> *Presence is proactive, intentional, in the moment.*
> *Presence is an attitude.*

Please indulge me for a moment. Reread Scenario 1 and notice the non-presence. Pay attention to how it alternates between past and future. Then reflect on your own life. Notice how you too teeter between past and future. Similar to walking on a tightrope, maintaining balance and being present requires practice. Here's the *good news irony*, noticing your non-presence is your way into presence.

A main difficulty in being present, analogous to staying on the tightrope, is dealing with life's gusts of wind. Because these gusts are comprised of past events and future happenings, such as the comment made by a co-worker, the anticipation of your upcoming review, conflict with a team member, or your job status, it is easy to fall off. It does not matter how aware you are. Knowing is not enough. This is a tough pill to swallow for business people who have built careers on their cerebral prowess. Practicing and building the muscle of presence, no matter how woo-woo it feels, is how we overcome life's gusts and flurries.

And yet, countless people spend their time attempting to control life's gusts of wind. Can you imagine trying to control the wind? It is rather futile. I would suggest spending your energy working on your balance versus trying to control something that cannot be controlled. Pause here for a moment to take that in. There will be many unexpected, unwelcomed gusts of wind in your life, varying in strength, size, and duration. Rather than focusing on influencing events/situations/people, you would be better served to focus on your own reactions. The more grounded and stable you are on the inside, the less likely you will trip on the outside.

As you practice presence, balance, and awareness, you will feel the once tenuous tightrope of life become sturdier and sturdier. As you practice and incorporate grounding, gone will be the disequilibrium and lightheadedness you feel from the tightrope's height. The intimidating distance will shrink and you will feel the ground widen beneath your feet, as if on a walkway or a sidewalk. The more you ground and secure yourself this way, no matter the situation, your walkway will get stronger, and will transform into the welcoming, sturdy, and supportive Mother Earth. When you are present, you will discover and enjoy calmness, awareness, and confidence.

If it is helpful, I offer a few personal examples below, depicting experiences when I was totally, unequivocally, present. There are a few big events for illustrative purposes, and hopefully as a result, they will trigger recollections of your own totally-present moments from which you can draw your own examples. I also included a few smaller, more easily identifiable moments as well.

- I was refinishing my wood floors, which as a novice required complete concentration to use the *big scary monster drum sander*. Time stood still as I worked—wood dust flying, the sound of the motor whirring, changing out the various grits. Suddenly it was early morning. I had been completely engrossed. Again while applying 1-2-3 coats of varnish and sanding in between in each new room, nothing else mattered. I even took a work sabbatical to stay on task. I was incredibly present—gratefully, I did not think of much else. The gusts of wind in my life did not have a chance to knock me over, or make their way into my psyche. This challenging all-consuming stressful task worked out because of my presence and became somewhat fun, creative, and satisfying.

- The week between my dad's sudden health decline and his passing was surreal. My sisters and I had the good fortune to be with him that final week. We tended to his every need, working in concert with one another to keep him comfortable. *Together, we were singularly focused on Dad.* I am so grateful for my awesome sisters. As Dad's time ticked away, I couldn't help but notice a *suspended in time* slow-motion-ness about our day to day. We basked in our togetherness and extravagantly ignored the rest of the world. Had our focus been on our anticipated grief of his impending passing, we would have missed the unfolding of a number of very special, memorable moments. In the most beautiful way, being present allowed us to truly witness him in his final hours. As his physical body lost vitality, he let go of his ego, and his essence/spirit/core/True Self grew exponentially. In the strangest way, this worst event of the year was also my favorite week of the year, experiencing the most beautiful presence with my family in such an incredible way.

- Another example is working on this manuscript. I know many writers discipline themselves to write X words per day, or write for X hours per day. My approach has been different. When my inspiration collided with a block of time in my schedule, which happened about once a week, I sat down, placed my fingers on the keyboard, and allowed the words to come pouring out. Time flew by. I didn't want the fun, creative, outpouring to stop. I felt satiated when finished. The only times it felt otherwise were when writing in a direction that did not feel right. Like, not coincidentally, the time I lost 4,000 agonized over words because I didn't hit save. Coincidental or subliminal? You be the judge.

- I'm making a weekend meal I really want to enjoy. It's not a how-fast-can-I-make-it Monday night dinner, and it's not a planned-out-intricate-requiring-brain-power Thanksgiving dinner or new recipe. I'm kind of on autopilot. I'm looking forward to the delicious food while my Spotify playlist is cranked up, and I am dancing around the kitchen feeling inspired, alive, happy—fully immersed.

- This final example is one I am witnessing in the moment as I work on this manuscript today, Sunday afternoon, here in my home. I hear a familiar sound. I look up and out the window to see a regular in the neighborhood, a young man with mental development disabilities. He walks by on a frequent basis, with his headphones on, singing at the top of his lungs. His speech is slurred, and his tone off-key, yet his unabashed authenticity, boundless in-the-moment presence, and expression of happiness offers me perfect joy today. As I write this and reflect on his spirit, I am humbled to tears.

Presence is a beautiful thing, and when you are in it, there is no better place. *Heaven on Earth.* I hope you understand how to find it for yourself in your own life. In a couple of the examples above, there were opportunities to fall off the tightrope. My son and I were having a conversation about this very topic. It is instinctual to turn away from these moments—to avoid them, get through them quickly, ignore them, or run away. However, there is so much more potential for transformation and joy when, instead, we lean in, and trust ourselves to be present.

Presence is not something we look for or find. We merely open up and allow it to be. *It is already within us.*

Positively Present

As human beings, presence is not our default mode. It is, however, for every other type of being. Your pets are neither in the past nor in the future. Rover is very present, letting you know when he is hungry, instinctively wagging his tail when you walk through the door, or jumping for joy when you grab the leash and head out. Buddy does not engage in the past, "I can't believe they went on vacation without me." Spot is not future-oriented, wondering, "Will they forget to feed me tomorrow?" Past and future thinking is only a human thing. Our special and unique ability to think and reason is exactly what takes us out of the present moment. This sometimes insufferable gift is the same gift that enables high-level reasoning and thinking. *How do we have our cake and eat it too?* The answer is to practice presence.

The present moment offers us many positives. When firmly rooted in the present moment, the tornado swirling around us, a.k.a. the worries and concerns of life, dissipate. When the tornado dissipates, we are light and unencumbered. When not weighed down, we feel secure in who we are. We are stable and sure of ourselves—our inner core unwavering.

Others feel our *presence*. They feel our inner strength and our aliveness. It translates into confidence. I've worked with a number of clients whose primary goals were to grow their confidence. As they worked on their core, focused on being grounded and present, their sense-of-self blossomed. When present, their ego (remember, the ego does not know how to be present) all but disappeared, which allowed the true and confident version of themselves to shine.

Likewise, others feel our *non-presence*. For instance, have you ever been in a conversation with a person who was not present or listening? Of course you have. It happens all the time. Know this. *Hearing* what is said is not the same as *listening* to what is said. When I hear the person on the other end of the phone clicking away on their keyboard, I know we'll be wrapping up very soon. They are neither truly listening nor are they fully engaged in our talk. They are distracted and will likely miss the intricacies and nuances of our conversation, and of our connection. My not-grounded self wants to be irritated and angry. And yet, because I am grounded, it is okay. *Truly*. I could take offense and lose my temper but then I'd literally *lose myself*. This is on them, not me. So I stay balanced and give them grace. Maybe their day turned upside down and they ran out of time, having to send a late-in-the-day email. Or a client texted, wanting to confirm an appointment for the next day, so they needed to respond right away. If I trust our relationship, it's all okay. Granted, I would rather understand the situation, "Hold on a sec, I need to respond to this." But it is what it is. For some, it is merely a bad habit. If it is, in fact, about not wanting to spend time talking to me, enjoying our conversation, by all means let's both save ourselves some time. I'm okay with that too. If not part of a dynamic conversation captivating both of us, I would rather not be on the call. Ending the call is a much better option than losing myself and compromising my authenticity. *It is all good.*

That having been said, if you are crunched for time and need to multitask, plan phone calls during mindless-multitasking chores like wrapping gifts, tidying up your desk, opening your mail (you can review the pile later), or going for a walk. One last comment regarding listening. If you think you're getting away with answering emails or responding to texts while talking on the phone, you're wrong. Even if the person cannot hear the keyboard clicking, they do notice your delayed responses and misplaced affirmations. *Please, end the conversation, I am embarrassed for you.*

LISTENING SKILLS

Years ago, in an effort to limit my travel and start a family, I became a recruiter. I found my success as a recruiter was directly proportional to my presence and listening skills. Because 98% of the interactions were over the phone, learning to absorb and translate a sharp intake of breath, a pause, a stammer, or a nervous laugh became a great asset to my career. Bonus for me as I transitioned into coaching.

EXERCISE: PRESENCE—Total Time: Open

As you move through your day, challenge yourself to be present. Maybe while washing your hands, notice how the water splashes, feel the temperature, and focus on the sensations. Or maybe while eating your lunch, notice the textures in your mouth, or how fabulously your digestive system works (starting with your mouth), or how the various flavors hit your pallet. My favorite is while driving, as mentioned in the presence scenario, feeling my hand wrap around the steering wheel, allowing all of the scenery to pass through me while keenly listening to the radio. That's when I find myself "car dancing."

"The Forest" Management-Leadership Metaphor

There is a fine, fuzzy line between management and leadership. These two words are thrown around carelessly and many leaders who do not clearly understand the respective nuances are challenged by the ambiguity. The distinction is important, especially when intentionally allotting time for management vs. leadership, and vice versa. In addition, understanding the differences is imperative in making sound decisions.

Leadership explained in the context of a forest is a powerful favorite client metaphor, as past clients launch into how thankful they are *to be consistently above the trees*. In this *leadership is a forest* metaphor, there is much activity happening on the forest floor, with hustle and bustle grouped by common activities and tasks. Some individuals raking leaves, some gathering sticks, some burning leaves, some planting new trees, and some moving piles of leaves. All are working independently while grouped in their areas of expertise (departments), not concerned with the others.

Perched on the branches just above the forest floor are the managers. With a more expansive view, they have full visibility of the forest floor activity. They are able to see everyone in their given activity jurisdiction, as well as a few fringe people in the neighboring activities. Because they are so close to the action, not only are they privy to a broader view, they are also within shouting distance of the forest floor. Although difficult to hear at times, they are close enough to provide feedback, course-correct, and lend support. They also have the ability to jump off of their branches onto the forest floor to help people with particular tasks, to teach, and to rally the troops. They also walk around the forest floor to stay connected, find out how things are going, and assess the work outcomes, as well as evaluate the level of talent. The time they spend on their branch versus the time on the forest floor varies by area, task, personality, rank, and tenure.

These managers are an integral part of the smooth, inner workings of the forest. Without them, their view, and their ability to grow the talent and expertise on the forest floor, the forest would be an overgrown mess. In that sense because they themselves are leaders, and their view and perspective is wider, they are able to make strategic decisions at their level, or at a minimum recommend strategic decisions, like two areas joining forces, say *raking* and *leaf burning*. In addition, managers also have access to higher-level leaders, reporting out events like the forest floor progress, efficiencies, and stand-out talent. Not every manager leverages this upward access; some are more focused on the happenings down below.

Whether individuals or managers, each leader has the ability to rise up within their given area with a broader perspective and have a more expansive impact.

The top executive leaders are within shouting distance of the *manager leaders*. Although they themselves manage people, more of their time is spent on the broad strategic view, substantially above the trees in the forest metaphor, deciding on best courses of action (with limited view of the forest floor). Clear communication between the branch managers and the top leaders is imperative. The managers must clearly communicate full understanding of what is happening at the level of the forest floor, and the leaders must also clearly communicate their expanded view. For instance, in this particular metaphor, unbeknownst to those on the forest floor, this forest is actually Central Park, located in the heart of New York. There are tall buildings, traffic, and millions of people nearby, in addition to rules, regulations, permits, and sanctions to deal with.

Sometimes leadership decisions feel arbitrary. Although leaders resist justifying their decisions, they would get so much more buy-in, traction, and leverage if they shared their vision, view, and thinking with those who cannot see what they can see.

For a smooth running "forest," optimally there is...

- a clear "*view*" from top to bottom

- a certain level of authority and *empowerment* at each level, outlined and respected

- a clear path of *communication* (up and down) from top to bottom

- a *communication spectrum* focused on honoring while respecting

- an inspiring *vision* vs. a mandated motivation, driving healthy behavior

- a *commitment to Whole-Leadership*—the three selves celebrated and encouraged within each individual leader: Authentic/CORE-Self, Operational Self, and Strategic Self

- a *culture* of openness, trust, and presence (not past- and present-bound)

- *ego equalizing* (no human being better than another despite their titles and the hierarchy, meaning shame and fear are not motivational tools; treating each other respectfully)

- a *growth mindset* striving for continuous improvement, which sends a healthy message regarding mistakes and lessons learned

Additionally, a smooth-running forest has excellent, healthy, and authentic top-talent at each level, in every department. Every individual in the organization should be able to:

- see (what is going on around them),

- speak (up and down levels to keep communication open),

- hear (be open to what is really being said—able to take in areas of improvement and discover blind spots),

- feel (the pulse of the forest floor),

- know [have inner confidence (not ego confidence) about moving forward in the spirit of the overall bigger picture],

- act (the courage to course-correct, drive toward the ideal, and inspire), and

- be (the best version of themselves in every situation)

Section II:

The Spotlight

The Inspiration

I purchased two very cool legit Hollywood studio spotlights, taken out of an actual big-name studio in Chicago, to be used as lamps in my living room. Although intended as everyday living room floor lamps, make-shifted to utilize regular bulbs, the necessary wattage turned out to be too much for everyday use, and now, while still cool statement pieces, I use them to highlight pieces of art.

I have to laugh at the perfect metaphor of these lights. Bright, larger-than-life lights shining on one or two items. Direct and singularly focused. Designed to make the focal point the center of attention. Difficult to not notice. Not exactly great for everyday use.

Could the ego have a more apt description?

Imperfectly Authentic

The Hollywood spotlights perfectly parallel the ego's allure. Captivating and seductive, we are easily blinded by its bright lights, fooled into thinking something is, when often it is not. Our ego's glamorous brightness boosts our shine factor, lessening our natural sparkle. At times we are addicted to the artificial light, *losing perspective of the beauty and wonder of our natural light, thinking it not enough.* The ego messes with our ability to be in the moment.

Recently, an old friend sent me a few photos I had not seen of myself, from back in the day. It was as if I was looking at a different person. I barely recognized her. She was so much more than I had given her credit for, and I was taken aback by this realization. I had been hard on her, my younger self, judging and withholding, *because she was not perfect.* She paid for that judgment for a long time—until I did the work to liberate her.

In an attempt to capitalize on a gorgeous end of summer day, I spent an afternoon hanging out on a Lake Michigan beach—one of my very favorite things to do. Taking a break from my computer work, closing my eyes to breathe in the gorgeous sunshine and the (salt-free) water, I felt something hit my leg... like a crumpled piece of paper. I looked up and saw a butterfly. Sitting on my leg. I was stunned. *Seriously, when was the last time a butterfly sat on your leg?* I inched my way up to grab my phone/camera a foot away and take a few pics, amazed it was still on my leg. This phenomena lasted for a full five minutes. After the shock of *there's a butterfly on my leg,* I noticed it had a torn wing which was almost half the size of the good wing. *Was that the reason it was hanging around?* Maybe it couldn't fly? But alas, with a bit less grace than a typical (perfect) butterfly, it eventually flew away and was beautifully (authentically) still a butterfly, having provided me with more joy than any other butterfly had.

Many leaders resist flying until they are perfect—hiding their imperfections, not risking exposing their metaphorical torn wing. Leadership, however, requires courage and risk. And vulnerability. Leadership gives leaders a wonderful opportunity, and responsibility, to touch others with their greatness. To light them up. And sometimes even instill a bit of joy.

Many have concluded the same, including best-selling researcher, lecturer, and author Brene' Brown, PhD., whose life work is about vulnerability, a topic she includes in her Leadership Manifesto and is the focus of her acclaimed *Daring Greatly—How the Courage to Be Vulnerable Transforms the Way We Live, Love, Parent, and Lead.*

Anderson/Adams' *Mastering Leadership* states, "There is no safe way to be great. Transformation requires courage. Authenticity is highly correlated to Leadership Effectiveness (.80), to Purposeful Visionary (.82), to Teamwork (.68) and to Business Performance (.50)." Neither transformation nor great leadership allows you to play it safe. Great leadership requires risk.

In *The Truth About Leadership*, leadership gurus Kouzes and Posner rank self, credibility, values, trust, commitment, grittiness, and passion (they call this love—seeing the greatness in others) in their Top Ten. In a leadership workshop brainstorming exercise, I ask business leaders to list important qualifications of great leaders. Answers almost always include 15+ years of industry experience, management experience and, most importantly, an MBA. Imagine their dismay when they realize soft skills like belief in self, credibility, values, trust, commitment, grittiness, and passion are the most highly rated indicators of great leadership.

What gets in the way of authentic leadership is ego. Remember the idea of less than and greater than? This is what happens when leaders use comparison or achievement to measure their leadership. The result is often perfectionism and misguided paradigms, leading to other ego-based emotions like fear. The fear of being less than is very common. In my experience, the number of leaders who are afraid they'll be found out (as less than) is probably 99.999%. You might be familiar with the popular label *Imposter Syndrome*, a label closely related to perfectionism and the fear of not being enough.

By the way, ironically, when a person/leader expects others to be perfect, it is almost always because they are dissatisfied with themselves. They have high demands, and basing their own wholeness and healthiness on those expectations automatically takes them out of alignment, triggering their own inner self-worth and imposter issues.

What people expect and crave from leaders is not perfection, but actually *authenticity*. In a sense they are craving the same authenticity found in the torn-winged butterfly. Fully and genuinely a butterfly, *while not perfect*. I hope my encounter with the real life torn-winged butterfly inspires you to say, "Yes, I want to be more authentic." If so, yay! Let's dive in.

The biggest challenge is moving from inspiration to action. If your gatekeeper brain has control of the wheel, your ego is probably the backseat driver. If you hit a green light, you have permission to move forward. A red light, you'll hear very unsupportive comments like "Oh, that's silly," "I don't have time for that," and "That is so woo-woo."

EGO OVERRIDE

The thinking, rational self dismisses anything instinctual. This is your ego at work, making sure it maintains dominance.

One time, while conducting an assessment debrief, I was unintentionally provided with a brilliant soundbite I will not soon forget. The assessment measured important sales attributes, one of which was "instinct." The gentleman had scored "0." This was especially odd because he was successful and one of the top producers, and quite frankly, *I just couldn't imagine anyone actually scoring zero on "instinct."* As a detail-oriented, sensitive, and facts-based guy, his M.O. was to overanalyze. I questioned his results, and his response was, "It's not that I don't have instincts, I just don't listen to them." Mic drop. He was so sensitive and tuned into his inner voice that he knowingly and actively shut it down and chose not to listen to it. A brilliant self-observation and a hilarious contradiction. It probably also explains his frequent bouts of *analysis paralysis*.

I've watched for this in clients ever since, especially when they seem outwardly devoid of instincts. The question isn't if we have instincts—we do. The question is, do we use our instincts? And if not, is it because we don't trust them? Since our instincts emanate from within, does that mean we don't trust ourselves? I'm sure there is something deep within us that we instinctually do not trust.

Sure, you might be thinking, *I trust myself just fine. Being a logical person does not mean I am not tuned in.* Fair. Kind of. I too am logical as well as instinctual and I get it. Since most people take an *either/or* approach, the work is to realize they are not mutually exclusive, and learn to use both simultaneously. Do not forego instincts while being logical. Develop both muscles. Leverage your logic while simultaneously accessing your intuition. Growing in self-trust and incorporating your intuition is a bigger game-changer than you might think (pun intended).

Some people call it a "ping" and others refer to it as an "aha." *Intuition?* Yes, of course. However, I propose it is something bigger. These are the moments when you are fully connected to your inner wisdom. These are the moments when you experience yourself on a truer level—with your Authentic/CORE-Self. I call this *Ego Override*—when your inner-core strength and connection overrides your thinking-rational self.

Case in point. Have you ever talked yourself out of a "ping" moment? In a quick real-life situation, I am packing and I hear my instinct/true inner-voice say, "take your X" (not to be confused with the fear you'll forget something). My head ego-voice says, "why in the world would you need that... nah, you do not need that—you always overpack. Forget about it." Well, first of all, no thank you for the judgment, and secondly, I did actually end up needing it.

What happens when you do listen to *your* ping? I fully honor my "ping" and consequently experience remarkable outcomes because I trusted the illogical. My youngest sister called to tell me our father, who had gone to the hospital for a simple treatment, had been admitted, not telling anyone. He was suddenly doing very badly and they weren't sure he would make it through the night. Needless to say, I was in shock. It was late afternoon and he was three hours away, so I scrambled to pull myself together and quickly pack my bags. I ran downstairs into my laundry area to retrieve a piece of clothing. As I headed back upstairs, I passed the downstairs refrigerator and stopped cold in my tracks. I had no idea why. Out of pure instinct, I opened the freezer door—my thinking-mind was saying, "What the heck are you doing? What are you looking for? This is so weird, even for you. C'mon, you've gotta get moving." Thankfully, my instincts had the final say. Within milliseconds I grabbed a favorite dessert stuck in the freezer door, ran upstairs, and threw it into my bag. On my way to the hospital, I called my middle sister, who was sitting at his bedside, and told her of my brilliant find. "I found a poppy seed coffeecake in the freezer, you know, the one from that bakery in Ohio—I brought it with me… we can all have some." She responded, "Heidi… Dad's not eating anything tonight. You'll see when you get here." I arrived around 9 p.m. Stunned, with tears welling up, I reached out, "Oh my gosh… Dad?" I glanced at my mother and sister, both somber.

We got our bearings, and at 10:00 p.m., they headed home for some much needed rest. I would stay with Dad through the night. Between his erratic breathing, my discomfort, and the shock of not being able to communicate with him, I was wide awake for hours, jumping up in response to his slightest sound or movement, and at times needing to call in the nursing staff. At 2:45 a.m., after the nurses had jostled him for 15 minutes before finally leaving the room, my father opened his eyes. I was shocked. My logical mind said, "It's 3:00 a.m., get him settled and go back to sleep." However, thankfully my instincts were driving, "*So what if it is 3:00 a.m., let's do this.*" I instinctively turned on the lights, pulled up a chair, and said, "Hi Dad, we might as well talk, sound good?" He shrugged his shoulders and nodded his head ever so slightly, indicating his willingness to play along. After reorienting himself, he whispered, "I really thought last night was my last." We were both silent, taking in the gravity of the moment. "Well Dad, your stomach has been growling for the last five hours, and I know you didn't eat dinner… you should eat something." Without an appetite, he wasn't interested. Then I had a "ping" idea. "Dad, do you remember my favorite bakery treat you made? Poppy seed coffeecake? Well, I brought the one I had in my freezer. We don't have knives or forks (or plates for that matter) but how about I break off a few chunks and we can both have some—*it'll be fun*. How does that sound?"

He nodded as a co-conspirator to my zany idea. And then, at 3:00 a.m., while engaging in a powerful father-daughter chat, we were delighting in the delicious poppy seed coffeecake I had "instinctively" brought with me. That's when he hoarsely whispered, "Well, it's good, but it's not as good as mine." We both smiled. *There you go.* I couldn't have logically created this beautiful moment, for which I am so grateful. This was the beginning of his last big rally. We had one more amazing week with him.

EXERCISE: INSTINCT—
Total Time: 5+ minutes

Using your Leadership Journal, write down a time when you did not listen to your instincts but wish you had. Do not overthink—write down whatever first pops up for you. This will be quick. The after-the-exercise exercise is to start being more aware of "instinct moments." For extra-bonus development points, keep track of your instinct moments. Doing so will speed up how quickly you strengthen your "instinct muscles."

PERFECTLY IMPERFECT

Back to my encounter with the beach butterfly. In addition to the beautiful metaphor it offered, and lessons learned, I was humbled by this elegant creature's courage. The courage to expose itself to me; the courage in being perfectly imperfect, while sitting on my leg, open and vulnerable; and the courage to be fully, authentically itself.

If the butterfly were a human being, which should be renamed "human thinking," its self-talk would sound something like, "I can't show my face on the beach, I look awful. I am missing half of my wing for heaven's sake. What if they notice I'm not perfect? I am not good enough to go out there—the beach is not for me. I'm so imperfect it is embarrassing, especially this half-wing of mine. For the rest of my butterfly life, I know I'll be less than, never good enough."

But since the beach butterfly is NOT human, thankfully, the hypothetical butterfly self-talk might sound more like this: "I love being a butterfly. I am free to flit around. I sit on, and drink in, beautiful flowers. Nature's landscape is gorgeous. I am the luckiest creature around. I am radiant. I'm so perfectly myself, I have the confidence to hang out with other non-butterfly creatures. A mirror once told me I was different from other butterflies, but I'm not sure why that was important, because I already know this truth. Of course I am different. We are all unique and different, and I like who I am. I am special. I plan to enjoy the day and look forward to spreading my wings on the beach."

Self-belief, self-image, and self-talk affects our entire being and all of our complicated layers. Because we do not live in a vacuum, the potential for outside dirt and debris to pollute us is great, soiling our inner sense-of-self. Our ability to reject these unwarranted opinions and judgments is based on our inner-core healthiness and cleanliness. Presence, awareness, and balance give us strength and power to ward off contamination.

When not present, not aware, and not balanced, we essentially give others permission to define us. *We hand over our power.* When this happens, we deny our true identity—our mind, body, and spirit, and how we operate in the world. We give those thoughts and opinions our power, creating limiting beliefs. This is when we cover up, hide, and get energetically small.

PRESENCE AND AWARENESS

I received a call to work with a female client who lacked confidence. The top brass wasn't sure she had it in her to lead a 90-person technical team, so they put her into the role on an interim basis. In six weeks' time, she was to give a financial update presentation to the company president, and if successful, the promotion was hers. We rolled up our sleeves and got to work. I had been instructed to help her with Presentation Skills, a two-day training program I had delivered many times. But, in fact, this was not our starting point. I believed that she did not believe she was good enough to lead this team of PhDs, engineers, and other really really smart people. It was critical we work on this core issue before transitioning to anything related to presentation skills. We spent the better part of four weeks working on her sense-of-self. Her mindset. Her worthiness. Her worthiness to be in this role. Her worthiness and sense-of-self to be okay leading a team of 90 technical people. She had neither a technical degree nor the IQ to measure up, and since literally education and intelligence were her measuring sticks, she couldn't help but fall short. "How in the world can I lead these people?"

This deep off-balance sense-of-self was derived from her limiting beliefs, primarily fueled by her own self-talk. Her ego, which questioned, judged, and critiqued her every move and decision, acted as an inner voice of doubt—second guessing how she handled herself, made decisions, and what her relationships were made of.

Our work began with silencing her inner-critic/ego, and rediscovering her Authentic/CORE-Self. After intense reframing work, armed with a new measuring stick (a stronger sense-of-self), she understood how her all-important EQ/EI (Emotional Quotient/Emotional Intelligence) skills could/would benefit the team. Her healthy foundation was rediscovered and cleaned off, and her energy ignited, creating upward momentum. With new self-talk in place, we lastly tackled the nuts and bolts of presentation skills. By then, her mind, body, and spirit was ready. Her Authentic/CORE-Self was intact and good to go. She gave a stellar presentation, *knocked it out of the par*k as some later commented, and yes, received her promotion.

Over time, she continued her self-development work. With a strong foundational layer, she incorporated new management tools and techniques to grow her Operational Self. She stabilized again, and found new space and energy to grow her Strategic Self Layer. This imperfectly-perfect authentic leader had the courage to show up with her metaphorical torn wing and successfully lead 90+ people while impacting the bottom line.

EXERCISE: PERFECTION/IMPERFECTION Part 1—
Total Time: 20 minutes

List out your "perceived imperfections" in your Leadership Journal. Be sure to write out why you cannot be successful due to these imperfections.

EXERCISE: PERFECTION/IMPERFECTION Part 2—
Total Time: 15 minutes

Did you find yourself resisting the idea that you could not be successful because of your perceived imperfections? Often we instinctually adapt and figure out work-arounds or ways of overcoming problems. If you are still in "I can't be successful due to my imperfections" mode, write out the silver linings to these qualities, and/or how you positively impact others despite your imperfections. It's like turning your frown upside down—look at it from another perspective.

The Backpack

I love the element of connection most in coaching, whether in person, virtually, or by phone—each type of interaction working perfectly for that particular client in that moment. Within the first few minutes I size up their energy—reading their personality, mood, spirit, troubles, etc.—to understand our starting point.

I had been working with an executive in the British Virgin Islands for six months exclusively virtually, when he learned he would be in town for a meeting. We met in person for a drink. *It was so perfectly anticlimactic.* With no surprises, other than height, the ability and efficacy of picking up energy had been proven, and I became a big fan of virtual interactions.

Many Michigan clients opt for in person sessions, loving the energy of our one-on-one interaction. Quite frankly, I am always surprised and flattered the distances they travel to meet me in my office. Not surprisingly, my favorite part is the first few minutes when their energy is revealed—I feel their mood, spirit, troubles, etc., and we begin.

When clients enter the coaching session, I immediately see the weight of their burdens—"oh, you're doing well, I sense a lightness about you" or "hmmm, what is going on that is causing you such heaviness?" We all have antennae and the ability to pick up these kinds of vibes within seconds. Do you recall picking up on a person's energy, speaking volumes before a single word was spoken? I recall meeting a client for coffee, who walked in with what I perceived as heaviness, confusion, and spiraling energy. She was a buttoned up, show-no-emotion CEO who, when I shared my observation, burst into tears and blurted out, "I almost cancelled today, because I knew you were going to see right through me." *Well, yes.* But it was because her metaphorical backpack was so big and obtrusive, and hard to miss.

If you are familiar with the phrase *weighted down by the burdens of life*, you understand the concept of the backpack. What I see is *the heaviness of the soul.* Whether not aligned, or not handling a particular challenge or interaction with the grace they know is within them, the burdens are heavy. To me, lightening a person's load by helping them raise their Whole-Self capability is success.

Rolling Stone guitarist and songwriter Keith Richards must also subliminally understand this concept. He acknowledged, on some level, the initial inspiration for writing "Beast of Burden" was a tribute to famed Rolling Stones icon Mick Jagger for picking up the slack when he was not present for himself to carry his own burdens.

The idea of carrying heavy burdens is not new. I suggest we see those burdens contained in a metaphorical *backpack.* This visual helps clients understand themselves and their heaviness more clearly. *I think the bigger value of this visual is understanding it is a separate entity over which we have control.* But this takes time. The starting point is growing the awareness of the backpack's existence and heaviness.

The beloved backpack stores our most precious, life-altering, and memorable moments. We keep, save, and store our most emotionally defining moments—as long as we can. Forever, if unaware. Attached to our person, the backpack protects and carries our prized hurts. Our most negative self-defining wounds, slights, and wrongs provide hours and hours of entertainment as we unzip, reminisce, reorganize, share, retell, and relive each story. Going through life, we collect more, giving each their due power, securing everything back in place, zipping it up, strapping the backpack on, and continuing through life. Totally unaware of its power.

Subconsciously we love our backpack. *Correction.* Our ego loves our backpack. As we are mostly unconscious, we do not realize the weight of the emotional hurts, slights, and wounds, but do feel the heaviness of its contents and burdens. When conscious, we realize it is too much. Too full, too cumbersome, and too heavy—negatively affecting our mental and physical health. Over time, as we grow increasingly tired and exhausted with life, and continue to add to the backpack, its size becomes overwhelming to us, causing us to lose our vitality. The backpack grows and our zest for life shrinks.

WHAT'S THE MATTER?

The backpack contains items such as misunderstandings, twisted childhood perspectives, beliefs created by others and passed down to us; judgments; ancestrally handed-down values, priorities, and traditions; hurts; pain; lessons learned; fear; comparisons; what-that-person-said-to-me memories; self-incrimination; etc., etc., etc. All serving as source material for some serious self-talk.

To be clear, positive experiences make their way into the backpack as well. To accompany the ego-defining wrongs, we slide in a few ego-defining *rights. But if they are positive, why are they going into the backpack?* Our ego tricks us into reveling in behaviors and patterns not necessarily in our best interest. If our poor self-esteem is boosted by a label, a comment, positive feedback, or some other ego-pacifying tribute, our ego tells us to save it… and into the backpack it goes. Harmless. Or so it seems.

The backpack plays a major role in our sense-of-self. *And like my purse, sometimes it needs a good clean out.* The challenge is, your backpack items are buried, intangible, and often you are blind to them. While oblivious and subconsciously grateful for the security of your metaphorical backpack, you appreciate the comfort it brings. Securely strapped on, you wear it always, keeping your very important worldly hurts from your past very present. Every stored emotional scar is prepped for the journey into your future—ready to provide context in any situation. Your ego is on standby, ready to play *backpack historian and futurist*, prepared to defend, protect, and highlight.

To best understand the matter contained within the backpack, you can draw on the Tree metaphor—root beliefs grow into the bark, and then up and into the thousands of leaves, affecting the situations, interactions, and events of your life-tree. If you do not take good care of your root system—feeding it with presence, balance, and Core Self principles, some leaves will be unhealthy. Those situational and out-of-alignment leaves collect on your mesh body frame and eventually transfer into your metaphorical backpack. Over your lifetime you will collect more and more and more, and the backpack will grow increasingly crowded, cramped, and heavy. With little or no space to breathe, the contents decompose, their shape no longer recognizable.

Your decomposing backpack leaves are turning into a concoction of self-doubt, fear and unworthiness, comparisons, resistance, critical comments, and other strongly held beliefs. This concoction feeds your system and fuels your thoughts. While wearing the backpack, not operating consciously, you underestimate its pervasiveness and influence, allowing the mixture of underlying beliefs, resistant thinking, and unworthiness to be absorbed into your system, changing who you are and/or could be. Your inner essence, tainted, grows new leaves, and thus, a newly tainted version of you. New parameters, new limitations, and new self-talk—all hiding your Authentic/CORE/True Self. Although subtle at first, this altered False Self state is your new normal. Over time, you forget the backpack's separateness, as it is so comfortably a part of you. Remember, as difficult as it seems, *you do have a choice*.

Option #1:

The decomposing matter stays in your backpack. Totally up to you. The leaves/situations decompose, it gets gross inside, and the matter becomes indiscernible. It changes your essence and your identity, and becomes the new you. The longer you wait, the more difficult and overwhelming the task. In truth, if the comfort and safety of your backpack is greater than its heaviness and burden, you'll keep everything the same. Status quo.

Option #2:

Use the decomposing matter to grow. We are all flawed and not perfect in some areas of our lives. Realize whatever it is that caused the heaviness made you who you are—*Yay!* Plus, it usually does serve a purpose. Just like a real compost bin, we can use the scraps to fertilize and encourage new growth. A heavy backpack filled with decomposed matter serves no purpose, but if you do the work, you can repurpose your backpack matter to your advantage. Acknowledge its contents. Lean in. Use it for your better good, making you a more interesting, richer, deeper, more complex person, full of experience and wisdom. A person who is fresh and clean and emotionally unencumbered.

Retain control of your backpack and your self-identity. As they say in the airport, *do not leave your backpacks unattended.* Be more discerning of its contents by asking this self-reflective question: "Is my backpack and its contents serving my best, long term interest?" If the answer is no, unless you want to keep it for nostalgic purposes, *let it go.*

THEMES

A childhood backpack exercise I use with clients to uncover big overarching messages and themes might benefit you as well.

EXERCISE: BACKPACK BELIEFS Part 1—
Total Time 20-30 minutes

What childhood messages in your backpack no longer serve you? Reflect on "lessons," fears, and protective conclusions you took on and believed to be true. Write them in your Leadership Journal.

EXERCISE: BACKPACK BELIEFS Part 2—
Total Time: 30 minutes

Did you discover an overarching belief in your backpack? How did it serve you as a child? As an adolescent or young adult? *Because at some point it did.* Does it still serve you today? Are you able to step back and realize its original purpose? Have you moved on? Are you able to view the belief through your adult eyes?

If so, what does your adult self say about these beliefs? Do you have a new perspective? Write your findings in your Leadership Journal.

Drowning in unworthiness, one of my clients used these two exercises to breathe again. Having become a different person after his parents' divorce, now nearing retirement, his old beliefs have kept him stuck in the perspective of his 12-year-old self all these years. These beliefs and perspectives spilled into all areas of his life, and most recently, professionally. We discussed this event from his adult viewpoint—how did your father's actions impact your sense-of-self? Was he cognizant of his impact? What would he say about it today if he knew? How has the belief from your 12-year-old self impacted your adult self, and you in the workplace? How does it parallel feeling taken for granted? From these questions, an underlying belief of *not being important* emerged, and was, as is often the case, deeply rooted in feelings of unworthiness.

With new awareness and complete surprise that one single situation had the power to contaminate so much of his backpack, he said goodbye to his old perspectives and refreshed his beliefs. In his words, he replaced his childhood views with his new enlightened adult view. He reframed this particularly life-defining time, and as a result, literally lightened his load by letting go of whatever no longer served him. With this perspective shift, he repaired many of his personal and professional relationships. He had newfound energy for projects and tasks he'd been putting off for years. Feeling appreciated and revitalized, he responded to new requests with energy, engagement, and enthusiasm.

EXERCISE: CORE BELIEFS—
Total Time: 20-30 minutes

CORE beliefs are versions of the childhood messages you worked on in the backpack exercises. Use your responses to see if you can identify an underlying theme or overarching message. Then think about how other decisions in your life were impacted by this. For instance, how you lead today.

STOP THE INSANITY

My call to action is for you to raise your consciousness and self-awareness. Be aware of your underlying beliefs. Understand your inner workings and your drivers. Know how you operate, not on a surface level, but at the navel-gazing level. *Those limiting, paralyzing, underlying beliefs that became self-talk.* They have so much power. Take your power back. End the entire cycle. *Do this incredibly powerful work.* Take action toward being centered and balanced, leading you to your core. Operate from this place of authenticity while renewing the quality and positivity of your self-talk to be the best version of you.

THE BACKPACK CHALLENGE

Before opening your metaphorical backpack to see what is inside, let's imagine life after a clean out. Just like when your bedroom is out of control, messy and disorganized, you feel the chaos. Now, with your eyes closed, focus on that room right after a good cleaning. Feel your ease and sense of calm. Personally, I love a clean house and thrive in that environment, and am almost giddy afterward. It also gives me a sense of freedom. *Can you imagine life without the weight of your backpack?* It is a similar feeling— very liberating and freeing. Can you imagine it?

As you unpack your backpack, look at each item and acknowledge it. Thank the belief for serving and protecting you at some point in your life and then, respectfully, let it go. This is the same process used by the pop-culture Japanese tidying expert. You have the power inside of you, available and ready now, at your discretion. You get to decide. You'll have complete control of the process, which I will tackle in the third section of the book. For now, know at a high level that the process is stepping back, creating space, having a sense of *curiosity,* providing *context,* and *reframing. You can be free.* Do your work, clean out your backpack, and unleash your power—the power to propel you to new self-heights and extraordinary growth.

You will be doing your spirit a great service by removing the beautifully preserved negative moments from your backpack, and thus your consciousness. *Take back your power*—use their absence to positively transform. Your newly clean backpack will be instrumental in any noteworthy future endeavor.

Self-Talk

When you are present, your backpack is zipped-up, resting. However, this is not your normal state. Being out of balance and not present is. In this state, your backpack is wide open, spilling its contents into your psyche, creating an endless stream of self-talk, full of limiting beliefs, resistant thinking, unworthiness, and fear-induced emotions.

This struggle for worthiness keeps the ego alive and energized. This is the ego's end-goal. However, when one identity lives, the other dies. The thriving ego suffocates the Authentic/CORE-self. The False Self reigns superior, keeping the True Self hidden in the shadows, all the while nourishing thoughts of insecurity and self-doubt as the undercurrent, feeding the steady stream of self-talk.

We typically think of self-talk as unsupportive, critical, and derogatory. And it usually is. But given your unexpressed underlying needs, your actual self-talk can be overly negative or overly positive.

I can't do that
I can do absolutely anything

I'm not smart enough to go to that school
I'm so smart I will be accepted at any school of my choosing

I'm not pretty enough to get asked out
I'm so gorgeous, you're an idiot if you don't ask me out

I am neither a psychologist nor a therapist. *My view and approach is as a coach.* The difference, in my opinion, is that therapy tends to look backward, and coaching looks forward—there is value in both. Although we do not spend a lot of time reviewing the backpack's contents, it is helpful (and to some degree, imperative) to have a general awareness of the facts behind our false beliefs. This allows us to pull back the layers to uncover what is underneath. When beliefs surface, we connect the dots, create awareness, reframe, and let them go.

Clients believe they understand their own root cause driving their actions. But when I do not believe it to truly be the true *root cause*, I dig deeper. My most favorite and effective question is "What's underneath?"

When a leader says, "I can't do it." I ask, "What's underneath?"

"Well, I'm uncomfortable with it."

"What's underneath?"

"I guess I'm concerned I'll hurt their feelings" (a common response, by the way).

"What's underneath?"

"Ummm… I don't want them to feel bad."

"What's underneath?"

"…"

At this point there is a lot going on. The backpack is providing a *heavy duty ego-pacifying soundtrack* to get them out of their conundrum. Here are a few unstated self-talk sub-editorials:

- "I'm a good person, I don't want to hurt them"

- "My identity is as a kind/humble/generous/considerate/you-name-it type of person, and making them feel bad makes me feel bad"

- "They are more important than I am" a.k.a. "I'm not as important/good enough" which really means "it is more important for me to care about them than me"

- "I'm strong… I can handle the hurt/failure/disappointment/injustice" which really means "I am strong, and I can take it, my feelings are not the priority—protecting the other person is"

- "If I tell them what I am really thinking, I cause conflict, and conflict is bad" which really means "conflict is bad, approaching them will result in conflict," "it was drilled into me to let it go and keep the peace." And so much more...

This is a great question to use on yourself to uncover deeper meaning. As you lead others, use the "What's underneath?" phrase or something similar to be a more conscious leader—modeling insightful self-processing while elevating those you lead. I'm not suggesting you dig in inappropriately, but rather help those in your care uncover potentially valuable insights and barriers that are keeping them stuck—saving precious time and energy.

Ultimately all of these layers emanate from the backpack, your unconscious psyche, and what I refer to as the *mini-brain*—polluting your self-talk, and thus, your true, Core Self. By way of self-talk, it is easy to convince yourself of untrue truths. Motivated by the fear and shame of your underlying beliefs, *your self-talk pretends to intend to protect.*

This is not protection. You do not speak to your loved ones, or even casual acquaintances, the way you speak to yourself. Unsupportive, critical, and derogatory. Pointing out flaws. Reminding yourself of these subtle imperfections repeatedly gives proof to the subliminal ego-derived sense of "I am not good enough," which fuels a lifelong effort to earn, win, and be enough.

EXERCISE: SELF-TALK—
Total Time: 15-30 minutes

Journal your stream of self-talk. Although you already know what it sounds like, it is helpful to see it on paper to appreciate the magnitude and tone.

Getting In Your Own Way

Whether it is stubbornness, hanging onto your backpack contents, resistance, fear in revealing your blinds spots, your refusal to accept you might be wrong, or a myriad of other self-imposed behaviors, over and over again you *do* get in your own way.

Years ago, I was working with a CFO who demonstrated this beautifully. We met weekly for three months before he reluctantly entertained the idea he might be, very possibly, *perhaps*, part of the problem he was having with his leadership team. He saw them as a group of liars—braggadocios, not honorable, and making promises they had no intention of keeping. His lack of respect for their talents and his perception of their low work ethic sent him into a tailspin. Not to mention the annoyance of their constant chatter. Most problematic, since he had been sent to work with me by the CEO, he was losing credibility with organizational leaders—marked as a *difficult to work with employee* and dragging down the group energy. We had our work cut out for us. We rolled up our sleeves to get to work using a variety of topic strategies:

- Assessments

- Blind spots

- Openness to a perspective shift

- Reframing

- Trust

- Rebuilding relationships

- Education—communication tools

- (Re)Setting Expectations

I administered a few basic assessments to convince him of what I already knew to be true. Since he wasn't likely to take my word for it, I needed proof. On DiSC he was a High D, High C—a formal, structured person who had a blunt, candid, forceful way of communicating, with a high priority on accuracy. On the Reiss 16 Motivators Assessment (which measures top motivators), High Honor was #1. Equally telling was his lowest score, #16—Social Contact. The leadership team members were primarily High I on DiSC (creative, positive, high energy, out of the box thinkers), and most-likely High Social Contact on the Reiss. *Complete opposites.*

We incorporated the assessments into our coaching conversations to create new perspectives and reframe—illustrating his black and white thinking, and how prone he was to a right-wrong/good-bad mindset. The assessments revealed his harsh judgment, which explained his perception that their "chitchat" was wasteful and due to their laziness. He was blown away that the results indicated he might be part of the problem.

We worked on understanding and reframing the team members' contributions and their value-add. Because of his disdain for the team (I believe because he instinctively knew they did not like him), he did not readily accept their positive traits. While focused on rebuilding relationships and trust (a common blind spot—"I'm a nice and good person—it can't be me"), he got stuck and could not take action. He was sure his impressions were accurate—believing they were inherently not good people. The #1, biggest, over-arching hurdle from the very beginning was his openness, or lack thereof. Although it took three months of intense coaching to turn around this single factor, one day, he walked into my office laughing and I knew he had opened up. He sat down to tell me about the most recent team meeting. "During our last leadership meeting, something happened to me. I sat back and was able to 'put on my DiSC goggles'—I saw them. I really saw them. I get it. Suddenly, everything was clear and made total sense through the lens of the DiSC assessment." Despite his initial resistance, *he did do the work.* And then one day, as if he flipped a switch, he got it. He understood they were not bad people, just different. Once he got out of his own way, he was able to extend grace versus judgment.

I'M GOOD

If this client had initially trusted and let go of his need to be right, or asked his ego to step down, or opened up his perspective just a little, we could have saved three months' time. But that was not possible. It had to happen this way for him to experience the shift he eventually had. This is quite common, actually. *This is how people get in their own way*, and is a frequent occurrence, especially when leaders are married to their own perspectives, or have naturally resistant personalities, which he did. Career success and advancement often solidifies the I'm-all-good-there-is-nothing-to-work-on mindset—very typical in senior leadership. Just because you've spent a lot of time managing and/or leading does not mean you are good at it. You don't get a hall pass just because you've been at it a long time. Saying no to development work or bettering yourself is almost always an ego-based decision. Which is unfortunate. Since I interview and work with those who report up to these leaders, I am privy to insider perceptions. When a leader does not want to do his/her work, it sends a deflating message that he/she is beyond reproach, or that the team is not worth the effort. Neither message is a good one.

GOODNESS

At one time or another, we all manage to get in our own way, typically *giving in* to our ego, which prevents us from operating authentically. On some level, leaders know when something within is off. And yet, sometimes it seems so trivial, or uncomfortable, that it is easier to avoid, which is just another form of getting in your own way. Hopefully, you understand this by now.

Do you remember one of my earliest assertions?

At the core of everyone is goodness.

This perspective creates space for every client to grow. To expand. To be the best version of themselves. Every person is assumed whole at the core, and begins with a clean slate. *We only need to pull back the layers hiding their awesomeness.*

No matter what strategy speaks to you personally, whether it is the concept of cleaning off the leaves or the visual of emptying your backpack, whether you focus on being present and balanced, understanding intention vs. impact, or perhaps delving into your personality tendencies via the assessment dossier, I challenge you to figure out the technique(s) to best help you get out of our own way. Find your core goodness and allow yourself to BE.

EXERCISE: PULLING BACK THE LAYERS—
Total Time: 15 minutes

How do you get in your own way? What is the overarching theme of *your challenges*? What technique (so far) could you apply to get out of your own way?

The Unknown

Within five minutes of awakening, I step outside, barefooted, to connect to the Earth. What started out as a little intentional practice in grounding has turned into something bigger. I live in Michigan, where we have a very robust winter season, so maintaining my practice means going out into the snow. Yes, today in fact, I walked out onto four inches of new fallen snow. Every day, just prior to stepping outside, I take a deep breath, set my intentions, and have a moment of truth. I must decide—*will I* or *won't I?* By now, it seems like it is an easy decision. I know I'll be okay. *But it does not get easier.* And every day I have a brief moment of hesitation and an opportunity to reconsider. It is a choice. I actively and consciously choose to put myself out there—choosing discomfort and vulnerability over comfort and ease. As I stand on the cold ground, I feel the snow melt beneath my feet and the Earth rise up to meet me, vibrating. Tuning into the Earth's pulse every day is a reminder to step into my power. If I take the time to tap into my energy throughout the day, I feel the positive benefits of *getting outside my comfort zone.*

My ego is not very happy about this. On the contrary. My ego is happiest when I behave and act within my *already established identity.* I am this kind of a person or that kind of a person. Being present or trying new things rubs the ego the wrong way, and as I head out into the wintery morning I hear it whisper fear-based warnings like, "You better not go out, you're going to freeze," or "Remember how cold it was yesterday?" and "Just stay in, nobody will know." The only way for the ego to be excited about this morning ritual is if a new, bigger identity emerges as a result. Then and only then will the ego settle down and welcome my actions.

The ego loves the past and the future, and does not take kindly to being present. The more whole, grounded, and present you are, the less your reliance on it, the ego. *Your insecurity gives the ego job security*—when you are seeking and wanting, and not content. In other words, if you are good with YOU at your core, full so to speak, the less you need the ego to fill you up. As you become full and *enough*, the ego starves. *And the ego does not want to die.*

The ego feels most alive when you are past- or future-based—fear and worry being its two favorite emotions. When there is an unknown it happily scares you into submission. Very sneaky in its approach, using every underhanded scare tactic in the book, the ego loves it when you are stuck. Stuck is the opposite of change, so you can imagine how the ego avoids any kind of transformation.

Thank heaven that nature cannot think as we humans do. If nature had thinking brains, egos, and conscious choice, imagine the chaos when a flower decided not to bloom because it was fearful of opening up. Or if it never rained because raindrops were afraid of falling and hurting themselves. Or a butterfly said "absolutely not" to heading into the chrysalis. Thankfully nature cannot resist what is.

RESISTANCE

I know you know what resistance looks like. Simply based on your encounters with others, you have experienced the halting, dragging, and grinding of gears. You, wanting to move forward, dancing in impatience, attempt to pull them along. Their resistance makes it impossible. *Are there times when you too are resistant?*

I have a great visual for you. As an avid horse rider in my younger years, I can tell you it was incredibly infuriating when the horse I was riding decided to not move forward. Feet firmly planted, not moving, the horse was suddenly stuck, not going anywhere. "C'mon... please? Please! Move! Argh... C'mon, what is your problem? Let's go!" Despite my coaxing/frustration, it did not move.

Upon further inspection, looking literally and metaphorically beyond myself, I noticed *an unknown* up ahead. A body of water—a puddle—scaring the horse. Horses are known for their fear of water, and because they rely on instincts vs. logic, *their resistance to water is grounded in their inability to see or perceive what's ahead.* It's not stubbornness. *It's fear.* The reflection of the water blinds the horse to what is ahead, literally. Without the ability to perceive, see, or know, the horse backs up and resists.

Not only is this a great visual for resistance, it also represents our fear of change. The sheer strength of the horse represents the power of fear and the inability to move forward when afraid. Negative emotions are powerful de-motivators. The horse—a.k.a. our emotions—is stronger than our rational mind, and no "pep talk" can turn it around.

THE FIRST FLOOR

Have you ever seen a person who is happy, confident, excited, and joyful be resistant, sad, and fearful all at the same time? *You have not.* It is impossible. These emotional states are mutually exclusive.

When you get off on the first floor of the Emotional Elevator, you are at the lowest level and not able to communicate with other higher floors (emotions). People, situations, and opportunities located on those higher floors are not accessible. They cannot hear you. They cannot see you. If they stay on their floor and you stay on yours, you are energetically invisible to them.

There are two ways around this: 1. Do the work so you can elevate, or 2. Trigger people on higher-level floors to lower their consciousness so they can/will join you on yours.

Option #2 is the easiest, most common strategy. It is neither balanced nor evolved. You will not benefit from getting off on lower floors, and you will not benefit the collective by triggering others to join you on your lower floor. Exercise restraint, consciousness, and inner core presence to stay up on the higher level floors. *It is the awake thing to do.* As tempting as it is, it is important you not get off on the wrong, lower-level, floor, no matter how comfortable and inviting. Ultimately, however, *you press your own buttons.*

GETTING AROUND RESISTANCE

I did figure out a way through my horse's resistance. First, I had to halt my own downward spiral. I was hanging out on the bottom floors #1-3 (blame, discouragement, and anger). This was neither helpful nor the best approach. In this state, I was incapable of thinking creatively. Next, I actively chose a new floor on my *Emotional Elevator* (grounding, reframing, and getting off the tightrope are helpful tactics). I chose to go to floor #15 (optimism and hopefulness). If you've not been to the top floors, be patient, they are difficult to reach and require special keys reserved for the VIPs—Very Intentionally Practiced. With work, focus, courage, and intention, you can work your way up using a staggered approach. Take the first bank of elevators as high as they will go, then transfer to the next bank and so on. This means stabilizing every so often once you've reached the top floor of that particular section and before you get on the next bank of elevators.

Heading up to floor #15 gave me access to my creativity instead of anger. In this state, I was able to see things from my horse's perspective and help resolve this situation of stuckness. Eventually, I realized the horse needed a new sideview vantage point, so I led him in a big circle. This reoriented him to a fresh perspective... ultimately offering new clarity, increased knowledge, and a new perception of the potential threat, which lowered the risk of the unknown. *It worked.* Because the horse could see what was ahead, the unknown was eliminated, and thus imminent danger and fear disappeared. His instincts were re-engaged and he moved forward.

Had I insisted the horse enter the water my way, head-on, from the same perspective, fear and resistance would have won out, with potentially dire consequences.

Maybe you've experienced this leading other non-equine individuals?!

EXERCISE: UNKNOWN—*Total Time: 5 minutes*

Take a few deep breaths. Set your timer for 1 minute. Allow your instincts to kick in as you recall seemingly awful instances that turned out okay. Quickly jot them down in your Journal using a word or phrase to help you identify them later. Set your timer for another minute, and silently repeat phrases like "It always works out in the end," "I am courageous," "I have nothing to fear," and "I am excited to experience the unknown."

EXERCISE: NATURE—
Total Time: 5-30 minutes

Go BE in nature. *That's it.* Experience the wonderful non-resistance and easy-going acceptance of nature.

Energetic Health

Your energy is your own *radar frequency signature*. Much like a silent dog whistle, its incomprehensible pitch energetically blasts us on a whole other sense level. It is the nothing-ness that has the power to shifts moods, and is felt from head to toe. A speaker once challenged the audience to "take responsibility for the energy you take into the room." With that awareness in mind, I check my energy at the door, deliberate and mindful of my healthiness.

Energy is best described in *action*. You enter a room and feel an immediate heaviness in the air, giving meaning to the phrase *you can cut the tension with a knife*. There is an energetic spark between two colleagues, creating a *buzz* in the office. You enter the breakroom as the laughter is dying down, signaling the end of a shared joke, with uncomfortable stares confirming your *energetic intrusion*. You watch the sales team exit the conference room just after having learned their performance broke a quarterly record—feeling their collective energy, buoyancy, and sense of ease, *you know all is well*. No words are necessary; their energy is palpable.

The energy I take into a room is intentional. Personally, my goal is *authentically clean and fresh*. I don't always hit my target, but it is what I strive for, and requires I do my work. Tuning in with awareness, I clear my energy which sometimes requires emptying my backpack, letting things go, reframing, or making amends.

I entered one of my daughter's favorite boutique specialty stores, excited to find her perfect birthday present(s). Walking through the store, collecting this and that, the urgency to use the restroom became greater than my desire to shop. With arms full of merchandise, I asked the store clerk if, even though they did not have a public restroom, I could use their private restroom. She refused my request. I placed my items on the counter, left the store as directed, and crossed the street to use a bathroom in another establishment. My irritation was at a fever pitch. *How unfair that this other establishment was funding their neighbor's clienteles' use of the bathroom.* How crazy that I was directed to leave the store where I was obviously planning to spend considerable money. You can only imagine my state of mind as I reentered the boutique. I grabbed my intended purchases off the counter and resumed my shopping. Realizing my very low emotional state was hurting me the most—*seriously, how could I pick out awesome gifts for my daughter when I was feeling so negative?*— I repeated a few phrases over and over again to get myself back on track. Attempting a renewed sense of calm, I made peace with my anger. With a deep breath, I concluded my shopping and approached the counter to check out, addressing the young woman behind the counter, "I want to apologize for my earlier energy, it was inappropriate. I'm very sorry." She was surprised by my words. I pressed on. I wanted to make sure I owned my energy while respecting her, and also honored myself. Keeping the same calm voice, I continued, having processed through what was really behind my anger, "Being turned away from the store while in the middle of my shopping felt like rejection on some level, and I felt hurt." I saw the tension visibly leave her body as she understood my perspective. She nodded in appreciation as we finished the transaction, then I was on my way to enjoy the rest of the day.

What is your energetic intention and responsibility?

EXERCISE: PERSONAL ENERGY—
Total Time: 20 minutes

Journal your personal energy theme. Brainstorm words which describe your ideal energy. Quickly review the list and whittle it down to 3-5 words. Go through your finalists and see how they sit with you. Select the one or two words, or a phrase, which best resonates your personal energetic intention.

HEALTHINESS

If a person's radar frequency signature is silently blasting energy at others and shifting moods, you understand the critical nature of energetic health. For this reason, evaluating energetic healthiness in yourself and others is critical in maintaining balance, presence, and personal power.

Not-so-healthy individuals, with out of control egos and energy, negatively impact everyone—co-workers, managers, teams, friends, and family. As if navigating landmines, hoping not to detonate a bomb, individuals on the receiving end groove out patterns to get themselves safely through these unhealthy interactions. Over time, exhausted and worn down, hopefulness erodes while waiting for things (or people) to change. Despite numerous attempts at intervention—crucial conversations, personality assessments, feedback sessions, topical leadership workshops— *nothing changes*. The unhealthy person continues to get in their own way, and negatively impacts others within the organization. And yet, they remain in their role, which is often based on the misperception that their technical value supersedes the damage they cause other team members or company culture.

By now, you understand the complexities of transformation, as well as *healthy*, *unhealthy*, and *toxic* patterns. Most leaders interact with people on a surface level, and unfortunately do not have the skillset to assess healthiness. Knowing how to move individuals, a team, and/or the organization forward on a deeper level is an extremely involved process.

Leaders, although smart and talented, are accustomed to knowing. They (subliminally) shy away from these gooey, messy, people topics. Avoidance takes over because dealing with an unhealthy or toxic person is uncomfortable. As I'm sure you already know, avoidance exacerbates the situation, and *a people can't change attitude* takes root, which is such a disservice to those who *can* develop. Leaders might be better equipped to take on these people issues if they had a clearer understanding of what they were dealing with.

Actively evaluating individuals on a Healthiness Scale is my first line of defense. This quick assessment also helps leaders move forward. Am I dealing with a healthy person who is capable of change? Is this an unhealthy person, and if so, what is their capacity and willingness for growth? Is this a toxic person, and if so, what are my next steps? Finally, the most important question I ask myself is, *"What is my part in it?"*

The original coaching goal for one engaging, bright, firecracker leader I worked with was to very intentionally smooth out a few *people wrinkles* and grow her capability. She dug in, did her self-work and quickly turned her leadership issues into non-issues, which was fantastic. However, without big issues driving her growth, she pulled back from coaching, feeling complete. Happy she felt strong and capable, my sense was this might only be a pause. Capable and sharp, she was just about to head into what I call *nuanced leadership work*. Months later, she reached out, caught off guard by a new wrinkle. A few of her staff feedback sessions had not gone well, and she identified herself as the common denominator. (Thankfully she had the wherewithal to figure this out prior to *awareness avoidance*.) She wanted to nip the problem in the bud, and courageously leaned into the challenge.

HR had coached her to not color outside the lines. Ultra-professional, she presented the facts very unemotionally—short and sweet, as instructed. Because the facts were factual—there was no denying the information—she anticipated an equally short and sweet reaction, with total acceptance of their poor performances. She did not anticipate the anger, blame, and disrespect that ensued. Together we analyzed the play-by-play in our next coaching session, and her new awareness was, "Oh my gosh, I wasn't being authentic. I stopped being compassionate. I did not give them grace about their valuable contributions, only pointing out the flaws. The conversation triggered their ego(s), and the result was awful. *I get it*. I know to approach them more authentically in the future. This won't happen again—promise!"

Well, my client took on all of the responsibility for both parties. She blamed herself because it was her approach that had triggered the upset, after all. However, there was another person dancing with her in each of the meetings, someone who was not being held accountable for their energy. *First and foremost, evaluate and understand their healthiness.* If out of alignment, this *state of being* trumps all other factors. As it turns out, both individuals receiving feedback were on the bubble and facing termination. Ego, lack of awareness, and unhealthiness had already been identified and noted. My client's only wrongdoing was adding fuel to the fire—escalating the conversation vertically. A *vertical* conversation is when the exchange creates momentum *upward*, a spiral widening as it ascends, representing the increasing emotional charge in the back and forth interaction. Visually this looks like a spiraling tornado and energetically it feels out of control, a.k.a. *spiraling out of control.*

She committed herself anew to operating from her Authentic/CORE-Self while inspiring *horizontal* interactions—smaller wider waves of up and down peaks and valleys, representing varied intensity while moving forward.

OPENNESS

If you recall, openness was a key success factor in a previous client example I cited, which was directly related to core healthiness. The ability to see new perspectives, have self-awareness, and implement new strategies and thinking is who we are at our healthy Authentic/CORE-Self core level.

In the early days when clients were sent to me for coaching by their managers, many of these clients were closed-minded, *perceiving development as punishment vs. an opportunity to grow.* Visualize this typical scenario. A client walks in, sits down, and shuts down by folding their arms as if creating a barrier to entry, defiantly saying, "You're not going to change me, you know." To which I'd respond, "You're absolutely right. I can't change you. You are uniquely you, and all I can do is help you be a better version of you. You'll learn new perspectives, tools, and techniques. People don't always see the best version of you, which is unfortunate. This will be our focus. You will still be you, but the better version of you, not to worry." Their bodies would visibly soften and they would breathe a sigh of relief. Then we were ready to begin the search for the Authentic/CORE-Self.

You are who you are. Period. You cannot drastically change who you are, what is important to you, your personality tendencies, your motivations, or your values. I am willing to bet that people do not truly see your inner goodness. Whether they aren't paying attention, they've not made the effort to know you, they're unaware, you are too confusing, or something else, the bottom line is that you are not seen. Another perspective to consider: *Have you courageously dared to show up, fully and authentically, as your True Self?*

When not seen, rigidity and close-mindedness result. Withdrawal, contraction, and anger are often the consequences. Your ego emerges, assuming authority and decision-making power over you, making sure to protect you from identity loss. With your core in hiding and out of sight, the ego dominates—measuring, comparing, and judging. You are stuck. If unchecked, this growing unhealthiness turns into toxicity.

THE HEALTHINESS MODEL

I love using experiential models and exercises to bring leadership development workshops to life. Crafting a personality model on the floor using ropes, the participants interact *with* and *in* the model, grateful for not staring at a sterile one-dimensional model via PowerPoint. Incredibly active, present, and engaged, participants take responsibility for their own learning experience.

In one particular workshop, while analyzing the various personality tendencies, a participant was incredibly resistant—emphatically rejecting his DiSC – High D personality type. As you can imagine, resistance to being typed is not unusual, but his outward, repeated insistence he had been *mistyped* was. Singlehandedly, he brought the workshop to a screeching halt. Although it was clear to everyone in the room he was perfectly placed, he continued to fight the categorization. As is often the case, he was extremely triggered and required immediate attention. In an effort to get the workshop back on track, I turned to him to help unpack his concerns. As it turns out, there was another person in the organization with the same profile, who was known as toxic. "How in the world can we be the same pattern when he is such a jerk?" Knowing he was not like this unhealthy person caused the impasse. I spontaneously shared the Healthiness Scale with the group but directed my comments specifically at him, explaining what I believed to be the disconnect. He was healthy and his counterpart was not, which made all the difference in the world. As if releasing air from an over-inflated balloon, he got it. We were back on track. Although the workshop was focused on personality tendencies, the *Healthiness Scale* proved to be extremely helpful in this situation. It helped him understand why he was so different from his colleague despite the similarity in their DiSC profiles. Ultimately it helped him lower his resistance. The Healthiness Scale was a helpful tool that allowed him to measure his energetic healthiness, even though the workshop was focused purely on personality tendencies.

Originally, I didn't realize The Healthiness Scale model was even a model. It was merely a mental structure that helped me assess situations and people, functioning as an internal flow chart. When I shared it with clients, they found the perspective helpful to isolate, understand, and take action on some of their most challenging people issues. The mindset became a model.

The 5 levels of healthiness:
1. Evolved

2. Healthy

3. Neutral

4. Unhealthy

5. Toxic

EVOLVED AND HEALTHY

Evolved and Healthy is when you are at your best and in flow. Your communication is open and honest. You receive constructive feedback, albeit uncomfortable, with gratitude. Teams welcome your input, collaboration, and participation. Optimism prevails, and you are on the upper floors of your Emotional Elevator.

Because we are human, life presents the occasional hiccup. When "healthy," these blips are minimal and minor, smoothed out straightforwardly. Even when deeply embedded backpack artifacts are triggered, and lower level emotions and behaviors emerge, if developmentally Healthy/Evolved, *awareness*, and then *recovery* is swift. Once developmentally Healthy or Evolved, *you can't unknow what you know.*

There are areas that potentially cause the Healthy and Evolved to get stuck, however; conflict is one of the bigger stumbling blocks. Expressing opinions, showing their true selves when opposed, feeling undervalued or not acknowledged, desiring others to be as motivated and engaged as they are, and working with others who are lower on the scale are common tripwires. Often, a binary mindset is at play. Expanding to a 10-point scale and learning skills to balance between *honoring self* and *respecting others* will help immensely.

Fortunately for leaders, healthy individuals feel easy to work with, especially in comparison to others on the lower end of the scale. As a result, leaders expend less attention, thought, and energy on those who are "healthy," pouring resources into those who are more difficult. What is important to remember is that *the Healthy are healthy*. Their concerns, observations, and feedback are for the greater good. The Healthy and Evolved serve as your organizational eyes and ears—not to be treated as organizational squeaky wheels. It is easy to overlook the honest but negative feedback from these solid individuals because you're tired of negative feedback from the not-so-solid ones.

THE PROBLEM CHILD

The problem child. We've all had one, been one, or seen one. You know one when you encounter one. The *problem child* is disruptive, painfully obvious, and awkward for everyone involved. Years ago I saw a graph indicating managers/leaders devote 80% of their time to the problem child, hoping to take them from problem to good. In discussing this with a business colleague, the observation was, "Most leaders aren't ballsy enough to address the behavior. Healthy people watch the leader to see what the toxic person can get away with... as a result, the message is that it's not a safe place." I encourage leaders to shift their efforts, spending 80% of their time and energy growing their already *good* to *great*, and leaving 20% for the *problem child/children*. In working with leaders on their problem children, I suggest maxing out the 20%. Make the time count. Up your skillset to facilitate impactful non-triggering feedback sessions. Find your inner balanced best self so that you can be compassionate while still holding the problem child accountable. Be so strong in your own abilities that you can coach them through rough spots, minimizing team upset. Then use the extra time for strategic endeavors. Reserve your energy for those *moving the ball forward.*

Back to my colleague's comment. I don't think it is about *not being ballsy* necessarily. I think it is about not knowing how to handle a given situation. If leaders were capable and proactive in handling the problem child, which requires more than basic management skills, they would have more time for the other team members. When covering for the unhealthy/toxic person, you take your eye off the ball and lose sight of the whole. When fearful of losing a person due to their *short term impact*, you miss the *long term negative effects* on yourself, the team, and the organization. I cannot stress this enough. Problem children, a.k.a. unhealthy and toxic people, affect everyone on the team. *You cannot cover up enough to make it all right.*

One optimistic client announced his goal to me at the beginning of the year: 0% turnover, *no matter what.* I challenged him but he was resolved that this would be the year of no turnover. Despite his optimism, he spent an exorbitant amount of time with a new, high-level, experienced executive who exhibited a number of red flags, such as repeated client-facing mistakes, basic skill gaps, and strategic misalignment. *Yep*, he was sticking to his guns about no turnover, *doggone-it.* At great cost, much time, energy, and resources were applied, me included. "You need to refine your goal. How about no turnover of 'A' players?" With new awareness, he pivoted. He realized this new person was not of the same caliber as the team he had already assembled. Within weeks, he executed on his decision, let go of his *no turnover* goal, and to his surprise heard a collective *office sigh.* He had not realized the impact on everyone but fortunately they were quickly back on track.

Don't get me wrong, problem children can and do make amazing turn-arounds, if they are open and willing to do the work. And if gifted with strong and *kind feedback*, and if able to own their part in the problem. *I'm a coach, I love development.* There's nothing more fulfilling than witnessing a remarkable transformation, of which I have seen many. My point is, do not lose sight of those who are giving you their all, doing a great job already, day after day. If you believe your problem child has true potential and is recoverable, join forces with a strategic HR person and create a proactive, *inspiring* development plan—versus a *punitive* performance plan. Whether professional development, mentoring, and/or in-house resources, give your situation a time expectation in which to see progress, and feel confident moving forward no matter what.

Because everyone has core goodness, I see the problem child as a wounded individual. They feel misunderstood, or not seen, or they're carrying around too much baggage, or they have been hurt and have consequently created a huge protective wall, or maybe they just don't feel like they fit in, or they feel attacked, or they are hypersensitive to feedback, or they feel overwhelmed and out of control, or they are just dialing it in, and on and on.

Using the previous sentence and inserting concepts already presented (which are fixes), you will understand my optimism in growing the problem child: they feel misunderstood, or not seen (Core Self model, Authentic/CORE-Self, Self-worth, Ego), or they're carrying around too much baggage (Backpack, Leaves, Self-worth), or they have been hurt and have consequently created a huge protective wall (Leaves, Feeling Naked, Core Self model), or maybe they just don't feel like they fit in (Self-worth, Self-talk, Ego), or they feel attacked (Ego, Healthiness Scale, Emotional Elevator), or they are hypersensitive to feedback (Binary, Ego, Emotional Elevator), or they feel overwhelmed and out of control [Presence, Grounding, Amygdala Hijack (discussed in a later chapter), Circle of Control], or they are just dialing it in (Inspiration vs. Motivation, Imbalance).

Determine if your problem child is worth the investment, and if so, which resources are to be applied. Then determine if you are able/willing to provide the necessary, clear feedback, and how the new expectations will be implemented and measured.

UNHEALTHY

To be clear, the problem child is not a healthy person who has made a simple mistake, or a person who needs additional training or skill development to be a better contributor. The problem child is a person who is *energetically unhealthy*.

The unhealthy person is closed-minded—unable and unwilling to hear feedback. They rationalize their behavior as positive. *They are unaware that they are unaware.* Their ego is out of alignment (quiet people also have out-of-alignment egos, by the way). They operate to protect their egos and advance their own agendas with little regard to others. They are stubborn. They blame and play the victim. They are the person you don't want on your team—not because they are different, but because they are unhealthy. People feel disrespected and stepped on by them. Conversations are contentious. Despite all of this, the unhealthy person is often blind to poor intent. They believe in their misguided intentions of heroism and sacrifice because they are battling for the greater good.

Their ego is highly self-protective and cannot hear you, blocking out anything that messes with their sense-of-self. The only way to *deal with* or *motivate* an unhealthy person into awareness or action is by attaching actions to consequences. In my experience, it takes a lot to get through to this person. But once you do, they are devastated to find out how misguided they were. And wounded, hurt, and shocked to find out they are in fact the problem, hence the term *blow to the ego.*

However, deep down they are usually a good person. The work can begin when there is the slightest crack in their exterior. *Do you have the time, energy, and patience to take this on?* If not, be honest with yourself. Turning this person around requires a big commitment—feedback, patience, technique, and time. Does the organization have the trust capital to give this person yet another chance? Evaluate the team/organizational trust and patience for growing this person. Identify the person's intent, willingness to atone (out of true desire, not fear of job loss), and where they are on the scale—unhealthy, very-unhealthy teetering-on-toxicity, or just plain toxic. These are major determinants in moving forward with an unhealthy person. Most importantly, and often forgotten, you *must* maintain trust and healthiness with those you lead while turning around this one individual.

A hopeful SIDE NOTE: As previously mentioned, leaders often enter the coaching relationship unaware of their own understated internal funk. As they do their work and get closer to their Core/True Self, they in effect rise up on this scale. No matter where they started, they move upwards. This is hopeful news for developing unhealthy individuals. Using healthy optimistic strategies to raise a person up is exactly why my business is named UPwords Inc.

TOXIC

Like the unhealthy person, the toxic person is not happy. Although they are experienced by others as grouchy/sullen/withdrawn/easily triggered/burned out/unhappy/easily provoked, it is not necessarily how they see themselves. In denial, they challenge. Difficult to work with in the team setting, they infect others, and are known as cancerous. This know-it-all who is condescending and disrespectful might be a good person at the core, but their exterior is so thick and tough and impenetrable, there is no way their light can shine *out* or *in*.

Their malice is visible on the surface, despite inner core goodness. Unlike the unhealthy person, the toxic person is *ill*, and the ill-ness is *ill-intent*. Unconscious, unaware, and drowning in ego, their backpack is heavy. They protect—themselves, their knowledge, and their opinions. Strongly believing they are right, they lash out at those who find fault, call them out, or hold them accountable. Their outward behavior appears vengeful, which is the fine line between unhealthiness and toxicity. The toxic person's actions cannot be trusted. Their self-centeredness and self-saving instincts drive malicious behavior. Referencing the wounded child: when backed into a corner, they come out kicking, screaming, and biting. Determining unhealthy from toxic is as difficult and simple as, "Do I trust them?" "Do I trust their intention?" "Can I count on them to do the right thing in the end?"

If you've determined a person to be toxic, it is your responsibility as a leader to remedy the situation as swiftly as you can. No matter how superior their technical skills, they are infecting your organization. Have you given this person strong direct feedback? Have you provided clear expectations? Have they had an opportunity to change? Have consequences been applied? If so, you are "whole" in your decision to let them go. The only option left is to transition them out of the organization.

The president of a 300-person organization could not seem to let go of her CFO, despite repeated offenses, conversations, and warnings. As a strong leader, her hesitation surprised herself more than anyone. During our conversation, she realized she had not drawn the line in the sand with clear feedback, expectations, and consequences. Within the week, she initiated a tough and clear conversation. He quickly violated the terms, *and she let him go*. No hesitation, no regrets.

Because unhealthy and toxic people are unhappy, they usually know they need to leave, and have already initiated a job search. Sometimes their toxicity is situational, due to a personality clash, an unresolved slight, or an organizational change. Fortunately, in many of these situations, a simple job change turns them around, which is great for everyone. If the issue is a deeper, personal backpack issue, they will experience similar unhappiness at the new opportunity, continuing to get in their way unless they do their work (similar to a divorced person repeating the same partner profile).

When the toxic person *self-selects* out of the organization, despite the positives of them being gone, the leader is fortunately, but unfortunately, *off the hook*. It is a red flag that the leader may have waited too long to deal with this individual. These situations are opportunities to grow. If this is you, use the situation to learn—how to identify toxicity, how to provide feedback so a person hears it, to develop the person within reason, and to make the tough decision to part ways. After a toxic individual leaves voluntarily, almost always the client-leaders make comments like, "Things are so much better since person X is gone, I should have dealt with this a long time ago."

ORGANIZATIONAL HEALTH

I want to reiterate an earlier point. *You have a responsibility and an obligation to protect the healthy individuals in your organization from those who are toxic.* To some degree, others in the organization are counting on you to make the tough decision to cut out the cancer, and to keep them safe and healthy. If you do not, they will leave. Do not be surprised if you choose to not address toxicity and end up with morale issues, poor employee engagement, or a turnover problem. If you are, or are becoming, the leader I believe you to be, you know both unhealthiness and toxicity are intolerable issues for your organization, and a top priority requiring your attention.

There is a strong correlation between thriving organizational health and a culture rich in dynamic communication, productive robust dialogue, candid feedback loops, team-based collaboration, and self-confidence-based creativity and idea generation. If you take care of the basics—healthiness and morale—engagement and out of control turnover will be non-issues.

SIDE NOTE: There is a distinct parallel in a person's position on the Healthiness Scale and their connection to their Authentic/CORE-Self. Different language but similar concepts and effect.

EXERCISE: HEALTHINESS—
Total time: 10 minutes for Journaling, additional 30 minutes if you choose to include confidant feedback.
Evaluate yourself on the Healthiness Scale. Journal your conclusions. It need not be lengthy or complicated. Give yourself an honest score. If you dare, ask a trusted confidant for feedback. Give them permission to be honest, while being kind in their delivery. Then sit back, and listen without judgment or defensiveness. Take notes. *Thank them for their gift of feedback.* Actually, how you react to their feedback will give you additional information as to where you are on the scale.

SIMPLE AWARENESS
A colleague shared a story from her prior work experience related to unhealthy and toxic leaders. Her female upline was challenging and unhealthy. However, steering clear and working around her seemed to be a tolerable strategy, because in her words, "There just aren't a lot of great

leaders out there. There's a lot of mediocre leadership, and I just accepted the unhealthiness as one more instance of that." She went on to describe the organization's top leader—the one who was ultimately responsible for the organizational culture, modeling leadership for others to emulate. "She was just awful. SO TOXIC… such a toxic leader. It was really awful and it impacted everything. The culture was terrible. No wonder there was a ridiculous turnover problem. And yet, as a person outside of her role, she could be soft and kind… kind of a nice person. *I don't know, it was weird.*"

I suspect the leaves that needed to be cleaned out of this toxic leader's backpack were ones related to her *paradigm of leadership*. I encountered this same situation with a young, smart, ambitious, impressionable executive who watched her upline closely to learn how an established, esteemed leader operated. Then she absorbed and mimicked what she thought were amazing leadership skills from this person she respected and revered in leading her own team, not realizing her leadership role model was not the ideal leadership role model. *She'd learned his bad habits.* I remember the look on her face when she realized his kind of leadership was not the kind of leadership she wanted for herself—not as a direct report and certainly not as an *up and coming leader* leading others. Within seconds of this awareness, she had a huge revelation and completely transformed. Her growth was exponential. She intentionally decided on the kind of leader she wanted to be. Freed of her tightly held beliefs, she went on to do great things.

As my colleague and friend described the toxic leader situation from her former job, she was perplexed at the idea that this leader might have had core goodness within her. Based on her reaction to the insinuation a leader so awful might be a softie as a human being, it indicated to me that there might be a similar *paradigm of leadership* issue at play for this leader: *misguided intentions.* Based on her age and probable pool of leadership role models, her leadership lessons were most likely outdated and *cemented in* as beliefs, resulting in her bad behavior:

1. To make it in a man's world, you need to be tough

2. Feelings like compassion and sensitivity are a sign of weakness

3. Only the strong survive

4. As a woman in a man's world, I need to be extra tough, not show emotion—I need to be strong

5. The hammer is the only tool I need in my toolbox

6. I don't want to hear excuses

7. What I say goes—do not question me—I am the authority

8. Good leaders need to be strong

Mimicking the *"What's in your wallet?"* credit card commercial, if working with this leader, I would ask, *"What's in your backpack?"*

We all have backpacks. In my humble opinion, it is our responsibility to find out what is buried in them, and clean them out. However, this requires awareness. Which ego-based artifacts, *not memories*, are the most expendable and should be tossed? The more insidious and damaging are of course the main priority. If you are able, figure out the most lethal and toxic beliefs powering your operating system. Your longevity as a healthy leader depends on it.

HIRING FOR HEALTHY

Learn to identify healthiness. It is a true *talent strategy*. Reward *healthiness* and *self-growth*. This is an easy and inexpensive way to instill a mindset of continuous improvement and vibrancy in your organization. Promoting, rewarding, and hiring for healthiness positively impacts everyone on the team. In the end, you will enjoy phenomenal business success when hiring healthy people as a default *talent acquisition* strategy.

Equally impactful is a second level strategy that includes continued development for already employed individual contributors and leaders, including yourself. The #1 reason cited for job change/turnover is *my manager*. Healthy organizations and healthy leaders attract healthy new hires, and help retain healthy employees. Do your work.

The Healthiness Scale is a critical triage tool that has come to my rescue many, many times. I encourage you to use it as well. A CEO client was in the process of hiring a new leader for his leadership team, a crucial role organizationally. He asked for my input during our coaching session, "What is *your* feedback in hiring for this role? What do you think we should be looking for?" He was a bit taken aback by the simplicity of my answer, "Healthiness. Period. *It is a basic, fundamental, must have.*"

LIGHT UP THE WORLD

Your clean energy will light up the world. May you spark a revolution of healthiness, presence, and conscious leadership. May your actions inspire, influence, and guide others to great heights. May you plug into your true power—operating, leading, and energizing from your healthy energetic core.

Limits and Boundaries

Personally I prefer the idea of limits over boundaries. Energetically setting my limits originates internally and requires proactive intention. Knowing myself, determined from within, I choose how far out I want to extend myself. I decide what will and will not enter into my consciousness. Conversely, a boundary is merely a fear-based response to someone else. Protecting myself from intrusion reactively. Barricading myself emotionally and/or physically.

The words themselves do not matter as much as the subtle conceptual and energetic mindset they create. What is important is the deep sense of knowing within yourself—what you willingly allow or take in. When grounded, *your inner being knows when it has been wronged*. This sense that a line has been crossed is *personal resolve*. You know who you are, what you deserve, what you need to do to flourish, and how to always have your own back.

When you reach the point of enough is enough (it happens), check yourself. You already know/feel/understand the importance of staying high on your Emotional Elevator floors. As tempted as you might be to get off on a lower level floor, you will not benefit. Your ability to stay on the upper floors depends on your personal internal core strength. Knowing and exercising strength in establishing boundaries prevents you from dropping down to lower level emotions. You can prevent giving away your power by grounding, being present, reframing, and knowing YOU.

Fortunately for you, your physical body is more aware of your anger, guilt, despair, or other power-robbing emotions faster than your brain can register. Your body sends out a distress signal the moment you have lost your power to those lower level emotions. Any time you are out of energetic alignment, your body lets you know. You might feel tightness in your chest, your back might seize up, perhaps you develop hives or a tension headache, or maybe even a stomachache. When your body talks, it behooves you to listen.

I answered my office phone to hear a friend excitedly ask what I was doing Thursday. Ugh. Without context, and not exactly sure what I was getting myself into, I hesitantly responded, "Nothing that I know of." Was she talking about the day? The evening? Business? Personal? She explained she was having an evening get together (I don't recall which product, but think Tupperware™ party). I immediately felt tightness in my chest. Honoring this body signal, I said, "Hey, I am feeling a tightness in my chest, which is an indication something is off, so let me check my calendar. Oh. I see. I am busy every night except Thursday, so I really need to use that evening to keep my life on track. I hope you have a great time, and if my schedule opens up I'll let you know." Sunny disposition intact, she said she got it and that I should call back if anything changed. All good. I honored myself, and I respected her—with the truth. P.S. When I tell this story, people ask if this is really what I said… *yes, almost verbatim.*

I share this story as an example of the power to which I've been alluding. Pay attention and listen to your body's clues. Stay powerful by honoring yourself when something (anything) does—or more importantly, does not—work for you. Readjust. Balance. People give away their power all the time, foregoing what their body is telling them, to protect the other person and their feelings. *In essence we are knocking ourselves out of alignment to protect and respect other people.* Consistently foregoing yourself, choosing to respect the other person in lieu of honoring yourself, causes binary imbalance. Be mindful of your inner guidance—it tips you off when you are out of alignment.

Balancing within the *honor self while respecting others* spectrum gives you the power to expand. Honoring what is important to you. Listening to your inner voice. Doing what you know is right (for you). Maybe it's knowing you deserve better, not because you are better than anyone else in comparison, but because you are a human being. Period. All human beings deserve to be treated well. By others of course, *but first and foremost by one's self.* Hold yourself in high regard. If you do, wonderful things will result, like having the capacity to treat others with grace and compassion.

The LIMITS of the EGO

As you grow and expand, your ego will want to get involved. Particularly righteous, and exhibiting total dominance, your ego wants to help you feel *more*—stronger, better, smarter, etc. For instance, when you encounter a person who you perceive to be on a lower Emotional Elevator floor, your ego opens the door, allowing a satisfying sense of superiority to creep in, well because… per the ego, you are obviously on a higher floor than them, which means you are better and more successful. If aware, you catch yourself in this game of subliminal stack-ranking. But unfortunately once you notice, it is already too late. Awareness means you are already dropping down the elevator shaft. Your speed and agility to halt the descending momentum and turn yourself around is indicative of your core strength, the work you've done, and your energetic healthiness.

In a business setting, it might play out like this. You join an already established work team. You identify a member of the team who is, from your perspective, quite low on the scale. You consider him to be blame-oriented and angry. You don't like him because he's so negative. Instead of staying conscious and separate, you let yourself get distracted, detour, and end up joining him in *unconscious negativity*. You judge and label him *Grouchy Guy*. Perfect and so fitting. You share the nickname with a few people on the team. They laugh and think it's hilarious, because it is so true. This elevates you. It catches on, and you too are labeled, the new cool funny kid on the team. All while Mr. Grouchy Guy's identity is cemented. As harmless as it is, your impact on Grouchy Guy is quite damaging. Ironically, in the long run you end up being less conscious than Grouchy Guy.

Here's the crazy thing about Grouchy Guy, something you might not have considered. What if Grouchy Guy actually worked really hard to make the progress he is demonstrating? What if he'd actually improved? What if he had elevated himself from emotions like jealousy, rage, hatred, and despair a few months ago to today's emotions of blame and anger? Relatively speaking, for him, blame and anger are milestones and signify huge progress. He feels better since he has worked his way *up*. Fascinating, right? This means Grouchy Guy is doing his work. Yay for him! And you just derailed him with your judgment. You and the team have made it extremely difficult for him to stay on track and continue his progress. As a matter of fact, this new nickname might send him back to square one. While you might have been on an upper floor when you joined the team, you are about to descend. You've literally lowered yourself by judging him. This can be prevented with both conscious and conscientious choices.

Our goal is to be on the upper floors of our Emotional Elevator. Not understanding the process, we attempt shortcuts. We expect to get to the top in one giant leap. Can you imagine standing on the bottom rung of a ladder, willing yourself to get to the top rung in one giant heartfelt and intentional step? All the intention in the world can't do that. As much as I appreciate the desire, the ambition, and the can-do attitude, this cannot be done. The same holds true for this process. It requires time, intention, awareness, focus, and patience.

STRATEGIES unLIMITed

What happens when you run into real life red-hot situations? These situations unfold in a blink of an eye, and if unprepared, send you spinning. If not practiced, you will not have the wherewithal to handle these situations in the moment. Well, not with your desired outcome anyway. Reacting in a healthy way requires proactive practice.

Despite the desire for clarity and resolution, clients, often, *often*, opt for paralysis versus moving into action because they are afraid to offend. This is another backpack souvenir, by the way. This binary mindset releases us from proactively practicing tactical strategies, thinking we do not have real options. But we do. Work through your immediate real-life situations to develop muscle memory. With competency, you will experience relief and resolution when future situations occur. Trust builds. Awareness and capability grows. Challenging situations will be less intense or hopeless, and issues will turn into non-issues. Once you've arrived at this place, new considerations will arise: "What is the best outcome for all involved?" and "What am I willing to do to achieve the desired outcome?"

Despite our old beliefs of nonconfrontation, a real conversation emanating from the Authentic/CORE-Self is one of the healthiest and kindest things you can do for another person. However, this is often a critical moment when leaders hesitate, allowing their old beliefs to take precedence, which does not serve as an effective catalyst for change. Initiating a real conversation requires courage, capability, and introspection.

The assumption is that the hesitation in initiating a real conversation stems from not wanting to offend. I believe the real issue is about *not wanting to feel uncomfortable.* Or lacking the skillset to have a sticky conversation. It is awkward and risky, and requires finesse. Something to consider, if you choose to forego a real conversation, *you* are the one carrying the ongoing burden of tension and misalignment within the relationship. This means you have already accepted un-ease about the situation. If you can own your feelings of discomfort in initiating the conversation, you will see they (you and your feelings, not the other person) have become the priority. Your discomfort has trumped peace. If you really respect the other person, care enough for yourself to not carry around the extra weight, believe you are able to do the right thing, and want to be in alignment, be courageous and give the gift of being real. If the other person, your relationship, and YOU are worth it, you will take the risk.

An authentic conversation is usually all it takes to reset a relationship, which often results in a resounding and collective sigh of relief for all parties. I encourage you to literally use the words *intention* and *impact* while having this real and kind conversation. These words provide a template for you to dive in, deal with, and move on, with your relationship intact. Down the road you might even chuckle over the misunderstanding.

When out of alignment, swirling in and around the topics at hand, your mind is on hyper-speed. Your human-ego-self and your inner-spirit-self are not in sync. They are swirling and stuck in a particular storyline. This is as exhausting for everyone to whom you tell the story as it is to you. You have options.

As a reminder from Section I, one of these three options will help you move forward:

1. Make peace with the story—let it go, it no longer matters

2. Change the story—move into action and change the outcome

3. Leave the story—sometimes you do not see a way out despite attempts to resolve the situation, and you need to extract yourself

I've recently added a fourth, which to me is the healthiest of all, a combination of the previous three…

4. *Reframe the story*:

   a. Make peace and find the positive silver linings

   b. Change the story to see things from a new perspective with a new level of understanding. Maybe even feel gratitude for how it turned out

   c. Leave (make peace with) the original story/talk track because it no longer has the same dire ending you originally anticipated. Understanding the intention, not just the impact, helps you see things in a new light. As the perspective changes, the new vantage point helps you let go and move on

My daughter worked a small, part time, non-career job while looking for her bigger career job. When she finally landed her very cool Social Media Manager career role (for a company she loves) she was so happy. The only catch was that the new opportunity was only part time. She suddenly felt very trapped by the small job. Unable to quit, she was angry and irritated every time she went in. In addition to feeling trapped, she was simultaneously and rapidly dropping down her Emotional Elevator. Overall, she was crabbier. *Blech.* Fortunately, she realized this was happening and did a quick reset. She acknowledged her energy was not good, which did not benefit her while searching for another freelance gig. Fortunately, her turnaround did not take long. She called me to say, "You know what? I did some reframing. You want to hear it? I can live the way I've been living with the new job, which means I can quit the other job if I want to. But because I really want to save some money to upgrade my life, this offers me a perfect opportunity to do just that. So I choose to work there for now. Yes, it is my choice, and this will help me start saving for my other goals. I'm approaching it with a new perspective." I was bursting with motherly pride!

KNOWING YOU

Breaking old habits is hard. You might still be living with long-ago created boundaries instead of *new you* honoring limits. When you do your work and find your true limits, share them with others. Stand up for yourself when something feels off. Be kind in the sharing. Stay on your higher floors, knowing others approach you from their own perspective.

Sometimes, their perspectives are misguided and judgmental. If you are not strongly rooted in who you are, you might accept their perspective. It is *their* perspective, not yours. Know and share your limits so you do not give away your power or erect boundaries defensively.

Your limits may flex depending on the situation, where you are in your life, or based on the person with whom you are interacting. The rigidity of your limits is based on your backpack's contents. As you clean things out, limits will change, or disappear altogether. Actually, my hope for you is that you become unlimited. *Clean and fresh with unlimited potential.*

EXERCISE: LIMITS—
Total Time: 30 minutes

Review your initial responses to the sense-of-self exercise in the beginning of the book. Based on those responses, what are your limits? When/where are you strong in your convictions, and when/where do you waver? Is there a pattern? A theme? Journal your thoughts.

Intention vs. Impact

I excitedly answered the call when I saw my best friend's name on the Caller ID. Foregoing her warm greeting, she cut right to the chase and asked me to repeat something from a previous conversation. She must have sensed my blank stare, because she continued, "You know, that thing you said about our intention and how we view ourselves. It was life changing." *Oh. I knew exactly what she was referencing.* She was right. This simple concept is easy to understand and difficult to exercise. However, mastery will provide you a lifelong ROI.

Intention vs. Impact.
We judge ourselves based on our intention.
We judge others based on their impact.

The greater the gap, the greater the rift,
the bigger the hurt, the pain, and the conflict.

It bears repeating.

We judge ourselves based on our intention. When someone insists we've hurt them, our standard wide-eyed response is, "No That was not my intention." We expect total forgiveness. It was their mistake for underestimating our intention.

We judge others based on their impact. When someone hurts us, and they say, "No! That was not my intention." With admonishment, we respond, "But, you hurt me, c'mon." We expect an apology. Their mistake was doing whatever it was they did, underestimating the pain they caused.

Do you get this? Do you see how incongruous this is? If not, please reread the definition above. It's important you understand this concept before moving on.

The world, our world, would be a much better place if we judged ourselves on our impact vs. our intention. No matter how good or pious our intention, owning our actions and the impact on others would be a giant leap forward for mankind. *Do I impact with joy and light, or hurt and pain? What was my role in that person's experience? Did the impact match my intention?* I am not suggesting their reaction is your responsibility or your fault when intention and impact do not align. I am suggesting that, if you are a strong, grounded, authentic, and aware person, attempting to be the best version of you, when a communication gap is identified, you should address it. Check for understanding. Clarify. Restate.

Holding yourself accountable for impact will be a total game changer.

Likewise, the world, *our world*, would be a much better place if we judged others based on their intentions. Regardless of our feelings and reactions, stepping outside of ourselves to understand the other person's true intention is equally powerful. *Did they really intend to hurt me? Am I able to get outside of my own experience to view the situation from a different perspective? What was their true intention? Did the person truly intend to inflict pain, evoke guilt, or shame me?* A perfect example of this is when you are cut off on the expressway. Your reaction (anger) is based on the impact to you. What happens to your anger if you consider their intention? What if their intention was to get to the hospital to say goodbye to a dying parent, or had just found out their child had been hurt. You never know.

Giving others the benefit of the doubt by considering their intention would again be a total game changer.

By now, you know I believe every being has goodness at their core. The same holds true for intention. *Most people are in fact well-intentioned.* More often than not, despite the impact, most people do not intentionally set out to cause pain.

The greater the pain (impact), the more blind we are to true intention. It is too difficult to get outside of ourselves. As we focus on our wounds, the other person's intention is not in our awareness. Only when grounded and whole are we able to look outside ourselves and extend grace to a person who has hurt us, to repair the misunderstanding.

Awareness of intention and impact helps us to be conscious. And when conscious, we have choice. And with choice comes responsibility— to ourselves, and to those with whom we are interacting.

Here are a few *conversation starter* examples regarding intention and impact.

Template Conversation Starters

Use a variation of these template phrases to share a misunderstanding.

1. "What was your intention when X happened, because this is how it impacted me..."
2. "This was the impact X had on me, but I'm sure that was not your intention... "
3. "What was your intention regarding X?"... "Oh, I thought so. Because this is how it impacted me, but I figured it was not what you meant."

As a follow up to our intention and impact conversation, I asked my BFF, who I've known since high school, if I'd ever done anything to upset her. I loved her response. "No never! We have so much trust between us. I would never believe you had anything but my best interest at heart. We talk about everything so proactively and directly, there's really not an opportunity for a misunderstanding."

It's true. With a full "trust bank," we easily extend the benefit of the doubt when it comes to intention and impact. If the gap grows, you know there is a bigger trust issue that needs to be addressed, a.k.a. calling out the elephant in the room.

It is my intention that you learn and use this simple concept/technique to quickly impact areas in your life, as it is one of my very favorite client tools.

EXERCISE: INTENTION VS. IMPACT—
Total Time: 15 minutes

Attempt an intention vs. impact conversation using one of the template conversation starters above. Later, Journal the outcome.

Pendulum Syndrome

As I purchased and remodeled my new house and thus my life, I found a need for a few new pieces. By following the serendipitous trail of breadcrumbs I ended up connecting with a guy who referred to himself as a vintage picker/artist/reseller—taking old things and breathing life into them again. Not a fan of old necessarily, I do like the clean lines inspired by mid-century modern as well as the coolness of *functional becomes art* simplicity, so I was intrigued.

I had an interesting run with this guy, securing some beautiful pieces—like the two refurbished Hollywood studio lights taken out of a legit studio, a one-of-a-kind lamp, and my 1960s super-cool barware set. Many wins. And unfortunately, a few noteworthy losses, mostly stemming from his cut-off-your-ear moody artist guy energy, which I quite frankly chose to overlook, because I was focused on the finish line. My bad.

When he went into a downward spiral, I was over-intentionally kind and understanding of his intentions. I extended grace. Lots of it. This can only happen when grounded, present, and interacting from the Authentic/CORE-Self, so I was grateful I was in this state of mind. I stayed out of ego mode even as delivery deadlines were missed and agreed upon next steps were forgotten.

I bring this up to share a valuable point. Not everyone is in a position to receive and give back from a place of authenticity (for a variety of reasons mentioned in the Worthiness, Self-talk, Energetic Health, Getting in Your Own Way, and Backpack chapters). As important as it was that I stay grounded, present, and aware, it was equally important I be aware of my boundaries, or rather, my limits. *Limits* are the outer edges of me intersecting with the edges of another, not allowing those edges to blur, maintaining what is important to me, not settling, and honoring self. What is happening inside of another person is on them. Not my responsibility. I can only be the best version of me, while extending grace and respect to them during our interaction.

As mentioned in the Energetic Health chapter, my first step in triaging any situation is to assess a person's healthiness using this scale to determine next steps.

1. Evolved

2. Healthy

3. Neutral

4. Unhealthy

5. Toxic

CAUGHT IN THE SWING

Ultimately, people show you who they are, and it is critical you pay attention. In the above situation, I made the same mistake as many leaders, extending the benefit of the doubt despite red flags. Giving the benefit of the doubt is great when dealing with healthy or evolved people, not necessarily unhealthy or toxic people. Because I was conscious (which is a good thing), and very intentional about staying grounded while also high on my Emotional Elevator, I thought I could handle the situation and work around his unhealthiness. In effect, I ignored the red flags and over-extended grace while working with him to get the results I wanted. There were many pieces in the works, and as a result I extended grace a little too far. *Sound familiar?* Walking on eggshells, extending grace beyond reason, stifling what I was thinking and feeling, and finding and referencing only the positive (even when there were very real negatives). With much at stake, I inadvertently compromised myself.

I reference my then *state of mind* as the *Pendulum Syndrome.*

To counterbalance my angst and concern, I swung in the opposite direction, to kindness and grace. Because of the pendulum effect, I overcorrected and over-swung, settling and compromising my SELF. Like an algebraic equation, I hoped the factors would cancel each other out in my effort to stay the course. Instead I fell out of balance.

Imbalance

On some level, we all desire inner knowingness and personal power. I remember the first time I saw *Maslow's Hierarchy of Needs* back in college—its impact significant as it awakened a desire in me. Looking at the pyramid, *basic needs, physiological and safety*, are at the bottom layer (think: food, water, rest, and security/safety). *Psychological needs* such as belonging, love, and esteem (think: love, relationships, friends, and sense of accomplishment) make up the mid-section, and at the top is *self-actualization*—achieving one's full potential. In my language it meant being the best version of one's self. I had an instant desire to reach self-actualization, the holy grail. I have no doubt *the achiever* in me was triggered, but it also triggered a hunger, deeper than my egoic nature. Inspirational and Peaceful. Fulfilling and Evolved. Another seed for inner growth implanted into my young subconscious. Since Maslow's theory was just that, a theory, versus a validated model, with little research or further explanation, I was on my own.

I'm not sure when my personal search began exactly, but I have always had a desire for connection, consciousness, and transformation. Even as an angsty teen, I walked to the wooded 10-acre parcel at the back of my parents' 80-acre farm. I would walk and walk, taking in the awesomeness of nature. Finally, finding a spot that felt right, I would sit on a fallen tree trunk, contemplate, and *be*, long before I had any awareness of what I was doing. I cherished those moments of peaceful wholeness.

Over the years, I learned that merely wanting wholeness wasn't enough. It required work and was not for the faint-of-heart. The prerequisite was openness. Specifically, openness to a mind transformation, which for me came later in adulthood.

During a coaching immersion weekend after I first started my business, I learned of a psychological concept that initially confused me. During the program, the facilitator made an off-the-cuff remark that everybody in the room, with the exception of one participant, was *object-identified*. Based on his tone, I knew immediately this was not a good thing. And I was not the one who had earned his gracious observation. My ego was especially agitated. Wondering how I could grow out of this state of mind, feeling trapped in a weird way, I had the same suspended Maslow moment I had had in college. I wanted (needed) to expand. Yes, I'm sure, initially this (again) triggered my goal-oriented inner achiever. But I realized in hindsight that my harsh and misplaced self-judgment originated from his judgment, *which was exactly the object-identification to which he was referring*. Hilarious! Even with this awareness, I was not ready to fully grasp the concept of subject/object identification, or to get out of my own way, for many more years.

As the nucleus or subject of our own lives we are *subject-identified*. Cast as the central figure in our life drama, we enjoy our own unique existence, consciousness, and (inner) experiences, as well as the ability to observe what is going on around us from the central perspective, much like the center pole of a merry-go-round. Although this makes sense logically, and seems easily attainable, as humans, subject-identification is actually quite challenging. It is neither our default mode nor our natural state of being. Growing this way requires focus and practice, and an intentional shift in thinking toward expanded consciousness.

Object-identification, on the other hand, is our default mode. Thanks to the ego, object-identification is a mental orientation that assigns power to objects around and outside of us. *We give power to objects to define us.* When other people/other people's opinions/stuff/the tornado around you/ material objects and possessions become your central orientation, they in essence become your sun and your moon, your compass, and your sense-of-self. Without realizing it, when object-identified you forfeit having a say in your identity or sense-of-self. You willingly open yourself up to the judgment and opinions of others. Note: If you feel resistance about object-identification like I did, know it is not the same as materialism. When object-identified, because you are not centered or at the center, you are off balance and imbalanced.

OFF BALANCE

Daily challenges, situations, people, and objects constantly test your inner strength and balance. To some degree these little things are even more threatening than the big things, because they are so insidious.

- Your non-stop internal mental chatter
- An overheard conversation (about you) at the water cooler
- Self-talk and feelings of self-doubt (i.e. prepping for a big presentation, looking in the mirror, avoidance of any kind)
- A reaction to a material thing (your neighbor's new car, and the resulting pressure to buy a new car to stay relevant etc., etc.)
- An unhealthy or toxic person on a lower Emotional Elevator floor attempting to drag you into a negative conversation
- A very heavy, filled-to-the top backpack, causing exhaustion and an easily ignited short fuse
- Another person's ego-based reaction about a comment you made, making you feel guilty and responsible

At this point your ego is strong but not necessarily healthy or wise, and with much (ego) imbalance and immature footing, you get knocked off, over and over again. A wise quote from the Karate Kid's Mr. Miyagi, "Lesson not just karate only. Lesson for whole life. Whole life have a balance. Everything be better." A great visual for this *whole life* balance is the Karate Kid practicing his Crane Pose atop a tree stump on the beach. It is here he learns to maintain physical balance by way of his own inner strength. The same goes for you. When not accessing your inner strength, in subtle and slight ways *you are giving away your power*.

TOPPLE MOMENTS

When problems arise, we often rely on a few learned, default mode, go-to emotions. Quickly accessed and overleveraged, without awareness, these emotions overtake us and cause *topple moments*. We lose our footing and thus our balance, causing us to get caught in our own chaos. The natural internal tendency is to blame and justify the imbalance on a situation or person, solidifying the I-am-a-victim mindset. Be careful, with artful self-deception you might even convince family and friends to support you, justifying bad behavior and encouraging low-level emotions like retribution and immature outbursts, all designed to protect you from perceived wrongdoings, causing blind spots and the very undesirable consequence of being off balance. This is when you are not conscious and at the lower end of your Emotional Elevator.

Ultimately this state of being infects other areas of your life. If comfortably stuck in this loop for too long, without awareness or intention, you learn to function in this *well worn groove*, a.k.a. rut.

The good news is that with *conscious awareness* you have choice. You can wallow in the current state of being, or you can rise up, ground yourself, learn the lessons, and flow within the bigger picture. There are great lessons to be learned in these topple moments, if you take the time to focus in to see what else is there. For instance, one of those positive lessons might be discovering the theme of your default, negative emotions.

DEFAULT EMOTIONS

Default emotions are our go-to emotions when out of balance. We typically use (and overuse) the same few in every sticky situation, even when different emotions would be more appropriate. Identifying your default emotions is understanding what causes imbalance, more than it is an actual emotion. Is there one you intuitively know is your default negative emotion? Personally, my favorite has always been *anger*. It is so very handy in so many situations. And it masks my true emotions. With easy access to anger, I didn't need to be vulnerable or varied in my emotional range. Illustrated below are examples of how this go-to emotion applies to previously presented concepts and models.

1. *Intent vs. Impact*: The intention is to show seriousness, force results, and ultimately protect others… using anger. The intention is for the better good. The impact, however, is that others experience fear. Fear that they will be on the receiving end of the anger in the future.

2. *What's underneath*: What is underneath this pretense of anger is hurt, damage, and negative impact, triggering (without realizing it) shame and guilt. You can see that many emotions are masked by the emotional anger catch-all.

3. *Ego*: In an effort to uphold and feed the identity belief of the protector, anger is used to intimidate and encourage better behavior in others, on behalf of those we are protecting.

4. *Motivation vs. Inspiration*: Anger engages to motivate performance and prove oneself, especially when challenged. "I'll show them what I'm made of—argh." And one does.

All well-intended strategies, this demonstrates the limitations of our toolbox. Rather than trying to turn two wrongs into a right, a better strategy might be to expand the toolbox.

COUNTERING IMBALANCE

Sometimes, when consciously attempting to stay whole, you can overcorrect. Especially early on, in an effort to maintain balance (and not topple over), while still very wobbly, there is a tendency to misuse and overuse variations of *binary mindset* and *Pendulum Syndrome*. Because you are working to stay grounded, see new perspectives, and open your awareness, you can swing back and forth through trial and error before settling into the center. During this period, it is easy to accidentally absorb others' unhealthiness.

Here is how it happens:
1. We give the other person the benefit of the doubt, which means

2. We let them off the hook, and as a result,

3. We do not hold them accountable. Ultimately,

4. We allow the other person to act out in a way that is detrimental to our psyche. In that instance, on some level,

5. We dishonor and betray ourselves by standing there like a human sponge, as

6. We absorb their unhealthiness, usually in the name of being nice.

There were times, especially in toxic situations, when I lost my footing because, while intentionally grounded, balanced, fair, and gracious, I listened and gave credence to my old *I am strong enough to take it* beliefs. It caused me to overcompensate. I think on some level I thought the other person not healthy enough or strong enough to handle *kind feedback* (unhealthy/toxic), so I took it in versus handing it back to them. In these moments, thinking I was standing in my power, I put my head down to get through it, staying cool and level-headed. I didn't realize my imbalance and allowed myself to be walked on. Even now, if not conscious, I can overextend kindness because I understand their intention. It requires self-evaluation and awareness to balance in these moments.

This is an example of *short circuiting our own power line*—stepping over and extending a disproportionate amount of grace while dishonoring ourselves, taking in and accepting poor behavior and tolerating poor treatment. This is often an after-the-fact awareness, but once we have the awareness, *we can't not honor it.* We would serve ourselves well to pre-determine our limits in such instances.

In the early stages of my development journey, I had been metaphorically holding my breath—waiting, watching, reacting. Needing a cathartic outlet, I had to release my breath. For me, that meant releasing emotions, starting with breath work and ending in cleansing tears. This proved to be an excellent private physical outlet, not necessarily the best in public. It is important you figure out your preferred and best way to release and get unstuck. A few client favorites are loud outdoor screaming, aggressive physical workouts, meditation, hot baths, journaling (one of my favorites as well), and a technique I use in the coaching engagement, called E.F.T. (Emotional Freedom Technique) or tapping.

THE TOLL OF IMBALANCE

There was a particular past situation which caused me imbalance. It was exactly as I described above. My view of this particular person was personal fragility and unhealthiness (unhealthy/toxic). I went into *since I can take it, I should* mode, and put my head down to get through it. In my effort to stay cool and levelheaded, while standing in my power, I overextended kindness (*do you see a pattern?*), allowed myself to be misunderstood, and worked around the unhealthy behaviors. The more I interacted with this person, the more and more imbalanced I became. Metaphorically speaking, my backpack was full, heavy, and burdensome. Obviously triggered, I started emptying out and reviewing the old hurts and pains and saved leaves. This was when I realized those artifacts no longer served me, and in fact were harmful, driving rut-like behaviors and reactions in me. Instinctively, because of where I was in my journey, I knew it was time to actively and deliberately clean out my backpack. Sitting quietly by myself, reflecting on those blockages, slights, and hurts, I took in l-o-n-g deep breaths, released, and allowed myself to cry. Not forcing tears, but mentally opening up this particular faucet and allowing whatever was trapped to pour out. I knew the release of tension was important but hadn't realized how much I had compartmentalized over time until it was flowing out of me. It was... *and is* important to let it go and create space—space for self-honoring, self-forgiveness, and self-compassion. The tears gently flowed out—before bed and again in the morning upon waking. Then it was over. An emotional backpack clean out is a kindness from which I always benefit.

There is a direct correlation between the deliberate work of consciousness and the speed at which we rebound, shift, and learn lessons of silver-lining gratitude. Personally, the more aware and conscious I am, the fewer topple moments I have, and the less the need for a release. To me, this is *ultimate balance* and power.

What causes you imbalance? I'm sure there is a pattern. Maybe you subliminally know what it is. Perhaps it is a blind spot. Do you have a default emotion? And how does it get in your way? What indirect messages are you sending when you are out of balance or swirling? Specifically as a leader, how does this pattern erode trust? What communications are you missing (or twisting) because you are not grounded and present?

EXERCISE: BALANCE A—
Total Time: 50 minutes

You have a choice. Opt for this bigger general exercise (A), or go in depth in the following two exercises (B) and (C). If you are able to dig in and have awareness, I recommend this one; however, either option will benefit you.

Journal your thoughts to the questions listed in the paragraph above (*What causes you imbalance? Do you have a default emotion? And how does it get in your way? What indirect messages are you sending when you are out of balance or swirling? Specifically as a leader, how does this pattern erode trust? What communications are you missing (or twisting) because you are not grounded and present?*)

EXERCISE: BALANCE B—
Total Time: 20 minutes

What is your default emotion or pattern of behavior? Write your response in your Leadership Journal.

EXERCISE: BALANCE C—
Total Time: 20 minutes

What is your favorite way to let your default emotion *out*? If you don't have awareness around this, please contemplate what action might best benefit your release. Write your response in your Leadership Journal.

BE-ING AN IMBALANCED HUMAN

It's taken me the better part of my life to get to this place, where I am centered and calm when caught in a metaphorical tornado. It has been a very intentional practice to learn (*yes, it is learned*) to rise above. That's how I picture it anyway. The chaos is swirling and while I am tempted to drop down and swirl in those lower-level emotions, with realization, I cue up my internal visualization—levitating up and out vertically. I can see what's going on, while not a part of it. This has not always been the case.

I have plenty of *before* stories. Even today, if out of balance, particularly triggered, or not present, I can get caught. However, today the difference is when I do, it is a quick dip and a relatively fast bounce back, with an opportunity to reframe, and have gratitude for the lesson learned.

Allow me to share a *before* story that surely reveals my once-upon-a-time immaturity, and demonstrates the ease in which one can get caught in a self-imposed swirl. After work, a few of us decided to meet at the local watering hole located on the ground floor of our office building. I was in sales for a Fortune 100 company, which is only relevant to let you know we ran in a pack—*Stepford salespeople*, all 100 of us, females and males, carbon copies of one another, dressed impeccably, driven, wound tight, working together by day and playing together by night. To this day, these are some of my best friends. Anyway, this particular evening, while standing in the back of the happy hour section with a drink in hand, nursing my boyfriend issues, two teammates consoled me as I spun emotionally *out of control*. My female teammate left to use the ladies room, which gave my male teammate latitude to amp it up, step in close, lock eyes, and share his wisdom from the male perspective. It was intense, as were my emotions. From the corner of my eye, I saw two young professional women looking at us. *No, staring at us.* Staring at *me. My God, what was their problem? Were they staring at me because I was crying? Seriously? How rude!* My attention was split between them and my colleague's encouragement to dump the guy. They continued to stare and snicker, or so I thought. Emotionally immature and in a fragile imbalanced state, I couldn't take it anymore. I dramatically whipped my head around and said, "What is your problem, why are you staring at me?" Well, as it turned out, they had definitely been staring at me. They were waiting to get my attention. *To tell me how much they loved my suit.* They thought it was incredible. Silence. I attempted amends. And rightly so, they were having none of it. They gave me the cold shoulder and turned their backs on me.

First of all, this was a classic example of intention vs. impact causing a huge misunderstanding, resulting in a contentious situation. If only I had had the ability to get outside myself to understand their intention vs. assuming I knew what was going on. Ugh. So embarrassing. I shortsightedly focused on the impact it had caused me. Secondly, I was so wrapped in my own junk (think: backpack, worthiness, self-talk, and low level Emotional Elevator spiraling default emotions) that I could not see past myself. There was just no way. Given my low-level swirling, I did not have much leeway to respond healthily. Thirdly, it is easy to lose it when in the eye of the tornado; you are sucked in and out of control. We are human, and it happens. Please do not be too hard on yourself. However this might be another call to action to do your work—*grow, get healthy, and evolve.*

If the visualization of *rising out of the tornado* is too challenging for you, try one of the others, like *grounding*. Picture your strong hearty tree roots connecting you to the center of the Earth, grounding you as the chaotic tornado is swirling around you. Another favorite of mine exercises mental agility: Moving quickly to the center of the *merry-go-round*, taking a deep breath, and observing the chaos swirling around me, while I go unscathed.

As you grow, get healthy, and evolve, your ability to rise above the chaos, or stay grounded and solid during the tornado, or move to the center of the merry-go-round will become easier and easier. Earlier, you learned these balancing strategies also represented present moment awareness. Walking the tightrope is especially challenging when not balanced. Between constant and ongoing stress and the undisciplined mind, it is easy to fall off. Being grounded, focused, and practiced is especially important. Our perspective transforms, and the precarious thread-like balancing act turns into a confident walk on a wider, stronger support system. My favorite image of this extends 70 feet over the rim of the Grand Canyon, and 2,000 feet above the canyon floor. The *Grand Canyon Skywalk* is an unbelievably strong four-inch-thick glass support that has the strength to hold seven fully-loaded 747s. Tourists can see up, down, and around, while trusting its strength and sturdiness. The same holds true for you while standing in your power. You have the same unbelievable strength inside you. When grounded, focused, and practiced, you too will be supported by your own version of the Grand Canyon Skywalk.

Previously, I mentioned *anger* was a favorite negative default emotion in my younger years—a very handy tool for my prematurely mature, inner adult child. Anger helped me showcase big emotions like frustration, irritation, impatience, and strength. Anger filled in for my less accessed *seemingly wimpy* emotions like sadness, hurt, pain, and grief. In many ways, as I was walking my own personal tightrope, any little push or slight, hurt or injustice would give me just the right nudge and reason to fall off. All under the guise of anger.

As it turns out, getting angry in all of its various forms was a favorite way for me to give away my power. It had to have been, because I accessed it so often. I was comfortable in my own personal emotional rut. Losing control and allowing myself to swirl—not consciously staying grounded or rising above—was an entry point for anger, which sent me spiraling down on my Emotional Elevator.

Here is the tricky part. Giving away your power feels intentional and conscious, but it isn't. It happens when you are not conscious. Remember, power is typically associated with influence, decision making, celebrity, physical strength, control, and the like. This could be called *importance power* or *ego power*. I am referring to *personal power*—the power within. It is the inner knowingness we all possess, and that we rediscover when we know we are worthy and enough.

HIJACKED

I have only met a handful of people who are grounded and securely rooted in their own worthiness. It's not something we really think about. If we were truly aware, our morning self-talk might sound intentional, "My worthiness will stay high today—I intend to accomplish all the things on my list, experience joyful time with my family, and make a difference in the world." The reality is, we get up and stumble into our day—metaphorically (sometimes literally) in a slumber, with our eyes half-closed, allowing various situations and happenings to impact us in the moment. We react. Maybe when someone cuts us off in traffic. Or the person in the front of the coffee takeout line is super slow. Or whatever situation that sends us spiraling. Our mind, mood, and inner voice get the better of us, as we whisper expletives under our breath in our empty car.

This loss in consciousness is called the *Amygdala Hijack*. The amygdala, an almond-shaped emotion center in the middle of the brain, takes control and runs rampant when an extreme feeling emotion is present. Picture King Kong pounding his chest atop the Empire State Building.

Our emotions arrive at the amygdala milliseconds prior to the pre-frontal cortex, giving it dibs on how to handle a given situation. If the amygdala has control, the rest of the thinking brain is shut down—hence the word hijack. As a result, the *Executive Center*, as you would predict, ruler over executive-like decisions, is not functioning. It too has been hijacked. Your Command Center is non-operational. You are a hostage of the amygdala, and are relegated to rash decisions, out of control emotions, and potentially damaging actions, none of which are intended for your best long term interest. *Go King Kong!*

SIDE NOTE: If you have difficulty spelling amygdala, while in a team workshop, my then-client Amy shared a hilarious observation, announcing this little almond shaped gem was named after her for obvious reasons—Amy-g-dala.

While hijacked and unraveling emotionally, we go into self-worth ego protection mode. Driven by a victim mentality, we attempt to subconsciously save face, ignoring responsibility and accountability for the situation. "If I was wrong, that means I'm not perfect. If not perfect, I am less than. If I am less than, I am not enough. If I am not enough, I am not good." And down we go. Once the spiral and self-talk begins, it is almost impossible to turn it around. Just like a wild animal (or an unhealthy person) backed into a corner, acting on very basic survival instincts, we come out scratching, clawing, and spitting.

It is also imperative you stay grounded when interacting with a person who is hijacked and spiraling. You cannot follow them to their lower-level Emotional Elevator floors. You need to stay up high, and whole. Despite your strength, awareness, good intentions, grace, and desire to help them, you cannot be healthy enough for both of you. The best thing you can do for them and yourself is to stay grounded and operate from *your best self.* Then, with kindness and concern, you are able to understand and appreciate their out of control behavior. From your balanced state, you can extend grace. This neutralizes the downward momentum and sends it, slowly at first, in the opposite, upward direction. But it starts with you.

I have had many opportunities to practice this with new clients who were *sent* to coaching. Those who had not received solid feedback felt like they were being punished, consequently licking their wounds and wallowing in low self-worth. If I met the client at their wounded, unbalanced state, we would not make any progress. I stay grounded, of course, and then applaud them for feeling real feelings, understanding and relating. Then, I ask them if they prefer to go up or down. They have complete control. It is totally up to them. Funny, they always choose *up*.

EXERCISE: TREE—
Total Time: 5 minutes

Imagine a deeply rooted tree. Nearby, you see a newly replanted tree with shallow roots. They are about the same size, living in the same weather conditions. There is strong gusty wind (a.k.a. stress, crazy situations, toxic people, etc.). Which one is more likely to weather the storm? *How deep are your roots?* Journal your response.

AVOID Be-ing Hijacked

To avoid a hijacked amygdala, distract it. This is a muscle you can, and want to, strengthen and flex, if you want to keep your cool. It only requires an intention (to be the healthier version of you), a decision (to do the work of building up and flexing this muscle), and focus (to catch yourself in the moment while learning the art of redirection). A few favorite (very simple) techniques for yourself, your four-year-old, or any other person who is ready to spin out.

P.S. I don't often use the phrase *amygdala hijack*, I lovingly refer to it as an *adult tantrum*. It's a better visual, don't you think?

P.P.S. It is v-e-r-y difficult to master these techniques in the moment, especially the very first time. When you are aware of a tantrum, after the fact, reflect on which of the following techniques would/could have helped you stabilize, given the situation. Then practice using these long before you are triggered again.

1. *A drink of water*—this gives you a moment to pause and pull yourself together

2. *A physical body trigger*—I noticed a client leaned forward whenever he was ready to go off. Once he noticed his body giving him this advance warning during meetings, he forced himself back into his chair when triggered and was able to stay in control

3. *Deep breathing*—it only takes about 2-3 deep inhales to bypass the amygdala and give the Executive Center time to take control of the steering wheel

4. *Expand your awareness*—when heading down the hijack path, you'll notice your view/awareness/perspective narrows, as if losing peripheral vision. If you are able, pull back on your lens and get awareness of everything around you, literally seeing the bigger picture. Focus on the other people in the room staring at you, the temperature in the room, the seating arrangement, your breath, that person's facial expressions when angry, any nature nearby, etc.

5. *Grounding*—this simple visualization works. When I started my coaching business I found myself extremely exhausted after only 1 or 2 client sessions. As an empathic person, I absorbed a client's heavy negative issues, struggles, and angst. It was imperative I figure a way out of this, so I intentionally grounded before they arrived (picturing roots growing deep into the earth creating a strong unshakeable connection and sturdiness). It did the trick

Hopefully these techniques will help you avoid an amygdala hijack. However, you are human and it happens, let yourself off the hook. Work proactively to prevent it the next time by staying balanced while strengthening our own power. *Do*-ing your work is about *be*-ing!

Give and Take

Breathe in deeply. Hold your breath. Continue holding… Do not exhale.

Try it now.

How did it go? I'm guessing you were not successful.

Okay, let's try it another way. Instead, exhale forcefully. Push all of the breath out of your lungs. *Hold.* Continue to keep the air pushed out. Sustain this indefinitely.

I'm guessing you were not successful continuously keeping your breath out, or holding it in.

By now, you understand what a ridiculous request this was. I know, pretty silly. But I needed you to physically feel the futility of the exercise. The pure impossibility of inhaling without exhaling, or exhaling without inhaling, is a metaphor that needs to be experienced for the greatest awareness.

I conduct this same simple exercise with clients. I observe their faces, seeing the light *turn on* as they realize how pointless it is to deny the natural rhythm of inhaling and exhaling while maintaining life. And then after the debrief, with new inner awareness, they realize the parallel to healthy and real relationships. Sometimes for the first time, they understand the necessity for relationships to inhale and exhale to survive, and how this simple concept represents balanced and healthy *give and take.* Their realization is that every relationship requires life-sustaining balance. If out of balance, they grant themselves permission to expect the same, for themselves and from those with whom they are in a relationship. Both parties need to inhale and exhale, give and take, to thrive.

Without balanced *inhaling* (receiving) and *exhaling* (giving), death occurs. The same holds true for a relationship. It takes two healthy people, both willing to give and take. Whether personally or professionally, if either party is unwilling to participate, to give as well as receive, an important decision needs to be made. What's important, the survival of SELF, or the survival of the relationship/situation? Think about that. If either party is unwilling to give and take, but only take/inhale or give/exhale, life-sustaining balance is ignored. One party gives/inhales and the other takes/exhales. Certainly you understand this is not healthy in the long run. Are you able to advocate for yourself? Are you ready to make YOU/your life a priority?

If you decide to save yourself, you may be criticized with an insinuation you are being selfish. Here's an interesting point. When a person says, "You're so selfish," they are really saying "you are not paying attention to me" and "you are not taking care of me"—emphasis on *me*—or, "We are not doing what I want to do." In essence, their expectation is for both of you to focus on them, and their needs.

All that to say that *out of balance* relationships suffer. I use this particular example of selfishness because I work with many leaders who cross their own line, overextending themselves in the name of being *not* selfish. Metaphorical leaves stuck on their mesh, or already stashed in their backpack—most likely well-intended lessons from a well-intended caretaker, urging their child-self to be considerate and think of others. Many clients think it noble to sacrifice themselves (to the point of exhaustion and loss of vitality), having heard this looped message countless times. Every relationship and situation varies in the give and take ratio, so I am not suggesting you *not sacrifice*. I am suggesting you take care of yourself and balance as you do. Like the flight attendant's instructions announced at the beginning of an airplane flight, "place the oxygen mask on yourself first before assisting others." Taking care of yourself is the only way you can give to others.

CONSEQUENCES

The consequence of living *out of balance* hurts you, and in the end, others. In the example above, you give and you give, forgetting about yourself until you are literally spent. Then, the aftermath: an adult tantrum, passive-aggressive behavior, withdrawal, funk, losing your essence, or the avoidance of life. All outcomes of ignoring and not honoring your SELF. In this state, you are empty, with nothing left for others.

Many leaves stick to you without your awareness or permission. These leaves are yours for a lifetime, exist in your backpack, and are unbeknownst to you, providing an endless stream of subconscious messaging. A few examples of labels intended to make you a better person include responsible, strong, and nice. Do you see how these labels could result in the overextension and foregoing of SELF if not balanced? *What labels define you?*

Yes, relationships and situations intersect, requiring give and take—with balance. Like a *Venn diagram*, individuals have their separate space, awareness of their limits, with a sizable portion of intersection for the relationship. In this space, they actively consider the other. Collaboration and compromise are energetically agreed upon while in the intersection, creating thriving relationships with one another, both personally and professionally.

A Whole-Leader vs. A-Hole Leader

In an effort to illuminate unhealthy and healthy leadership behaviors, the following binary list depicts two extreme types of leaders. Gauge your actions—are you more of an *a-hole leader* or a *Whole-Leader*? At this point, if you are thinking you might be leaning more toward *a-hole leader*, congratulations, the awareness alone lets you know that if you thought you were, you no longer are. Not completely anyway. You are on the path to wholeness. You must first acknowledge your a-hole-ness to get to wholeness. With concerted effort, you can turn it around. People will understand and forgive.

On the other hand, if you are honest with yourself, and you know yourself to be more of a Whole-Leader, congratulations! Here is a test of wholeness. Is there room for improvement? Do you have a sincere interest in strengthening weak muscles? If yes, you are on your way. For best results, ask others to provide feedback (anonymously?) on your behalf.

The binary list of a-hole vs. a Whole-Leader behaviors is endless. Here are a few examples:

- Talks AT the team vs. Talks WITH the team

- Takes calls during a conversation without excusing him/her self vs. Mentions he/she is expecting a call and to please excuse the interruption

- Requires everyone be punctual to the team meeting yet often arrives late vs. Holds him/her self to the same rules as everyone else

- Leads by authority vs. Leads by example

- Meetings start late vs. Meetings start on time

- Acts like he/she is all-knowing, even when not knowing vs. Is healthy enough to admit to NOT being all-knowing, shares limited perspective, and asks others for input

- Gives fake authority to others and in the end makes the ultimate decision, robbing others of their power vs. Gives true authority, allowing others to make the decision, while offering guidance and perspective along the way if needed

- Believes their own story without question vs. Asks for feedback to verify beliefs regarding their story

- Makes assumptions regarding team members' behaviors which guides future career decisions vs. Understands the core/nature of a particular behavior to make the best career decisions, in everyone's best interest

- Scoffs at development opportunities ("I've already learned that stuff") vs. Welcomes the opportunity ("I can always learn more")

- Presents veneer—inauthentic version of themselves in most situations (hiding what they are truly thinking/feeling/believing) vs. Offers authentic version of themselves (speaking truth and being real) no matter the situation while delivering their message in a way that is respectful and understood by the audience.

- Spends much of their leadership time in the weeds micromanaging vs. Practices out of the weeds big-picture strategic thinking and action

- Has a binary mindset vs. Has an expanded 10-point mindset/perspective

- Carries a heavy backpack vs. Feels light and healthy

- Doesn't trust others to do the job vs. Trusts, trains, and guides

- Dictatorial vs. Collaborative

- Team meetings are silent vs. Team meetings are engaging

- Spends a lot of time in their head vs. Is often in the moment—accessing information, making decisions, collaborating, building relationships

- Avoids sticky situations vs. Courageously pulls back layers

- Defensive vs. Open

- Behavior extremes vs. Balanced behaviors

- Needs to be right vs. Open to being wrong

- Spends most of their time on the Emotional Elevator's lower floors vs. Spends most of their time on the Emotional Elevator's higher floors

- Leverages formal authority vs. Leverages informal authority

- Hears vs. Listens

- Distracted—cleans out their inbox during a conversation vs. Stops other activities for 100% engagement

- Takes shortcuts vs. Does the right thing

THE GOAL: A WHOLE-LEADER, not an a-hole leader

You've read through the list. What kind of a leader are you? If you started this book as an a-hole leader, I know with complete confidence, if you've read this far, you cannot still be that same kind of leader. Perhaps those were your unenlightened prior tendencies, but now, closing out the *Spotlight on the Ego* section, you know for a fact, deep inside, you have core goodness within you. I wish you well on your journey to rediscovering it, finding it, and expressing from your light within. *Plugging into your core power.* At the end of the day, the goal of the soul is to be whole.

Section III:

Your Core Light

The Inspiration

When I first learned the song we chanted to close out our Kundalini yoga practice, I focused on memorizing the words and staying in tune. The words were coming out of my mouth but I had not yet internalized their meaning. I wasn't ready to take in the fullness of the message.

Today that same song, "Long Time Sun," sung on the right day, brings tears to my eyes, the message so powerful. Although it is a short and simple song, it's message is full and intricate, filled with hope, blessings, and inspiration. To me, the most meaningful line of all, my favorite, is "… the pure light within you," referencing the beauty of your core goodness. And then, the finale. A prompt. That we allow ourselves to be guided by our beautiful core light.

If you take on the challenge of wholeness, you'll soon realize it to be a lifelong journey. Messages, meaning, and lessons early on that might have passed right by you, only to impact you profoundly later on when you are ready to receive them. As was my experience with this song. At some point, the line "pure light… guide your way…" took on a whole new meaning.

I was designing a workshop for female leaders and wanted to share a visual representation of this pure inner light concept. I entered a few key words into the search bar and within seconds the most splendid photo popped up. The image from the promotional poster based on a movie, aptly named, The Core, 2003, was exactly as I had imagined my inner core light might look. This picture was the perfect grand finale for a talk I was giving about core power. When it appeared on the screen, there was a collective audible gasp as the participants took in the visual brilliance of what stepping into your power really looks like.

Power

The *inner core light* image is stunning. A blue-black nighttime view of Mother Earth in all her glory, with a piece removed, allowing the display of red-orange-yellow core brilliance, pouring out and illuminating the cosmos with her inner light. *I love this image.* It is a perfect representation of our inner essence and reminds me of my own journey.

Remember that conversation I mentioned earlier with Robert? *That profound message he gave me?* Well, Robert and I were finishing up our first in-person meeting over dinner in Jackson Hole, Wyoming. We had been working together in the coaching immersion program, virtually, for months. As we walked out of the restaurant, Robert, a newly retired CEO and a very interesting, experienced, wise man, said something that changed me forever. He stopped, turned deliberately toward me, chuckled with a twinkle in his eye, and said, "I can't wait to see you step into your power."

I looked at him indignantly. "But I am powerful. I have had a great career. I've won trips and trophies. I have my own business. I make my own decisions. I have two beautiful children. I've been successful…" My voice trailed off. My mind was searching for the right answer, not truly understanding the nature of his statement. With his slight Texan drawl, he said, "That's not the kind of power I am talking about." I was perplexed. "So… what exactly do you mean? What kind of power are you talking about?" Again he chuckled and said, "When you figure it out, give me a call." "Awww, c'mon Robert, just tell me!"

Over time, my friendship with Robert grew. During our phone conversations, I would occasionally test his resolve to withhold the meaning of his statement, "So, what kind of power were you talking about exactly?" Again, he would defer to a future moment in time when I would magically have the awareness he suspected I already had within me.

A few years later, finally, I called him, and gleefully jump-started the conversation with, "Okay, I get it. I finally get it. I understand the kind of power you were talking about, in every fiber of my being. I feel it. I am there!" I let out a breath it seemed I had been holding in for three years. Relieved and excited, I awaited his response. Expecting a verbal pat on the head, he instead responded with his classic chuckle and lazy drawl, "Well, that is really terrific. That is great. Okay, now what about the rest of what I said In Jackson Hole?" Wait a minute. *What?* "What are you talking about, Robert? I have no idea what you're talking about." "Well, there was a second part to what I said that you must not remember. What I said was 'I can't wait to see you step into your power and light up the world with your beauty.' So what do you think about that?" All of my proud bubbly exuberance was quickly replaced with deflated confusion. "What? What does that even mean?" He told me to call him when I had figured it out.

It took me another year or two, but I did eventually figure it out. But not with my brain, *in my soul.* Looking back it seems ridiculous it took so long, but since I was working through this on my own, it was as if I was fumbling around and developing in the dark, while simultaneously juggling my life. I tell you this so you understand it doesn't happen overnight. It requires patience. Which is why I hesitate to share the answers. I want to shortcut your process, *but not your progress.* My intention is to provide a beacon of light so you are not walking alone, or walking in the dark. However, you will need to do the necessary tough inner work of walking the path, on your own. No shortcuts.

You cannot rush this tough inner work. Quite frankly, it would be easier if you turned and ran away. Easier, not better. Funny, I just had a realization. Although not an original or conscious intent, it has certainly been a subconscious motivation: The contents of this book are my attempt to help you answer Robert's question, and move beyond.

When I returned home from Wyoming, with Robert's challenge loosely planted in my psyche, life sucked me back into the day to day. Between life, life's lessons, and my coaching business, the focus on *finding my power* took a backseat. Fortunately, between my appetite for leadership and self-development, the curiosity for clarity, and an excuse to sit on the beautiful beaches of Lake Michigan, I eventually dug in and filled numerous journals with self-reflections and the resulting personally subtle yet seismic shifts. My aha's lit up, next steps were illuminated, and needed-to-be-removed layers were highlighted. I sensed something was happening, but I wasn't sure what exactly.

As I became more aware of my evolving growth and awareness, the work spilled over into my client projects. I had just begun a really cool assignment with a coaching client responsible for a 400-person downline and an 18-person three-level leadership team. "Time to grow this team," she said. However, her desired starting point was my facilitated LIVE 360-feedback session. *The Open 360° Feedback Process*™ is not where I would normally begin. This process requires high levels of trust, which were not yet established since we had not yet worked together. To honor her intention to jump right in (she was quite insistent about this), I designed a *work around*, spending our first hour on exercises paving the way for voluntary disclosure, vulnerability, and the heavy-duty lifting necessary to do this work. I had the team's buy-in.

During the entirety of those initial two days, each leader courageously dug in and forged through much personal work—exercises, giving feedback for their 18 peers, and receiving personal ego-wounding feedback. The outcome was fabulous. What started out as a *one-time event* turned into a quarterly two-day session for the next two years. They got dirty, did their work, and grew.

In fact, their corporate surveys reflected what we were witnessing: growth and transformation. All of the vulnerability, feedback, and disclosure paid off. The team raised their delivery model standards, elevated their connection, and had each other's backs in a new and meaningful way. Their teamwork, deepened levels of trust, and increased engagement was evident to all. This team truly lived the *honor self while respecting others* mantra, which served as an ongoing checkpoint for balance and healthiness. Gone were the days of extremes and unhealthiness.

SIDE NOTE: This team's customer satisfaction scores were far superior to other organizational teams, which incited my client to write a professional journal white paper based on our development workshops and the incredible follow through and accountability work done by this very strategic leader/client.

This team was at the right time/right place personally and professionally. Open and ready, they combined leadership topics with *personal power* work, creating a perfect platform for development. Using their own personal development examples to augment the leadership topics, their learning, team bonds, and speed of progress came alive—digging in individually, each finding their CORE, and of course, benefitting the team. Personally for me, the correlation between personal development and leadership growth in the business setting was so apparent and advantageous, it set a new standard for UPwords Inc. *I couldn't not do this work.* Our initial goal had been self-awareness and communication skills, which, in the end, barely scratched the surface.

Upon reflection, the inner sense-of-self work was absolutely the catalyst for each leader's growth. Unfortunately, this type of work is often minimized and disregarded when allocating development dollars. Because it is soft, intangible, and difficult to measure, the investment often feels too risky. Fortunately for this team, their fearless leader had experienced her own shifts, followed her instincts, and knew the true benefit and investment payoff was in the exponential power of developing every individual, and the team collectively. Bravo!

This was an excellent case study for UPwords Inc. The inner core work outcomes increased individuals' self-confidence and the overall team bond, which had a domino effect on the participants' ability to engage in robust dialogue, advocate for themselves, conduct candid conversations, address conflict, improve teamwork, and lay the foundation for confident decision making.

What I was witnessing was an increase in their power—their personal power. *Robert's version.* I was so honored that this team courageously journeyed to find their inner personal power, *the kind of power when we know we are worthy and enough.* They opened up, dared to be vulnerable, and shared themselves. Their true selves. On a level they had not dared before. They were good people and a good team, and discovering themselves at the core level took them to greatness. This is the outcome of discovering and building your personal power muscles. Knowing you are great at your core, just the way you are.

This is the inner goodness I referenced earlier. The inner goodness I know resides in every person, every client, and already within you. It is your task to recognize it, acknowledge it, build it, use it, grow it, and release it. When you finally recognize your personal power, plug in and let it fill you up. It will radiate from within you and flow out of you, fulfilling Robert's message to "step into your power and light up the world with your beauty."

Your brilliant, personally powerful, radiant inner core light will illuminate the cosmos.

Letting Go

Do you enjoy beautiful autumn leaves? The brilliant gold, orange, and red hues create a breathtaking landscape. I know people flock to Michigan to witness the spectacular colors of fall. The funny thing is, those gorgeous vivid fall leaves, of which we never tire, are nature's grand send-off. Those leaves are actually dying. But they do not know fear. Not afraid to age, or change, leaves thankfully do not resist transitioning from emollient green to dried-up orange. Their incredible maturity creates the brilliant and spectacular display we call fall colors. *Aging never looked so good.*

Nature's existence doesn't require control. It just is. If only we would take our cues from nature, trusting in the cycle of life. Wouldn't it be amazing to have the confidence to let go?

EMULATING NATURE

Always looking for opportunities to sneak in lessons learned with my adult children, I had a moment with my son as he was heading off for his final semester of college. I don't recall the subject matter exactly, but I certainly recall the nature of our conversation. We were talking about the tendency of human beings to turn away—run away—in the face of the unknown. Specifically, his tendency to turn away in the face of the unknown. How our long ago adapted fight or flight instincts betray us in modern day moments. How running away thwarts our own growth. How much richer life could be if we leaned in and allowed ourselves to live through the unknown. Like nature. It was a simple and short conversation, and yet I saw the impact it made on him. The lesson settled into his being as he internalized its meaning. My son grew stronger and more centered in that moment.

I am grateful for nature's example, helping him step into his own power.

I am grateful for nature's example, providing the best example of trust and letting go.

I am grateful to nature's example of be-ing.

Leaning In

When we encounter negative emotions or situations, our tendency is to literally and figuratively turn and run away. This flight response is a smart option when chased by a tiger, but in most modern day instances, the impulse to run actually thwarts growth. If you are truly interested in developing into a better version of you, you would be best served to not turn away. *Leaning into the unknown is scary.* Relying on yourself to be in the present moment, facing the unknown head on, is an act of bravery and the only way to conquer it.

Conquering *lean-in moments* reminds me of playing in the waves along the Lake Michigan shoreline, with wave jumping as a favorite metaphor. Standing in the water, scanning the horizon for the biggest, most exciting incoming waves, kids screech in delightful anticipation of the unknown. Boldly facing the waves head on, daring the water to oppose us, we resist what is. We are not prepared and we naively ignore the water's power, getting knocked off balance. When we turn our backs on the incoming and run away, we quickly find out there is no way to outdistance the looming wall of water. The waves crash down, reminding us of their dominance, claiming victory over our bodies in a moment of disorientation as we attempt to regain our balance. Eventually, our bodies tire of resisting, and we instinctually turn in and face the waves. I now realize this is always the order of wave jumping. Giving in and being one with the water is the finale. Diving in and leaning in, we are newly empowered. By working with the wave, it is as if we give ourselves permission to be one with it—anticipating its grand arrival and timing our immersion—we lean in, we prevail, we conquer. We are one with the problem and the solution simultaneously. Gone is our fear, and its power over us. One by one, little faces emerge from the water, beaming with satisfaction. The squealing quiets to peaceful confidence. By leaning in and being one with the water, we are all happy, joyful, and at peace.

Although easier to lean into courage, trust, and in-the-moment excitement, while playfully frolicking in the water, real life *leaning in* offers us similar access to the already-within-us traits. Whether heading into a difficult conversation, dealing with an uncomfortable situation, experiencing change, or engaging in *new and different*, drawing on courage to move forward is our first course of action, and already within us. Trusting ourselves to tap into and access this courage to handle these little lean-in moments gives us confidence to advance and metaphorically dive in. What unlocks it all is *presence*. We generally rely on our experience, which takes us out of the present moment, and throws us into the past or future. Which causes imbalance. There is no way to conquer the unknown when out of balance.

The following example isn't presence per se, but it is a relatable image you can access as a reference point. Have you ever gone to the movies by yourself? Viewing a movie with a friend, or a group of friends, is the norm and our societal comfort zone. As a shared experience, each person is focused on the reactions of others—comments, laughter, and group think, all creating closeness, a wonderful outcome of watching it together. As fun as it is to watch a movie with friends, the distractions prevent us from being truly present. Sitting in a movie theater by yourself, completely focused—no talking, interruptions, or splitting your attention—changes your experience. Being totally engrossed in the minute to minute unfolding of the story is a wonderful experience in presence. Granted, you are present in the life of the character on screen, not your own, but you get the gist.

CONTROL

It is our nature to choose the familiar. I'm sure you can relate, noticing it in yourself as well as in others. The crazy part is that we opt for familiarity and comfort, even when it keeps us *stuck in a rut*. It seems counterintuitive, but sometimes, choosing *not great and familiar* is more acceptable and comfortable than choosing *great and unfamiliar*. Unfortunately. Not conscious and operating in this default mode is a perfect example of getting in our own way. Giving up control is scary. The ego, head-centered part of us, is convinced, "If I know everything, I have control, and I can keep myself safe," with a subliminal message of "If I do not know, I cannot control, and therefore will not be safe." The need to control aligns with our basic survival instincts, protection, and safety, which is incredibly motivating.

Being in flow is a beautiful outcome of leaning in, which offers a huge incentive to give up the need for control. But for many, this is not a very strong muscle. Actively leaning in and flowing requires work, and over time strengthens your ability to consciously choose. Tapping into your own internal courage, trust, and presence gives you access to new and extraordinary parts of yourself.

Stephen R. Covey, author and businessman, is famous for his perspective on controlling our mental energy, which at a high level is "we are what we focus on." His famous Circle of Influence features two concentric circles: the inner circle depicting what we can control and what we have influence over, and the outer circle depicting what we cannot control and we have concerns over. Based on this, I call them the *Circle of Control* and the *Circle of Concern*. If we focus on the inner circle, the things we can control, our mindset is more proactive (less stressful). If we focus on the outer circle, what we cannot control, what is outside of us, our mindset is more reactive (stressful). Our focus drives our perceptions. Covey's work on change and control is in essence summed up in his quote, "I am not a product of my circumstances. I am a product of my decisions."

Circle of Control

Circle of Concern

Despite valiant efforts, we cannot completely control *change* or the unknown. We cannot know enough, plan enough, worry enough, or control enough to fully prevent or protect ourselves from change or the unknown. I posit self-care and self-clean-up will do more to help you weather the storm of change and the unknown than sheer control ever can or could. If you are clean and relatively debris-free, having done some emotional leaf clearing and backpack dumping, you stand in great power to face the unknown. Self-care and self-clean-up allows you to be proactive, effective, resilient, and strong. Standing in your own power and trusting your SELF, you self-protect from unhealthiness by keeping your power/immunity strong. This is leaning in.

The art of leaning in is allowing expansion and flow. Hyper-focus constricts, which is the opposite of flow. Opening up and shifting your perspective is the first stage.

LEANING IN WHILE STANDING IN YOUR POWER

When standing in your power, your personal resolve is incredible. You are solid. Grounded. Unwaveringly authentic. You know who you are, what you deserve, and what you need to flourish. You have your own back and you take care of YOU.

In this state, you are intentionally up on the highest floors possible on your Emotional Elevator. It feels so good that dropping down to lower levels and out of control emotions is not an option. You instinctually know that nothing beneficial comes from lowering yourself. Only your ego is satisfied with your smart retort, last punch, or clever zing. When this does happen—*you are human after all*—you hand over your power on a silver platter. This is like giving your ego, a drunk driver, the keys to get behind the wheel—driving off balanced with low level behavior. Only your ego wins.

When caught in the ego's snares, you lose. Imagine the parent with an out of control temper at a Little League baseball game. The consequence of their low level YouTube-worthy Adult Tantrum results in gossip, embarrassment, and loss of power—for the parents, the kids, and the team. The collective consciousness has been lowered.

When clear-headed, conscious, and strongly standing in your power, you hold others accountable for their actions without your low-level emotions creeping in. With respect and kindness, you are able to honor your voice, saying what needs to be said, while respecting the other person. This powerful stance prevents conflict. An excellent conflict definition highlights the destructive quality of out of control emotions:

2 Diverse Ideas + Emotion = CONFLICT

When you remove the low level emotions, you are left with 2 diverse ideas, and no conflict.

Jim and I were office spouses, and at first glance, couldn't have been more different, setting us up for a great *conflict opportunity*. I was responsible for sales, and Jim, the technical solution. At that time I had two children under five and was averaging 4-5 hours of sleep. Working 60-80 hours a week at this IT enterprise job was like working in a pressure cooker. It was a tense time. Fortunately we were both committed to a healthy partnership. I can't imagine having the success we had, had we not worked on *us*.

Still close friends, Jim and his wife visited me in my home recently. While reminiscing about the craziness we had endured, Jim chided me about my stress induced emotional range—his kind way of saying he had to handle my tears. His wife followed up with two brilliant comments. First she told me that I made a delicious dirty martini. *Yes I do*. Second, she explained how much my tears had benefitted their marriage. As a result of our partnership, he better understood women's emotions and was unafraid to lean in. Yes, I admit it, there were times when my frustration was expressed in tears. And when this occurred, I made sure he knew it was a release and a sign of frustration, versus the often misperceived sign of weakness. This awareness was important for us professionally, and also happened to benefit him personally. Rather than avoiding *out of sync* emotions, he now leans in and hits pause, asking, "What's going on? Let's talk. Something is obviously bothering you. If it's me, just say so—I can take it. We need to clear this up." His ego isn't triggered. Healthy and standing in his power with the confidence to lean in, they talk. Just as he and I did.

LEANING IN STRATEGICALLY

Committed to securing the business, as was evidenced by our growing friendship, Jim and I were equally committed to healthy, real, present, and in the moment conversations. I remember a particularly defining interaction when we returned from yet another unproductive, endless loop, head spinning client meeting. As the sales part of our dynamic duo, I was feeling quite defeated, sensing we were no longer in partnership with the client. I didn't trust my instincts because as the non-technical person I didn't totally understand our solution. Fortunately, Jim, seeing my frustration, knowing our magic only happened when *in sync*, yanked me into a conference room where we spent the rest of the afternoon. Together we fine-tooth-combed the technology benefits for the client, the seemingly off-kilter dynamics, and our strategic approach going forward. We leaned in, balanced, and emerged with a plan.

By leaning into the issues with a magnifying glass, we cleaned up the underlying trust issues and presented an updated technical plan—a complete refresh. Our client partnership was restored, and together we secured a major piece of new business. By the way, as it turned out, the previous team had burned a few bridges, and the embers were still smoldering. Do not underestimate the need for trust.

At the time, I hadn't realized how much we were impacting each other on a personal level. By engaging in real communication, healthy interactions, and true partnership, it raised our respective individual expectations and our actions for the future in all areas of life.

LEANING INTO BEING

Having seen the conflict equation, you know great conflict also includes great emotions. Whether revved up reactions or an engaged ego, when emotions are triggered, low level behaviors result, i.e. shouting (with or without obscenities), vengeance, flipping people off, tattle-telling, gossiping, tantrums, rage, fights, and pouting. All of these low level behaviors are invitations, goading others to join in on the descent, taking down the collective energy. Obviously this is not good.

At a high level, what is happening is that the *need to be right* overshadows and justifies the unhealthy reactions. All of this havoc and mayhem is the result of a triggered ego. The only way to bypass the ego is to stand in your power—clean and fresh and whole, grounded in emotional integrity. When you are be-ing, you are conscious. When conscious, you understand you deserve the best, not because you are better than or less than anyone else, but because you are a human being.

As mentioned in Section I, I am grateful to instinctively know, see, and experience core goodness within each client. Within each person. And within you. Remembering, returning to, and plugging into that core goodness is your work. When you do, you are a complete and whole human being.

CHOICE

Leaning in is an active and conscious choice. *Choice* being the operative word. Choose to do your work, rediscover your core, and uncover your true essence for a complete refresh. With a refresh, you have the personal power to trust leaning in.

When you lean in, your body talks. Your body will let you know *all is good* by showering you with positive feelings when you are balanced and the best version of you. It will feel like fresh air and calm. Like grounded tree roots. It will feel like the stable center of the merry-go-round. Like basking in sunshine on the top floor of your Emotional Elevator. Your body's inner guidance system will let you know when you are connected and whole, and when you are out of alignment. You just need to pay attention.

EXERCISE: LEANING IN—
Total Time: 45 min.

Please Journal your answers to the following questions.

- Which situations cause you to turn and run away?

- Which emotions are the most easily triggered?

- Can you recall a time when you felt like you were standing in your power? Describe the feeling.

- Describe a time when you've actively leaned in. What was the outcome?

- Describe the feeling when your inner guidance system signals you are connected and whole.

Balance

By now you know how easy it is for us human beings to be imbalanced. The slightest upset triggers our ego. When off center, with the ego at the wheel, we are convinced it is not our fault. In that moment of erroneous processing, a few faulty perspectives arise. We do not/cannot recognize the true intention of the other person. We only see our own perspective (this is self-protection mode). And, because we are convinced we are right and good, our wrath feels justified.

It is in your best long term interest to avoid being emotionally hijacked. In this state, the amygdala gains control, and you are not strong enough to get out of your own way. Unless of course you've been working out and have developed your balance muscles.

Our flawed ego instinct is to build muscles on the outside—the muscles necessary for brute strength retaliation, threats, and intimidation. The ego loves these s-t-r-o-n-g and protective muscles. Strengthening the exterior muscles, and thus the ego, is not our goal. We want to strengthen the inner core muscles, where true strength resides. The muscles for being in—and returning to—balance are developed from the inside out. Think about that. From the inside out.

When you are strong inside, your inner core is grounded and supported and knows. Knowing decisions and actions emanating from inside you are pure, and grounded in joy, appreciation, happiness, enthusiasm, freedom, love, and understanding. This is where true strength lies.

Listed below are a number of exercises to strengthen your *inside out* core muscles. I use each of these techniques myself. As you regularly exercise internally and gain strength, you will notice healthier perspectives, a wider peripheral vision, and more balanced (re)actions. In addition you will return to balance much more quickly.

1. *Visualization:* (used for Grounding and the exercise I use to *Rise Up, internally, levitating up and out vertically*) As a starting point, create a mental picture of a house. See the details of the house. Pause. Then envision the word *house*. Pause. Complete this before continuing.

   I am guessing visualizing the mental image of the house was easier than seeing the actual word. The image of the house, more visually stimulating, evokes emotions, attachments, and memories. Visualizations are more effective when full-bodied and intense. When you practice visualization, focus on as many details as possible and, very importantly, feel the details.

   As I mentioned previously, in the early days of my coaching business, I was extremely exhausted after only 1 or 2 sessions. People brought their issues and struggles into my physical space, and dumped their heaviness and angst into my lap. As an empathic person, I absorbed it all. To counteract this, I started the Grounding visualization practice—grounding myself before they arrived—picturing my roots growing deeply into the earth, creating my strong unshakeable sturdiness. It absolutely did the trick. I also wiped away any lingering energy after they left. I literally wiped energetic junk off of my person. Another favorite visualization I continue to use is the one mentioned above, which I call *Rising Up*. I picture and energetically levitate out of the tornado of chaos. Because visualization is a proven and powerful technique and especially known to help athletes, I urge you to use it regularly.

2. *Journaling:* Journaling is a great way for you to have a real conversation with your Authentic/CORE-Self. When you start out, do not be discouraged by your resistance. It is normal. It often sounds like: I don't know where to begin… what do I write about? What should I say? Rather than listening to your self-talk, I recommend the Hot Pen technique, which I discovered when I began my own journaling practice, and then later suggested to my clients starting theirs.

Sit down with pen and paper (I again suggest buying a Leadership Journal you love—favorite color, texture, binding, line size, etc.) and start writing. Start out with self-talk, which might sound like, "I have no idea where to begin, but I'm going to start writing and see what emerges…" As you start flowing, your writing will shift again into something like, "I want to figure out why X" or "I should ask myself Y." Allow yourself to flow. Nobody else will see your writing. It is amazing what clarity you can get by talking to yourself through journaling. I highly recommend it.

3. *Meditation:* Meditation is a great practice for inner core muscle building. Ideally this should be a daily practice. The amount of time is not as relevant as the intentionality and the routine. When I first attempted meditation, between falling asleep and not being good at it (hello, ego), I was inconsistent and quite frankly not interested, seeing no clear benefits to motivate me. Later, when avidly practicing Kundalini Yoga, I fell in love with meditation. My gateway meditation "drug" was a 40 day Kundalini Yoga meditation challenge. It was a 30 minute meditation, which I eventually worked up to. The consistency worked. I managed to make this a daily habit for 18 months.

Today my meditations are inspired for the particular day. I might start out with quiet time, allowing myself to mentally unwind (I use a timer so I am not distracted by time), then maybe a Kundalini Yoga meditation, or something from Deepak Chopra, MD (thank you Deepak and Oprah, I have listened to many 21-day meditations). Sometimes I focus on prayer, intention setting, gratitude, or deep breathing meditations to a few favorite songs ("Returning" by Jennifer Berezan and "Odyssey" by Peter Kater are currently at the top of my breathing playlist). Commit to a week and see what happens. Find as quiet a space as is possible, set a timer, and meditate on what feels right for you. Give up expectations of perfection. Do the best you can. Bottom line, this is for you to feel more grounded and quiet inside. Shoot for peaceful nothingness—time for your Authentic Self to just *be*. No judgment.

4. *Intention vs. Impact:* Although this topic was presented earlier, it warrants repeating. Intention vs. impact is a great exercise/ technique for balancing and working your core. This technique can/should be used the minute you realize you are out of alignment due to a miscommunication. Emotions like hurt, betrayal, or being misunderstood are indicators. Remember, we judge ourselves based on our intentions, and we judge others on their impact. This is human nature. Personally, I like to go straight to the source. I make sure I'm grounded, and then I ask the person (with true sincerity, assuming good intentions) to clarify or explain their intention… "Despite how it impacted me, I assumed your intention was good." Their perspective is almost always illuminating. This is often followed by clarification and apologies, after which the issue disappears, just in the nick of time to avoid entrance into the backpack.

5. *Reframing:* This topic was also presented earlier and warrants repeating. Reframing is a tool you can and should use on a regular basis. Take any situation tempting you to be out of balance and reframe it. To better understand, study a piece of framed art in your home. What colors pop out? What feature in the picture stands out? Now imagine that same piece of art with a completely different frame—instead of an ornate gold frame, maybe a red metal frame. How does the art change? Just by putting a new frame around it, you get a new perspective. Try the same exercise with your perspective.

   Reframing is an important muscle to strengthen over time. Initially, this might be quite difficult. If practiced, however, it will become second nature. This is tied closely with "What is the lesson learned?" and "What is another perspective?" For example, "I am so angry she said I was a micromanager" can be reframed into "Although I was really irritated when she told me

I was a micromanager, it really helped me look at, and analyze, my management style. I think it was preventing me from being successful. I'm grateful for the feedback."

6. *Backpack Clean Out:* When we feel triggered, it is almost always an indicator the root cause is in our backpack. A great technique to help you clean out your backpack is the one described earlier—"What's underneath?" Using this technique, especially in conjunction with Journaling, you will figure out what is stuck, thus causing you to react. Remember, what you are carrying around in your backpack feeds your operating system. Your operating system lights up when this particular trigger is tripped. Awareness of the past situation/trigger allows you to actively let it go and clean it out of your backpack. (Then try reframing your trigger. "I'm so glad I encountered that particular trigger, it gives me an opportunity to get it out of my backpack.")

7. *Merry-go-round:* Another favorite mental visualization for quick grounding and balancing is the *merry-go-round*. Take a deep breath in and move to the center of your metaphoric merry-go-round. Lean up against the sturdy, unmoving, central pole. From this vantage point, observe the chaos swirling around you while centered as the observer.

8. *Moving from Head to Heart:* To some degree, I have saved the best for last. This particular strategy is one of my very favorites and at the heart of all of this authenticity work—pun intended. It is the one for which I have received the most positive feedback from the C-suite level. It is not difficult, but requires focus and intention. Without a real situation to work through, however, it will feel anticlimactic, so first things first. Select a situation/person with which you are presently dealing, or something in your recent past. Something that has or had the potential to get you stuck. In a minute, I'll have you close your eyes and talk it out for 30 seconds. Out loud or in your head, *talk out* the conversation you might

have with this person—*the conversation you have in the middle of the night that is keeping you awake*. I find clients make more progress saying the words aloud. While talking, picture everything you are saying, *the words*, literally shooting out the *top of your head*. Try not to think about it, just picture the words flowing out of the top of your head. Okay, ready? *Go*. Now that you're back, pause and take a deep cleansing breath, in and out. Use the same scenario for Part 2. This time picture the words flowing out of *your chest*—through your heart/soul and bursting out of your chest. *Go*. Did you feel the difference? It's amazing isn't it? I've done this exercise with many people. One CEO in particular, who was not really inspired when we role-played the exercise together, reported that he later used it with great success in a real life, rocky situation. Success he said he wouldn't have had otherwise.

EXERCISE: UP and DOWN—
Total Time: 10 minutes

Think of a scenario when you are UP, followed by a scenario when you are DOWN. Now spend a moment in each and feel. Do you sense how light the UP scenario is, versus the heaviness of the DOWN scenario? Spend some time distinguishing the differences. Do you notice yourself sitting up straight vs. slumping over a bit? If you are able to take it a little further, imagine your attitude and performance throughout the day if UP vs. DOWN. Although this only requires thinking, I recommend you jot down the outcome of your two scenarios in your Leadership Journal as a quick point of reference to inspire you positively in the future.

REAL LIFE

In theory, *grounding* and *rising up* is easy. The difficulty is putting the exercises into practice. In reality, like while in a real tornado, we are not equipped for the incredible force of nature. Reacting in the moment is challenging and unrealistic the first time around. Success requires that you build the necessary muscles in advance. Be proactive.

As you are heading into a situation from which you'd rather turn away, your temptation to ride the elevator down to a lower level emotional floor will be incredibly strong. Resist the temptation. Lean in with the intention of balance and wholeness. Stay strong, standing in your power.

Real Life Balance

Whether walking on a tightrope or your own personal version of the Skywalk, balancing is a daily practice. Although leaders do not want to hurt others, sometimes when they are not balanced, they inadvertently do.

Having received numerous complaints about a colleague within the organization, my client knew it was time for a conscious conversation. We prepped for the upcoming colleague feedback session, working toward his intention of providing honest, clarifying feedback, while maintaining the relationship. Fortunately, he knew being in balance was the only way to achieve the outcome he desired, hence our conversation—*Bravo!* From my perspective, the only thing getting in his way was his state-of-mind. Based on the complaints he had heard, as well as the behavior he himself had witnessed, he was quite irritated. However, he believed this colleague deserved his respect, and felt the weight of responsibility to be fair and balanced.

His own old-backpack patterns and tendencies were to downplay and sugarcoat, but he knew in this case that strong and clear feedback was necessary. The dance along his proverbial tightrope would be tricky.

SIDE NOTE: The intention to stay balanced while having this kind of conversation is very admirable for a leader. It is easy to get caught up in past triggers and emotions, not prep, and be out-of-balance... only honoring self (blurting out all of the wrong-doings) or respecting others (saying nothing or downplaying the situation).

So we rolled up our sleeves and went to work. His irritation coupled with his reluctance to initiate the conversation caused him to drop down a few floors on his Emotional Elevator, which revealed an older, not so healthy version of himself. While in this state, he was, *call it what you will,* out of balance/not grounded/caught up in the tornado/off kilter. "I don't know if I can do it. I'm so irritated with this guy. Doesn't he realize what he is doing to these people? I'm afraid to tell him what is really going on. I'm not sure how he'll take it. He'll be ticked off. At them, and me. So I have to be intentional, but I don't think this is a good time… maybe next week." On one hand, he is smart to realize he is not in a position to speak to his colleague at this moment, while not operating from his Authentic (and best) Self. On the other hand, delaying the conversation and expecting the intensity to die down is a missed opportunity, and naive. a) There is never a good time—seize the moment as a catalyst for change, b) The hesitation will take up space in your brain until you handle it, and c) Preparing helps you diffuse your angst and competently have the conversation, resulting in taking care of those in the organization while helping your colleague.

All that to say, yes, it is challenging to stabilize between honoring yourself and respecting others, especially when out of balance. Whether new thoughts and emotions or old tendencies and triggers, these stuck leaves are cutting off flow and creating a backup. When this happens, life is not flowing through you. Life is getting stuck *on* you.

A quick trick to rebalance and ground is to find a new entry point. You might think the entry point is about the other person—hoping for a positive topic or an upbeat moment in their lives that opens up an opportunity for you to initiate the difficult conversation. You know the thinking, "I'll wait until he's in a good mood, then I'll talk to him about it." *The reality is that finding an entry point isn't for them, it is for you.* You are the one who needs the new entry point. A new entry point allows *you* to make your way through your own swirling tornado to find them. Translation: When you are too close to a situation, your picture is distorted. With negative emotions about the person/situation, you are more likely to give them a piece of your mind while imbalanced—literally losing your mind while interacting with them, which creates more distance, and the loss of your better self.

Instead, pull back your lens for a higher level, bigger view. Find a connection. In this instance, it might be, "He is such a driven, passionate, and high-performance producer. This issue is totally expected given his nature—the other side of the same coin." With new awareness (usually, the complementary view), you are able to burrow a metaphorical tunnel through the swirling tornado of your negativity. The tunnel gives you a clean and clear path to a new connection so you are stable and balanced while speaking your truth.

FINDING AN OPENING

Your newly forged tunnel creates an entryway and an opening for connection. The connection gives you access to being centered, grounded, balanced, and stable. Now you are ready and able to speak your truth— truly honoring yourself while respecting the other person.

A few rules of engagement:

1. *Reiterate your goal* (to yourself)—With your goal at the forefront of your mind, you solidify intention and mindfulness. It might sound something like *give honest feedback while maintaining our relationship.*

1. *Ask permission*—By asking, "Are you open to feedback?" or "I would like to share some feedback with you, which I think will benefit you in the long run, if you're open to it," you are opening up a channel of receptivity.

2. *Let them off the hook*—If you are initially too direct, they will not hear you. Help them maintain their dignity while providing feedback, which increases the probability that they will actually hear you. Instead of blurting out the truth, "Your team thinks you do X," try a version which respects them as a person, "You are a passionate leader who is 100% in, and the flip side of this great quality is X, which seems to be getting in your way." Do you hear the difference?

3. *Do not quote or share soundbites*—Do not say, "Jack told me he felt X because of what you said/did." This will only create more agitation. What you can say is, "I had the sense in talking to Jack that he is feeling X." Now you, the person in the room, having the

conversation, is owning the feedback instead of pointing back to Jack (which by the way, is a lower level, less empowering way to handle this, which will cause more drama as you attempt to *pass the buck*).

4. *Be kind vs. nice.* Leaders want to be *nice*—telling people what they want to hear even if not true. Being *kind* is providing the advice and/or feedback they need to hear that benefits them in the long run. You're indirectly showing your care and concern by presenting feedback that helps them in a number of ways: grow/be aware/get rid of a blind spot/get promoted/be the better version of themselves. Being *kind vs. nice* is more difficult and requires great courage. It is literally a *gift* from you to them.

5. *Attitude of positivity.* You know how dogs sense fear? So does a person receiving feedback. Entering a feedback session with angst, ill will, doom, and/or any other negative emotion will make delivering difficult feedback much more challenging. The person will sense your fear and it will be awkward. Walk into the conversation positively. *Truly.* This might be the toughest part of the process. A few mindset examples are: "This is all good… with this little tweak you will be more effective than ever." OR "I'm interested in your career, and if it were me, I would rather know this info sooner than later." OR "I think you are an amazing leader—you need to know about this one little sharp edge… " OR "Great leaders want to grow, and you need feedback to grow, so this is an opportunity for feedback. I want to help you grow…" Finally, "I am so grateful I am the one who gets to give you this life-/career-changing feedback, it is an honor to be a part of your growth."

By the end of our session, my client shifted from foreboding to anticipation. While the magnitude of the conversation remained daunting, he felt better prepared and ready to help his friend/colleague move forward. Over the years, with many opportunities to provide tough feedback, I have found that, when delivered consciously, how it is received is humbling. It is a reciprocal gift to have the receiver express profuse gratitude for the feedback they received, knowing it was this gift that opened up their awareness. Even if they were subconsciously aware, for whatever reason their resistance caused a blind spot. *The only way to be rid of a shadow or blind spot is to illuminate the situation with the gift of light.*

FINDING REAL LIFE BALANCE WITH UNHEALTHY AND TOXIC PEOPLE

While my job is to decode and finesse unhealthy and toxic people and situations, in real life, I too bump into unhealthy and toxic types. Although not frequent, I have to finagle my way out and around them, just like everyone else, which of course requires that I be balanced. I want to share a couple of real life unhealthy and toxic situations, and how they unfolded.

UNHEALTHY

Truly healthy, strong, and real relationships are not tied to winning or losing, or fulfilling each other's needs. They are non-ego-based. Each person's healthiness and wholeness, and ability to stand in their own power, plays a part in their combined dynamic healthiness. Rather than two halves creating a whole, two whole individuals create a relationship exploding with potential.

At the time, I was young and not whole, and in a relationship with another *not whole* person. Together, our two halves made a whole, however, and it worked. As is often the case, life happens. Various challenges triggered his old, unhealthy patterns and thinking, and sparked his ego. Our relationship suddenly felt competitive and win-lose, like we were on a teeter-totter. When I was up, he was subconsciously down, and vice versa. The more I was my big self, the more our relationship suffered. In an effort to maintain the relationship, I shape-shifted, making myself X—enter in whatever this is for you—to preserve the original, agreed upon, subconscious relationship. In this case, *I made myself smaller.* We all do this to some degree. I voluntarily, although subconsciously, changed myself to maintain our equilibrium.

His backpack was heavy and full. And I understood the pain it contained, so I rationalized its unhealthiness. Young and not yet consistently my Authentic/CORE-Self, walking on my figurative tightrope, I easily lost my footing—not knowing my boundaries, limits, or myself really. When the backpack was triggered, resulting in irrational outbursts, I developed *work arounds* and accepted unacceptable behavior. Unhealthy people lack awareness, the ability to think outside of themselves, and self-accountability—our imbalance was not his concern. The gap widened until one day I had full awareness of my lopsided and compromised self. Although the relationship did not last long, it taught me a great deal, providing powerful insight for my future self.

THE GAP

When interacting with unhealthy people or in unhealthy situations, we can get out of alignment and disconnected from ourselves. The gaps that develop cause us to feel unsettled, imbalanced, and uncomfortable. If not tuned in, we disregard the subtle intuitive messages indicating when we've strayed too far, causing us to stay stuck in relationships and situations not in our best interest. However, the gap can also signal a huge opportunity for growth.

A real life example of a gap is when an individual considers leaving a career-long job. Something has changed and the job is no longer satisfying. Perhaps there is a change in the leadership regime, or a shift in the culture, or new dynamic personally. If this same person ignores their dissatisfaction, and continues on without action, a number of negative outcomes will likely result.

If aware, open, and ready, a gap offers valuable insight. Pay attention to the gaps. You'll instinctively know when you feel separation, distance, discord, or unhappiness. Whether for you individually or in a relationship, the presence of a gap signals something is off. I have seen this happen within organizations, when one person develops interpersonally and subsequently grows beyond the remaining team members or management.

The resulting dissatisfaction impacts and compounds many areas including performance, turnover, engagement, and teamwork.

Clients often talk about their gaps, which is good. Until it isn't. I'm sure you know somebody who has been stuck in a gap loop. Maybe you've been stuck in one yourself. This is tiresome for everyone involved and does nothing for forward movement or growth. When the same old story begins to cut a groove in their internal talk track, I suggest three main ways to get unstuck.

1. *Learn to be okay with X*—this is extremely difficult once the disparity is identified. With growing awareness of the gap, being okay with it is quite impossible if conscious. Unhappiness sets in, and only viable options are #2 and #3.

2. *Attempt to change the dynamic/relationship*—this is a tough but brave option. No matter the magnitude of the gap, courage, energy, and healthiness is required to address it. Then both parties need to be present and involved to close the gap. Acknowledging the gap, understanding each other's perspectives, awareness, openness to change, then having a candid conversation, a go forward plan, and action is required from both individuals.

3. *Leave the relationship/situation*—this happens after having exhausted options #1 and #2. If you are in growth mode, it is highly unlikely you'll be satisfied with #1—unless the situation no longer causes imbalance. Option #2 requires bravery, vulnerability, leadership, and a heart-centered mindset. Optimally this closes the gap and you are at peace and resolved about the situation. If #2 is thoroughly exhausted without success, #3 might be your only remaining choice. I'll expand on this next in *Encountering the Unhealthy*.

SIDE NOTE: There is great value working with an experienced coach at this point, finding and exploring completely new game changing options, learning and using new tools to remedy a situation, and considering enlightened perspectives to help you navigate #2.

ENCOUNTERING THE UNHEALTHY

Encountering an unhealthy person—a person is not grounded or centered, who does not have great awareness, is not self-accountable, and habitually responds from their wounded ego—tests you. How you handle their tantrums, lack of awareness, and insensitive remarks is an indication of you, your growth, and your personal power, even if you are whole.

When their thoughtless comments trigger you, you feel your blood pressure rise and your animal instincts kick in. You begin to lose yourself. If you follow your impulses, no longer operating from your core, you will have lowered yourself to their level. Lowering yourself to meet this unhealthy person on their lower level elevator floor is very tempting, and feels justified, offering you a satisfying momentary release. In this state, if you give this unhealthy person a piece of your mind, literally and figuratively, you are no longer whole. Maybe you've won the battle, but you've lost the war. You will have lost something most precious… you. Winning this round of verbal sparring but losing your wholeness is too great a price to pay. Remember, the goal is to be whole.

As unsettling as it is interacting with an unhealthy person, a practical strategy in staying whole is understanding their S.O.P. (Standard Operating Procedure). Knowing their S.O.P. reminds you they are operating from a wounded ego, carrying a heavy backpack, and engaging in mind-numbing negative self-talk. They are protecting and serving themselves, and as a result, block you out to the point of losing their senses—not able to hear your feedback, feel your extended hand of reconciliation, or see your kindness. They are just not capable in the moment. When my kids were young, I relied on natural consequences to grow their capability—realistic and fair consequences applied firmly and lovingly as a result of their actions. The same applies in dealing with an unhealthy person. Let the chips fall where they may. You can offer a healing hand, but you cannot save them if they do not want to be saved.

As you move to #3, the only remaining option, there is one last challenge for you. In an effort to stay whole, it is important you rid yourself of your residual negative emotions. This will be difficult. Are you ready for this crazy and counterintuitive request? I ask you to find it in yourself, deep within your core, on a basic human level, the ability to rise up. *Rise up to a place where you can love them despite everything.* I know, it is so strange to use the L-word, especially because it conjures up personal attachments, meaning, and images. Instead, think of the L-word as fully accepting them without judgment. I'm not suggesting you start hanging out with them, or accept their behavior, or even like them. I am asking you to trust me in this huge perspective shift, which is an incredibly important step on your path to wholeness.

During a developmental retreat in Sedona, Arizona, our facilitator suggested everyone with whom you are challenged or triggered, on some level, is acting on your behalf as your own personal teacher. I know, crazy, right? This thinking forced me to do mental gymnastics but once I got my head around it, I realized it was, in fact, the best thing for my true and authentic, Core Self. She pointed out the importance of finding gratitude in processing the lessons learned, in order to heal. Adding this exercise to client work has taken their shifts and growth to new levels. I now see it as a companion piece to reframing work—another step toward wholeness, which is ultimately amazing.

While standing in your powerful Authentic Self, know what is intuitively acceptable for you and *what is not.* Be intentional about who you are, and who you will be when encountering not-whole individuals. The goal for your soul is to be whole.

TOXIC

I was in another real life situation with a person I thought to be unhealthy. Honestly, I thought I could manage his mood swings, but it turns out he was in fact quite toxic. If you recall, the biggest difference between unhealthy and toxic is intention. His mean-spirited texts and emails ramped up, literally threatening me, and yes, his imbalance was a concern. The former me wanted to give into his demands and threats, sacrificing myself to make peace. One friend even advised, "Be the bigger person and walk away," which seemed reasonable on the surface, but not at my core.

There had been an assault on my soul and a threat to my safety. I suspected others with whom he had interacted had been similarly threatened. I was not interested in fighting—the toll to my personal well-being was potentially far too great. Yet, I had come too far to allow this to continue. I knew I had to lean in and figure out a way through this—to stay balanced while holding him accountable. This was particularly difficult because I had moments of fear, and anger, and hurt. So I asked of myself what I ask of others… work on being balanced. What I am about to say will (again) sound counterintuitive. While in the middle of this real life situation, I let go of my resistance and lower level emotions (it is natural to resist this strategy when you are in it as you have already lost perspective) to lean in and *balance*. I did this by meditating two times a day.

Diving into meditation helped me re-ground, re-center, and re-connect with my higher Authentic/CORE-Self. It sounds hokey, but intentionally and consistently elevating out of my egoic-self was the only way to find an entry point. In this True Self state, a new entry point, a mental/emotional tunnel through which I could connect mentally and energetically, emerged. Then, I sent him intentions of kindness, love, and gratitude. All based on the awareness that this was yet another powerful opportunity to grow. This experience proved to be another lesson about *standing in my power*, practicing my balancing act, and finding and honoring my voice in the face of a toxic individual.

I was ready when his texts dropped in. I felt amazing. With a sense of calm, I ignored them for days, keeping my wits about me. A friend who had also been tormented by him texted to see if I had read his messages. My response was, "Nope. Not until I'm ready. Or feel like it. I don't need to react. Or let it distract me when I'm doing something more important. Or when I'm not centered or ready to receive them. Maybe tomorrow or Wednesday…. But I will. When I'm ready." I didn't realize the ripple effect of these words. She responded, "That's so powerful," and later told me my actions inspired her to stop receiving his messages, no longer powered by fear.

As I worked through this situation, I plodded through his snowstorm of toxicity, repeating the mantra, "I will not allow his toxicity to enter my backpack." My metaphorical parka-hooded head was slightly bent, forging through the elements with ice and snow pelting my face. All the while, I knew I had to stay calm, maintain my balance, and move forward. Doing the right thing meant holding him accountable for his actions while being in balance—not punishing him *the person* per se, not berating him, or expecting him to be on the same page (this is often our expectation when we over-explain and defend ourselves). In this case, accountability meant *contract fulfillment* while staying in balance and operating from a place of wholeness.

Of note, there was a distinct moment after meditating when I felt my tightrope turn into the *Skywalk*. Overcome with calmness, I knew the tornado had subsided: *I've got this. I have the power. If I so choose, I can get the tornado twisting again by retaliating with wounding words.* But I knew doing so would only cause me to lose my power, because it is not possible to be in the tornado and simultaneously balanced. The most whole thing I could do was to get healthy resolution and closure while outside of the tornado.

REAL LIFE QUICK TIP: Let's say you are engaged in email banter that is spinning out of control. Before you fire off an email that drops you down a floor or two on your Emotional Elevator, try this:

1. Start with good intention—wanting to write a response that is healthy and whole. Write a quick first draft. Then, set your timer for 3 minutes, close your eyes, and focus on deep breathing until the timer goes off. Open your eyes. Feel yourself on your tightrope, and then visualize the tightrope expanding in width... like a sturdy sidewalk, bridge, or Skywalk. Feel grounded, whole, and balanced.

2. Make another attempt at a response, thinking of the lessons learned, and injecting a spirit of gratitude.

3. Then edit your response one last time.

4. Once the situation is resolved to your satisfaction, let it go. Release the toxic person from your consciousness and your life (if you are able). It is so much more beneficial to your Authentic/CORE-Self and the Best Version of You to move forward in balance.

This is a real exercise I share with clients when they are in the heat of battle—it requires true balance, strength, courage, and vulnerability. I wish you well. I promise this will help your soul to be whole.

A Balanced Human Be-ing

Your support system expands when you intentionally practice balance. What starts out as a narrow, *easy to fall off* tightrope widens, and turns into your Skywalk, giving you needed support, groundedness and, quite frankly, relief. The constant self-monitoring (fueled by fear and self-doubt) goes away, and you more confidently move through life. Then, your figurative Skywalk, although super strongly supportive with a full 360° view, transforms. Instead of a temporary walkway that you occasionally rely on for support, it becomes an everyday reliable reality.

The security and confidence you feel walking on sturdy Mother Earth becomes your new normal.

You are more self-assured—confident handling whatever crosses your path.

Life is more joyful and flowing when you practice presence.

This is a glimpse of your personal power.

The Truth About Authenticity

I've delivered many workshops over the years, and the title that has created the most intrigue is "Stepping into your Power." Everyone wants personal power, *but what is it exactly?* If you recall my conversation with Robert, he had suggested I had not yet stepped into mine. You might also remember my insistence that I had, and the resulting journey I began. Ultimately, it was all about personal power and authenticity.

If authenticity was my entry point into personal power, did Robert think I was inauthentic? Did he think I was a liar? Did he think I was not a person of integrity? As I am quite forthright and real, how did he arrive at this conclusion? This was all very perplexing. Initially, because I did not yet understand the depth and richness of authenticity, or its subtleties, his definition of the word escaped me. My understanding of authenticity was that it was about integrity, honor, truthfulness, and reliability, with sublayers of *being real*—"Hey, this is who I am, take it or leave it." I assumed I could check off the *integrity* and *real* boxes, which meant the need to work on authenticity was unnecessary. Or so I thought. As it turned out, there was so much more to authenticity than I had anticipated.

Here is another way to look at it. If personal power was coupled with authenticity and being real, it would be perfectly captured in the mantra "honor self while respecting others." This balancing statement focuses on *healthy BE-ing while in relationship with others.* If we operated on this balanced and centered 10-point scale, our world would be a better place.

Unfortunately this does not happen because our greatest challenge is when we are challenged. When we are challenged and stressed, we are out of alignment, and our 10-point scale shrinks to a very personal, constricted, binary 2-point scale, representing black and white options: honor self OR respect others. We've talked about this. Our work is to e-x-p-a-n-d both—honor self AND respect others, allowing for the many options within the expanded 10-point scale. This authentic personal power is the natural outcome of being grounded and present.

While in our authentic personal power, we quite naturally keep our spectrum open. We forget the tightrope ever existed because the ground we walk on is supportive and expansive. We stay out of the tornado, or at a minimum know enough to quickly get out of its way. I promise you, life is easier and more joyful on this expanded scale.

AUTHENTICALLY ME

I was watching a singing competition performance, a duet, with last year's winner accompanied by his seasoned mentor. I was taken aback by the seasoned star's performance. Not a fan of that genre, I wasn't familiar with his music, but in the moment I totally understood the reason for his fame. He sang from his core. Deep from within, while tapped into his inner essence, even as the glorified back-up singer he was during this duet, he was in the space where magic happens. The new talented star was wonderful, of course, but because he had not yet fully stepped into his power, he was only singing beautiful notes in a cool tone with his style and understated charisma. He lacked the connection to his core. He was still playing a role. I look forward to hearing him when he is authentically himself.

Being authentically yourself is the first step in being balanced. If you focus on the outcome rather than that first intentional authentic step, you lose yourself. For instance, the minute I got stuck in what Robert thought about me, I let his thoughts affect me. It caused me to wobble and lose balance. This will happen any time you overthink and give credence to another person's opinion of you. While developing your CORE-self muscles, like a young colt, you wobble, lose your balance, and fall out of alignment. Giving power to his thoughts about me, which defined ME to me, caused me to fall out of alignment. To compound the issue, he was right, I did not have the sturdiness and personal power he suggested I step into. The problem was not what he thought about me—he could think whatever he wanted. What *I* thought about *me* based on his thoughts about me was truly the problem. Pause for a moment. Take that in. It may seem convoluted, but once you get it, it is very simple.

THE FALSE SELF

When you fall out of alignment, you no longer operate from your Authentic/CORE-Self. You operate from your not so authentic False Self.

Operating from the False Self sends you on an unwanted downward spiral. The speed varies—sometimes it's a slow descent and other times a speedy plummet. Either way, falling into the lower parts of yourself causes your thoughts and emotions to descend. I'm sure you've experienced the lows of rage and vengeance—"What a jerk!" or "What the h—!" Surely you feel the downward spiral of these words. As the energy builds up, you drop down. The duration of your imbalance is up to you.

To be clear, imbalance is one-sidedness, unevenness—*a disparity within oneself.* Imbalance turns into unbalance. To be unbalanced is to be disturbed, unhinged, distorted, or destabilized. When you fall out of connection with your true Authentic/CORE-Self, space is created for your less-than self to exist. Your lower level self is full of misjudgment and mistaken perceptions, justifying low level behavior, and letting in outside comparisons. No longer operating authentically, you give others meaning-making over you, basing your opinion of yourself on others' opinions. This is how you give away pieces of yourself. Not consciously, but voluntarily… in the name of peace, being nice, not creating conflict, etc. This means that the resulting internal madness from imbalance is *potentially* incredibly detrimental to your Authentic/CORE-Self. In other words, if you are not balanced and centered, and listen and believe your own negative self-talk that is based on the comparisons and opinions of others', you will potentially lose your mind.

A friend had her resume professionally created, and afterward she asked me to look it over. She instinctively knew the finished product was off. The resume writer she had hired had created an excellent resume. However, it did not accurately reflect the wisdom, maturity, and depth my friend possessed. In the end, it was all good once she revised it, adding in her own essence. What wasn't good was that she had accepted the finished product as a representation of herself, not fully trusting her own instincts, allowing the influence and words of another to define her. Fortunately, in the end, she did listen to her gut, made edits, and created a resume that reflected her authentic self.

Hopefully now you understand why I am harping on the importance of staying grounded/centered/aligned. When disconnected from your Authentic Self, you dishonor YOU and give yourself away. I'm not suggesting you'll never lose your cool; of course you will. If you do throw an Adult Tantrum, know negativity, constricted awareness, and binary thinking follows. Automatically, *without question*. And then you infect others on the way down, and potentially (negatively) impact other (important) areas of your life:

- Snapping at a loved one and creating hard to undo damage

- Disengaging from your team, adding to a general lack of morale

- Withdrawing from your family and subliminally triggering your child to blame him- or herself for your lack of interest

The worst part of losing the healthy version of YOU is that you can no longer access your awesomeness, to be used in the other parts of your (important, wonderful) life. Losing the best version of YOU is a hefty price to pay and not worth the cost. Choosing someone else's opinion over you and yours is a form of self-betrayal and self-sabotage. The funny thing is, they have not asked you to hand over anything, especially not your personal power. They don't even perceive your internal conflict. If in a disagreement, their focus is on the impact you caused—not on your intention, not on your perceived sense of injustice, and certainly not on you. Unless highly aware and evolved, their ego is in *self-protection mode*— not tracking you. If the off-handed comment was taken too personally by you (triggered by your backpack), how can that be on them? You must proudly BE—owning who you are inside and out, from top to bottom. Otherwise you are a co-conspirator in taking yourself down. This is the meaning of not being Authentically YOU and giving away your power.

STANDING IN YOUR POWER

While present, standing in your power, and operating from your Authentic Self, your awareness broadens. Your peripheral vision sharpens and you begin to see others' perspectives, motivations, and potentially their pain. Your senses are heightened. *Are you aware of what is happening?* Your out of balance view of blame, anger, frustration, and vengeance has shifted to seeing them in a new and Whole-Self way. You see their core goodness. *How beautiful is that?*

You could call this new perspective Compassionate Accountability. I call it *grace*. You understand their brokenness, their shame, and their inner turmoil. You see their intention. You forgive. You are healthy in your response and treatment of them. Your anger, hurt, and feelings of injustice transform into inner strength. This is where true compassionate accountability resides, and the place from which grace is extended.

Just to be clear, this enlightened view does not mean you forget about yourself, what is right for you, and your limits, which is holding them accountable. Because you are balanced, your inner pendulum, resisting the urge to swing, is centered. Whether interacting with a person who is healthy or toxic, regardless, you exhibit Compassionate Accountability—honoring yourself (accountability) while respecting them (compassion). This is you operating from your balanced Authentic/CORE-Self, extending grace.

Finding Your Voice

If I could wave a magic wand, I would grant every person access to their authentic, *speaking from the core* voice. Speaking from that place of original wholeness would be like reverting back to a forgotten, natural, mother tongue language—before the outside was allowed in. Children naturally exist in this space—unabashedly themselves, innocently speaking their truth. No guarding, no posturing, no hiding.

While enrolled in a Master Coaching Program years ago, I quickly dismissed the instructor's comment, "coaching is good for the planet," assuming he was either in sales mode or boosting his own sense of esteem. Now I understand the genius in, and intention behind, his words. He simply wanted everybody to know who they were at their core, and to operate as Whole-Selves, accessing their authentic voices.

Speaking from your authentic voice is the purest expression of you, and how you best honor your*self.* The quality and healthiness of your voice is an outcome of your wholeness. When speaking your truth, you expand. Operating from wholeness, standing up for yourself, knowing your limits and boundaries, and caring for yourself is as Maya Angelou wrote, "I got my own back." When whole, you are full, and able to extend grace to others.

Conversely, when you do not speak your truth, you shrink. When not whole, there is a misalignment of what is desired and what is communicated, incongruous behavior and language being the result. It is difficult to give to others when not aligned and whole yourself. When not whole, we comfortably live in the ego's shadow. I recall a phrase that seems relevant here: *The shadow cannot exist in full light.* I love this. This means that when living authentically, fully shining your light, the shadow disappears, and the gap of incongruence closes. You are whole.

This is the essence of my client work, as well as the expectation for myself and others with whom I interact. Finding and using the authentic voice is challenging, however. It certainly was for me, especially as my younger self. I expressed myself with a strong physical presence, and did not feel the need to find my voice, per se, *because I didn't realize it was missing.* I had not yet unraveled or found the truth in my voice.

As I became more conscious of this truth, the more I acknowledged it, spoke it, and honored it. Honored ME. And to my surprise and confusion, the more I honored me and my Core Self, the more challenging certain relationships became. In an effort to figure things out and keep the peace, I conducted a little experiment. I was curious. *What if I was getting in the way? What would I hear if the people with whom I was in relationships had more opportunity to speak up?* I set out to hear the authentic voices of others and learn who they were at a deeper core level. I believed this comprehensive view was the key to unlocking my own blocks, and would potentially help me sort things out. I pulled back. I became a spectator and allowed things to unfold naturally. My normal intensely driving forward personality got quiet and listened. This is where I made a big discovery, and *stopped working so hard to make it work.*

Unintentionally, my energy and enthusiasm had masked reality. My natural confidence propelled me forward and covered up the inaction of others. I had taken on the responsibility for movement in every situation. Without realizing it, I was the *spackle* that filled in relationship cracks and gaps, smoothing things over and making it look nice. It didn't matter with whom, it was a pattern. While moving full steam ahead, I trusted the other person to let me know when we were not aligned. What I had not accounted for was their ability to speak their truth. Or should I say, *their inability to speak their truth.* They could not speak their truth if they did not know their truth and, therefore, I did not hear what was not being said.

By pulling back, allowing things to unfold naturally, and not intervening, I gained incredible clarity—seeing relationships and conversations more clearly. What was real and what was not. I identified misperceptions and misalignments on many levels in many situations—energy, boldness, agreement, vision, commitment, goals, and engagement to name a few. Yes, my little experiment revealed a blind spot. In me.

I had inadvertently used ME to fill in those cracks, covering up our incongruencies, believing it all was for the better good. I was like a runner who stops every few blocks waiting for the others to catch up. When we weren't on the same page, I waited for the other person to catch up, not registering my own frustration. Obviously, my own narrative was driving my actions. However, without wholeness or Core Self understanding in the other, there was no other narrative.

This was a lightbulb moment. As a general rule, I was practiced at the care, concern, and comfort of others (imbalanced on the spectrum of *honoring self while respecting others*), by not imposing myself (a learned *in the backpack* childhood message). *I made myself small to accommodate others.* As I danced in relationship with others, I fully gave of myself. In my exertion (and exhaustion), I hadn't noticed they were often standing still, contributing minimally to our shared dynamic dance. When others do not do their work, they do not know themselves on an inner, authentic level, and cannot give proactively. They react. *Their light and brightness is dependent on others.* In this case, dependent on me.

I implore you to do the hard work of clearing away your stuck leaves and layers, emptying your backpack, and reacquainting yourself with your core. Learn your various beautiful facets. Know your triggers. Value your value. Grow in your self-worth. Be authentically you. Be whole, and find your inner authentic voice.

I ask you again, who are you at your core?

PLOT TWIST...

As a result of my experiment, there is a bit of plot twist that may have escaped you—initially, it did me. On some level, my newly discovered awareness and perceptions sounded something like "Yes, my energy and enthusiasm drives action, and I often carry the ball for both parties in a variety of situations. With this awareness, because I have worked on myself, I can pause and take a breath. Whew, time to relax. After all of this hard work, I can pause and wait for others to meet me on this level—it's time for them do their own heavy lifting."

Well, what if, *maybe*, just maybe, I too got in my own way? What if I based my sense-of-self on others' reactions to me? What if my *not yet worked out* worthiness caused me to work harder to maintain equilibrium in relationships, hoping they would like and approve of me? What if I jumped higher, danced faster, spackled over, and did more because I positioned myself as lower? At this deeper level, I didn't matter as much as they did, and was okay being a casualty, even though on the surface I told myself I was strong enough for the both of us. In less-than mode, my ego was driving, my backpack was full, and my S.O.P. was the default. In ego mode, making myself *less than* and small to make others more comfortable was the only way I knew how to gain approval, and as a result, *be enough*. Because, after all, my personality was so obnoxiously big (or so I had convinced myself based on the reactions of a few important people in my life). This is the twisted logic of ego mode. *Didn't see that coming, did you?*

You have your own magic wand. Grant yourself access to your authentic, speaking-from-your-core voice. Speak from a place of wholeness and go back to your pre-ego, forgotten, natural, mother tongue language. Find your voice. Speak your truth. No guarding, no posturing, no hiding.

Worthiness

While at a neighbor's, I was offered a boozy cherry—a cherry marinated in booze with a tad of sugar. It was very boozy indeed. I had a sudden realization that people marinate too. (I told you I find metaphors in everything!) However, rather than marinating in booze, they marinate in their own stuff. Depending on their healthiness and backpack contents, people marinate and soak in their own unhealthy beliefs, self-talk, and unworthiness.

Whether or not you have taken the time to examine the contents of your own backpack, surely you know the general themes: misunderstandings, twisted perspectives, judgments from self and others, no longer aligned beliefs, hurts and pain, ego protective measures, lessons learned, fears, etc. Now imagine the guts of your backpack marinating. Then steeping. And finally seeping into you. Impacting your sense-of-self. Yuck!

Back to Toxic Guy. I knew he'd experienced serious life setbacks. Growing up in an unhealthy environment, he suffered from a very full backpack and a long list of mistakes. He rigidly kept himself in check, but when triggered, his old shame, guilt, and self-loathing—yes, self-loathing—took over. Down he would spiral, resulting in mean-spirited adult tantrums. My former less worthy self would have taken it, tolerating his bad behavior while helping him get out of his own way because I felt badly for him. My new and improved worthy self understood his toxicity, got out of the line of fire, and ran.

Most individuals are not so extreme on their worthiness spectrum. Having said that, only a few fortunate souls (who are born into extremely healthy, clean, *no baggage* families, or more realistically have *done their work*) are on the opposite side—grounded and rooted in pure, unadulterated worthiness.

In case I've led you to believe otherwise, doing your work is a journey, not a destination. I daresay it is *a journey of remembrance* vs. a journey into the future. Doing your work helps you remember the worthiness you had when you were born. On some infantile, subconscious level you knew you were worthy. You let everyone know when you wanted attention, were hungry, or needed to be changed. On some level, you loved yourself enough to demand the care necessary for you to thrive.

If you are a parent, I offer you another compelling worthiness perspective. When your child was born, did you withhold your love until they accomplished something wonderful? Did you think, "Once they roll over, or smile, or walk, I will love them. Until then, they are not worthy of my love"? No, of course not. Your child was worthy of your love the minute they were born. *Their beautiful pure soul was—and is—absolutely worthy.*

Your journey of remembrance is getting back to that sense of worthiness you had at birth, before it was tainted by the subconscious needs of others. Although well intended, as others attempt to self-heal and self-soothe, sharing opinions, messages, and fear-based lessons learned, they cause you to get dirty.

We all know parents who live vicariously through their children. This often subconscious act to live through their child's accomplishments to boost their own less-than sense of worthiness is outwardly intended for the child's better good, but internally sends less-than subliminal messages— *You are not enough or not good enough unless you accomplish…* or help, or are perfect, or are smart, etc.

When you are whole, you cease craving fulfillment from others. You no longer need someone to complete you. You are aware of your worthiness. It resides on the inside and the outside—in your sense-of-self and your actions. In relationships, nothing is more dynamic than when you, healthy and whole, join forces with someone also healthy and whole. Rather than needing two halves to become whole, since both individuals are already healthy and whole, you double your fun.

$$1/2 + 1/2 = 1$$

vs.

$$1 + 1 = 2$$

Ready!

As a first-born American named Heidi, with German heritage, it has been long suggested I drive a German luxury car. A sales manager first suggested it after a big sales win, subconsciously challenging me to up my game as I was still a newbie. My immediate reaction was, *Oh my gosh, there is no way I can pull up in a car like that.* My underlying self-talk was that it was too pretentious—what in the world would people think? No way. Over the years, others suggested the same, and my response was always the same. Funny, I have driven and enjoyed other understated luxury cars, but none as obnoxiously image defining. As I worked at emptying my backpack, I saw, tightly wrapped up in ego worthiness issues, the truth was that I had allowed others' opinions to steer my course, pun intended.

When I saw my neighbor's slightly-used German luxury car, not knowing the make or model, something inside of me lit up. My internal reaction was, "Oh. What a cute vehicle. Wow, that is so sharp for an SUV." Not being a car person, this was an unfamiliar reaction. When it came time for me to purchase a sport utility, I kept going back to the moment that vehicle sparked something inside of me. The same model was even older, and if I was logical (according to everyone else) I would buy something newer. But I couldn't let it go. Choosing to not buy it based on their opinions was more of that same *handing over my power* action I had done in the past, only this time the pendulum was swinging in the other direction.

So, after much research (to satisfy my own logical brain), I did in fact purchase the same make, model, and year. There is an ironic ending to the story. Because I bought it *out of state*, my daughter and I flew to pick it up and drive it home. It was great having her with me. Although I loved the car right away—it drove great, was in excellent condition, and very cute—something was missing. I missed the giddiness that typically accompanied a major purchase. In a weird way, it almost seemed like I didn't like it. My daughter must have picked up on my less than exuberant mood. As we were driving away from the seller, in her very articulate and emotionally intelligent way, my daughter lit up and said, "Mom, I feel very smiley for you." And yet her face had a question mark on it, as if asking me for confirmation of the emotion.

Upon reflection, because I had shifted, my reaction was healthy. I had let go of what others thought about the vehicle, or me purchasing said vehicle, and had grown. My ego was not in charge of this purchase. Ultimately, it was just a car. Albeit beautiful, fun to drive, well designed, and sharp, it was just a car, and it did not define me.

My less mature self would have shied away from such a purchase because I felt *less than*, or had a heady reaction because it made me feel *greater than*, but my updated self was ready to stand in my power and purchase it, just because I liked it. Period. I liked the car because I liked the car. *Functional utility meets indulgent frivolity.* My decision was authentic, pure, and real—reflecting me.

My sense of balance during the entire vehicle purchase process was a testament to the work I'd done. I was ready to own this car. No need to dig into my backpack. No imbalance, no shame, no embarrassment, and no explanation.

Pure joy!

Communication

Two days before my dad passed away, I asked him if he would have done anything differently. He was quick to reply. He'd obviously been thinking about it, "Absolutely," he whispered. I was surprised by the resolve and forcefulness of his response. "What Dad? What would you have done differently?"

His answer blew me away. "Communication."

I knew immediately he was referencing his relationship with my mother, and the many lost opportunities for a deeper connection, and to some degree, a nod to the three of us girls. We had all deepened our relationship with him as adults, but lost many years of connection as children. In those final days I believe he wished he had risked being vulnerable.

This was his last gift to me.

The fact that the last words of a man who had lived a hard but successful, interesting, and full life were about communication was astounding. In those last days, as his ego dissolved, acknowledging the need for connection with others, and the importance of communication in that connection, was the bravest I'd ever seen him. I was humbled by his vulnerability and wisdom.

COMPONENTS OF COMMUNICATION

Entire books are written on communication. Workshops are fully dedicated to the topic, and yet they only scratch the surface. I know I cannot do *communication* justice in one chapter. I can offer you a few bite-size takeaways, providing ideas for a path forward, which at a minimum will help increase your communication awareness.

1. When my clients work with the Communication Model, their first takeaway is every interaction has two sides, a Sender (S) and a Receiver (R). We often assume our own communication is pretty good, and breakdowns are the fault of others—we are innocent and the other person is guilty. However, both parties have culpability, which is often a surprise to most people. Both S & R have bias and their own perspective. I call these biases filters. Filters being the second takeaway, ranging from title, income, age, and personality type to the car you drive to your perception of how hard or easy your life has been. Courageously opening up to real conversations, with the intention of clearing miscommunications by acknowledging and understanding filters, is the third Communication Model takeaway.

2. *Intention vs. Impact* is such an important concept, an entire chapter of this book was dedicated to it. It is worth the repeat. We judge ourselves based on our intention, and we judge others based on their impact. The greater the gap, the greater the rift. The greater the rift, the bigger the hurt, the pain, and the conflict. I highly recommend that you use the words intention and impact in your communication to unravel those rifts. Literally. "I don't know your intention, but this is how it impacted me." And "I am sorry you were impacted this way, my intention was this."

3. The biases mentioned above, a.k.a. filters, that color our intention vs. impact perspectives are homegrown and sitting in our own backpacks. If healthy communication is your goal, a high level backpack clean out is necessary. At a minimum, your heightened awareness should prevent additional leaves from collecting and getting stuck on your mesh, thus stored in your backpack.

4. In my experience, words hold an electrical charge. Two words sitting side by side in a thesaurus indicate they are the same and interchangeable. However, they probably elicit different reactions. Pay careful attention to your words—how you use them and the charge they carry. I'm sure you, or someone you love, has pushed

your buttons—dropping a word bomb on you that detonates on delivery. We all know how to do this because even subconsciously we understand the power of words. Be aware of your intention and potential impact as you choose your words.

5.   I love assessments because they are incredibly beneficial in helping clients communicate with others. Facilitating a communication workshop with a personality assessment component for a large organization, I noticed palpable tension between two colleagues. It was unusual two co-workers would be in the same module; however, this exception worked in our favor. I rearranged the curriculum and colored outside the lines to help the group learn from their tension. After assessing their personality types, I added a segment so each participant would understand how they were perceived by others, followed by role playing—learning how to prevent miscommunication by learning to speak each other's language. This particular exercise continues to create *communication* and *conflict resolution* miracles. By accessing the assessment at the root of misunderstanding (and the corresponding bias), perspectives open up.

6.   Expand a binary mindset to a 10-point "honor self while respecting others" mindset. Scale up. Balance your communication. Quite frankly, if this point was universally followed, I'd be out of business.

7.   Maybe you've heard a version of the phrase, "Be responsible for the energy you bring into the room." (outlined in greater detail in the Energy chapter in Section I). Your energy is a reflection of your emotional healthiness and the starting point of great communication. A few elements that can get in your way, and cause you to drop, include a heavy backpack, ego attachment, object orientation, a low sense of worth, or an in-the-moment trigger.

8.   Courage to be vulnerable is a key element in healthy communi-cation. Just when you have the urge to ignore, turn, walk, or run

away, use the avoidance as an indicator of the need to lean in and deal.

9.   Trust. When we trust the other party, we give them the benefit of the doubt. We trust their intention to be good. We trust they did not mean to hurt us or negatively impact us. This is a foundational element of healthy communication.

10. Saving the best for last, the most important aspect for healthy productive communication is authenticity. Take your real self into every conversation. Be vulnerable. Points 1-9 are inherently included in this final point: When communicating from your Authentic/CORE-Self, the rest will fall in place.

HEALTHY COMMUNICATION

Julie and I have been best friends since 10th grade. Our healthy communication is certainly one of the top reasons we've stayed so close over the years. We had an opportunity to put our communication skills to the test recently. We planned a get together one weekend as we now live almost three hours apart. Because of weather conditions, after a brief text exchange, we cancelled our fun weekend. Both of us were incredibly disappointed.

Our normal modus operandi when issues arise (which is incredibly r-a-r-e) is to talk it out. I cannot remember a time when we needed space to get through an issue, so not talking the rest of the weekend was foreign territory. At some point I reached out. We both acknowledged the negative shift our cancelled plans had had on our psyches. As it turned out, we had a number of misunderstandings. In addition to meta messages and underlying meanings, I misinterpreted her reaction, and she, mine. So, par for us, we leaned in and talked it out, quickly sorting it out and laughing at the misunderstanding. We also grew. I confided a lifelong insecurity—not being worthy of time, attention, and effort—had been triggered during the process, causing a sublayer of hurt. She was shocked. And she had reactions based on her upbringing that I had not considered.

After all of these years, we were capable of learning more about each other, and shifting our behavior. Each of us heard the other and adjusted, taking care to prevent any future hurts. Our ability to communicate in a healthy way, and adhering to the 10 components above, allowed us to take our communication game, and our relationship, to the next level.

Scaling Up

Calling all leaders. Conscious expansion is required for you to be the best Whole-Leader you can be.

EXPANSION

Shifting out of a binary mindset, and opening up thinking, beliefs, and views that include the Authentic/CORE-Self, the Operational Self, and the Strategic Self creates alignment within the leader, and leads to wholeness. Whole-Leaders operate from an expanded state of consciousness, and are naturally more deliberate, intentional, and mindful. Clarity, calmness, and wisdom lead to upgraded decision making, resulting in operational healthiness. As trust and hope increases, employee engagement and morale is positively impacted, with strategic outcomes as the result of expanded and conscious Whole-Leadership.

As consciousness is expanded, so is mindset. As is often the case, concepts are easier to comprehend than execute. Whether one-on-one or in workshops, clients nod their heads, affirming the learning, believing they are ready to apply it in real life. When I ask them to verbalize it in the moment, they are at a loss. The required heavy lifting suddenly feels impossible with atrophied muscles, which are in great need of a workout.

PRACTICE

It is time for a workout. Broaden your binary thinking by expanding your 2-point scale to a 10-point scale. Let's practice using a simple business situation to illustrate the possibilities.

To help with our exercise, I am referencing a real client scenario. This particular client was defined by her silence. One day she entered my office visibly frustrated. Her manager wasn't giving her access to an important meeting she thought she should attend.

The first step in this process was encouraging her to express her pent up emotions, to get out what she was holding in—what she really wanted to say to him. I watched her struggle to translate her frustration into words, and finally, *finally*, in a relatively strong, assertive voice, she said, "I should really be attending those meetings." I was anticipating anger, cursing, and a shrill voice—needing to massage her "10 statement" into something more palatable, but I was mistaken. It was a great reminder to see how restrained a Stay Silent person can be, internally as well as externally. I looked at her and said, "Well, that's exactly what you should say to him." We laughed. It was quite comical. Her 10 language was actually a 4 or a 5 on the 10-point scale. Fast forward. She did approach him using the same statement, and his response was, "Oh, okay." Done.

For the sake of an easy demonstration, let's say we were asked to comment on something we did not like. Here are a range of sample responses based on the 10-point scale:

1. Nothing/Silence. [no honoring of self—over-respectful (and fear) regarding the other person]

2. Yah, it looks good. (not true; not honoring self)

3. It looks pretty good. (hesitatingly)

4. It looks good, and I think there might be other options that could work for you as well.

5. If you like it, then that is all that counts. Personally, it is not my style but I like your vision and how cohesive it is.

6. Although this isn't my style, I can see a lot of YOU in it. Terrific.

7. It's not great. I think there are other options that would be better.

8. This is not my taste. Personally, I wouldn't do it this way.

9. This is NOT good. Blech. Yuck. (not respecting others)

10. Omygosh, I hate this, this is awful, why would you use this? (honoring self, not respecting the other person)

This simplistic example works to demonstrate the evolving and devolving nature of the responses. Clearly, there are a multitude of response options at each number. The goal is to be somewhere in the 3-6 range, which is where responses are balanced—honoring what you need to say and want to communicate while respecting the other person by using tact to prevent hurt feelings and potential conflict.

To help my clients find balance, the starting point is:

1. *What do you really want to say?* What is the end goal of what you want to convey? You are likely heavy on one end of the scale or the other, hence a binary mindset. No matter how ugly, express what it is you really want to say… to yourself (not the other person).

2. *Assess where your thoughts are on the scale.* Do not make this difficult. Figure out if you are weighted too far on one end of the scale or the other. If you are…

3. *Change your wording to balance out the statement.* Binary mindset and the black and white responses on either end of the spectrum are rooted in negativity. Balance and ground yourself, and do your best to get out of ego mode. Then it will be easier to find the truest response originating from your Authentic/CORE-Self. When you are in *best self* mode, you will find yourself drawn toward the middle, naturally offering hybrid/balanced statements.

4. *Scale-up.* Instead of the only 2 response options available in a binary mindset, work toward healthy outcomes and reducing potential conflict by expanding to 10 possible response options. Exercising your communication muscles on the 10-point scale will help you gain communication freedom.

Backpack Clean Out

When you say *yes* to the backpack clean out challenge, you are honoring your core. By giving yourself the gift of *clean*, you remove negative backpack artifacts and experiences from your consciousness, and, ultimately, through this exercise, create space for transformation.

By now, you know your backpack is contaminated. Old hurts, wounds, and emotions pollute your core essence. In real life, emotions do cause bodily harm. For example, you might be surprised to know the detrimental effects of the emotion *shame*, a version of which is most likely hidden in everybody's backpack. Research shows that shame causes real life physical consequences, producing inflammation, which is the leading cause of illness, in the body. Since the human body hangs onto emotions in our connective tissue and fascia, *letting go* means both physical and emotional healing.

THE CLEAN OUT PROCESS

Admittedly, this particular exercise is challenging for you to do on your own. If possible, it would be helpful if you could lean on a friend, colleague, or loved one at certain points for additional clarity, but you can do it alone. The process itself flows quite naturally. Each step overlaps and naturally flows into the next. Breaking it down into the process listed below makes it seem more cumbersome than it actually is.

o *Intuition:* I suspect you already know the themes in your backpack. This probably isn't new news. What might be new is formalizing your knowing and acknowledging what you know. Tap into your intuition and give yourself the freedom to explore. It might be helpful to write down a few main themes in your Leadership Journal. If you have no clue as to what your big backpack themes are, have a deep conversation with someone who knows you well. What are a few repeated patterns? What's got ya? How and when do you get in your own way? A few additional guiding questions you can ask yourself, once you've discovered the big themes, are: "Do I need this?" "Am I keeping this for my ego or my soul?" "Does this define me?" "Am I using this to support my identity?" "How is this benefitting me?" "What can I learn from this?" Continue to access your intuition as you head into the next phase of observation. Notice when something feels off, or better yet, when it feels good and *right on*!

o   *Observation:* Now that you have a good sense of your general backpack themes, it is time to observe yourself in real time. Notice how the topics play out in real life. Pay attention to your decision making, and observe yourself with heightened awareness, looking through the lens of the themes. To some degree, be a detective, noticing when things are off or do not sit well with you. Despite good intentions, you will most likely not remember the particular situations after the fact (even if you think you will, I promise, you'll forget... clients forget their aha's all the time). Write your observations in your Leadership Journal.

o   *Wisdom:* After you've observed yourself for a while, review your Leadership Journal entries. Is there a theme to the themes? Access your inner wisdom and intuition to help you make sense of your findings. Is a picture forming? What big question would help you dig in a bit further to give you more clarity? You are at a pivotal point. If you have the courage and desire to continue through this process, take out your Journal. Turn to a fresh, clean page. Write an inner wisdom question at the top of the page. In other words, ask yourself something that gets you thinking. Trust yourself to know what this is. Set your timer for 30 minutes and start writing. Just go with it. It does not matter how you start. This is the

Hot Pen technique I mentioned earlier. Your pen just needs to start moving. Write down whatever comes to mind. By busying yourself with writing, your intuition will have a wonderful opportunity to tap into your inner wisdom, and will result in an outpouring of words. The best conversation is with your inner-wisdom self. Any new awarenesses regarding the themes? If you are on a roll and want to extend your time beyond the 30 minutes, by all means, go for it.

o *Awareness—Younger Self Clarity:* This huge turning point in your backpack clean out is one of my favorite steps in the process. You've done important prep work by diligently working through the previous steps, which makes this one more meaningful. Ready to trust the process? Go to a quiet private space. Get comfortable. Some people sit in a comfortable chair, either in a yoga pose or with feet firmly on the ground, but most people lie down for this exercise. Choose whichever position is easiest for you to concentrate. Close your eyes and spend a minute or two deep breathing. For extra fun and relaxation, hold the breath for three seconds at the top and bottom of each breath, before each inhalation and exhalation. Knowing in advance the topic you want to work on, in this super relaxed state, direct yourself to access your earliest memory of the theme/issue/wound. Can you picture the younger version of you? How old are you in this picture? What is your emotional state? Imagine your adult self crouching down to connect eye to eye with your younger self. Continue with the exercise by asking your younger self a clarifying question about this situation. Listen to the response this image shares with you. This is a powerful process. Allow yourself to fully experience whatever emotions rise up. You will most likely discover the nuances of this topic buried in the crevices of your memories. Your wisdom and intuition are now able to see your younger self situation as a neutral bystander. Thank your younger self for the assistance and clarity. You might even want to give your younger self a hug and let him/her know *you've got this*. I highly recommend you spend a few minutes immediately afterward documenting your awareness.

o   *Adult Eyes: Bravo for getting this far.* The last exercise was a lot. Now you are ready to move forward with new adult awareness. This is a big step, and another favorite of mine because it offers such huge growth. Given the last exercise you should have a new perspective of this situation as an adult. Looking through your *adult eyes* at your younger self situation, what is your new and enlightened perspective?

o   *Reframing:* As you have a new awareness viewing through your adult eyes, it is time to reframe the entire picture, even if the new awareness isn't totally new intellectually. Your pre-backpack clean out version might be: "My dad worked a lot to take care of us, so he wasn't around much." It is important you conduct a fresh, reframing reset. The deeper core awareness might be something like, "Wow, my dad was juggling so much, and had a lot on his plate. I get why he couldn't attend my games. I thought he didn't love me but actually he loved me and my family so much by taking care of us and never complaining. I feel that now. When we did spend time together, he was proud of me. I get that now. This new awareness will help me as a father, since I too can get caught on that same treadmill."

o   *The lesson in everything: This is what I know for sure.* There is a lesson in everything. Truly. If you take the time to see— and work through—a modified version of this process every time you encounter a *less than* or *greater than* moment, you'll find the proof that there is *a lesson in everything*. If you've successfully moved through the process and taken the time to reframe, this step is easy. For instance, years ago, I got intentional about reframing myself as a headache person. My years of daily migraine headaches, which at the time had subsided to once a month migraines, were instrumental in teaching me about my body. I learned how important it was for me to tend to the quality of *my fuel* to keep my engine running smoothly, as well as the harmful effects of non-natural additives, etc. This healing took a few decades, resulting in no more headaches (yay!), and an incredible education, as well as an influence on my family's health and welfare.

What are you ridding yourself of? Are those ego-defining *less than* and *greater than* moments stuck to your mesh body frame, creating *limiting beliefs*? After years of burdensome weight on your shoulders, this process helps you empty out your proverbial backpack and lighten your load. You can be free. You are not *less than* and you are not *greater than*. You are whole. Wholly you. Enjoy the renewed sense of *being*, my friend.

P.S. In case you appreciate a mnemonic device, try I.O.W.A. A.R.T. for remembering the steps of the clean out.

The Whole-Ness Workout

Imagine *working out* only one half of your body. If right-handed, based off the demonstrated dominance and strength most likely present on that side already, you leverage its superiority—focusing only on the right so it will be stronger. What a silly idea. Toned muscles only on the right side—your right bicep, your right calf, and your right pec? I am certain not one single person would intentionally build muscles on one side only, allowing the other side to atrophy. To maintain balance, the left side might require the same, if not more, attention and training than the right, right? Instinctively, we know a balanced approach is the best approach when working out our physique.

The same holds true for your inner leader. Overall leadership fitness requires a balanced inner workout. You owe it to those you lead to be in good, balanced shape.

Peeling back your all important complex layers and continuously striving for leadership healthiness is a workout. Just as you wouldn't expect the intense, physical workout from a few years ago to maintain your shape today, you know continual time and effort is required to maintain your musculature. The same holds true for your personal power workout. Uncovering and discovering You at your core and operating from wholeness is a journey rather than a destination, and a work in progress that requires ongoing attention and effort.

When whole, you create authentically with others as the best version of you vs. projecting onto others, masking the deficits within yourself. When whole, you move from false power to real power, knowing yourself and tapping into your inner truth, your inner strength, your inner wisdom, and standing up for that knowingness. Real power is being fully present. *Power is powerful when you don't try—when you are exclusively, authentically, unapologetically you.*

Listed below is a compilation of the Wholeness Workout exercises provided throughout this book to help you build your personal power. If you haven't already done your wholeness workout, now is your chance.

Your Very Important Layers:

EXERCISE: LEADERSHIP SUPER MODEL
—Total Time: 5 minutes

Rank the three leadership systems (authentic, operational, strategic) in order of your capability. What is at the bottom? Note this in your Leadership Journal to reference it later.

EXERCISE: THE AUTHENTIC/CORE-SELF
—Total Time: 30 minutes

What are the characteristics of your Core Self?
What are the characteristics of your False Self?

Self-worth:

EXERCISE: SELF-WORTH—
Total Time: 10 minutes

Quickly jot down what came up for you while reading the "handing over your power" questions. (*How have the beliefs of others shaped you? What arbitrary, innocently intended comments contributed to your sense-of-self? Was it your parents' belief of "when you're finished with your work, then and only then, are you allowed to play" that caused work/life imbalance or lack of joy? Or maybe when your favorite teacher demonstrated significant attention or pride when you achieved an "A," letting you know straight A's, a.k.a. performance, was the ticket to praise and admiration? Did playground bullying send the message you were not cool because you were too smart? How about basing your appreciation of your looks and attractiveness on a girlfriend or boyfriend's interest, or lack thereof? Maybe it was where you stack-ranked on the Hall of Fame? Or watching where others stack-ranked on the Hall of Shame, creating fear about future performance? Did comments about what was normal stir up feelings of not fitting in? Did a peer's conflict orientation, personality traits, or unhealthiness cause you to feel like you were less than? How about a neighbor's raised eyebrow or scornful view?)*

Can you identify any core messages that shaped you?

Inspiration vs. Motivation:

EXERCISE: INSPIRATION—
Total Time: Open

Set an intention to get a particular activity/task completed within a certain period of time (especially one you are excited to finish, but not excited to do), and then let it go. When it pops into your mind and you feel it is time to do it, a.k.a. inspired, do it. Record how you felt during the activity/task.

Core Development:

EXERCISE: CORE A—
Total Time: 15-30 minutes

Please use your Leadership Journal to answer the question: "Who are you at your core?" Do not use titles, roles, and/or responsibilities to describe yourself. Be honest. Even if you land on a description that is unflattering, please keep going. It might mean you have not dug deep enough, which you'll have an opportunity to do later.

EXERCISE: CORE B—
Total Time: 30-60 minutes

Again, using your Leadership Journal, further dig into the question posed earlier, "Who are you at your core?" Your follow-up question is, "What does my personal S.O.P. look like?" Record your thoughts.

EXERCISE: CORE C—
Total time: 10 minutes

Use your Leadership Journal to record your response to the following questions: How thick is each wall of your Core-Self model? Which circle is the furthest from your core? What are the primary reasons for the distance between your Core and outer circles?

Strengthen Your Core:

EXERCISE: GROUNDING—
Total time: 3-5 minutes

Stand with your feet shoulder-width apart and your hands on your waist/ hips. Set your timer for 2 minutes and breathe deeply. Imagine your feet rooting, and the roots growing deeply into the ground, planting you into the core of the earth. Imagine a string pulling up from the top of your head, causing you to elongate, stabilize, and feel supported. Imagine yourself grounding the entire time. You might even feel expansive once you're practiced in this exercise. When you are finished, take a few deep breaths, realign, and take a moment to assess how you feel. Maybe a combination of refreshed, centered, and powerful? Hopefully your Leadership Journal is handy to record your experience.

EXERCISE: EMOTIONAL ELEVATOR—
Total time: 10 minutes

What is your Emotional Elevator baseline? Please be honest. There is no right or wrong answer, it is what it is. Your response will not be judged. It is important to have an outside-looking-in perspective of you. Record your answer in your Leadership Journal along with a short paragraph about your rationale.

Ego:

EXERCISE: EGO—
Total Time: 45 minutes

- On what end of the *Honor Self vs. Respect Others scale* are you? Journal a quick paragraph about where you are with an example if possible

- List 5 positive *defining ego structures* you formed prior to age 20

- What does your *ego mask* look like? Or, who are you when you are wearing the ego-mask?

- Write "I am enough" on your bathroom mirror (or a sticky note in your car, message on your calendar, etc.), and whenever you see the message, take 5-10 seconds (*surely you have 5-10 seconds!*) to let it sink in

Positively Present:

EXERCISE: PRESENCE—
Total Time: Open

As you move through your day, challenge yourself to be present. Maybe while washing your hands, notice how the water splashes, feel the temperature, and focus on the sensations. Or maybe while eating your lunch, notice the textures in your mouth, or how fabulously your digestive system works (starting with your mouth), or how the various flavors hit your pallet. My favorite is while driving, as mentioned in the presence scenario, feeling my hands wrap around the steering wheel, allowing all of the scenery to pass through me while keenly listening to the radio. That's when I find myself "car dancing."

If you need extra help getting started, begin Presence Practice by spending two minutes in the Power Pose (hands on hips, feet apart—like Superman and Wonder Woman!) while breathing deeply and calmly—eyes closed. Allow yourself to enjoy this two minute respite being totally YOU… take two minutes to just BE.

Imperfectly Authentic:

EXERCISE: INSTINCT—
Total Time: 5+ minutes

Using your Leadership Journal, write down a time when you did not listen to your instincts but wish you had. Do not overthink—write down whatever first pops up for you. This will be quick. The after-the-exercise exercise is to start being more aware of "instinct moments." For extra-bonus development points, keep track of your instinct moments. Doing so will speed up how quickly you strengthen your "instinct muscles."

EXERCISE: PERFECTION/IMPERFECTION Part 1—
Total Time: 20 minutes

List out your "perceived imperfections" in your Leadership Journal. Be sure to write out why you cannot be successful due to these imperfections.

EXERCISE: PERFECTION/IMPERFECTION Part 2—
Total Time: 15 minutes

Did you find yourself resisting the idea that you could not be successful because of your perceived imperfections? Often we instinctually adapt and figure out work-arounds or ways of overcoming problems. If you are still in "I can't be successful due to my imperfections" mode, write out the silver linings to these qualities, and/or how you positively impact others despite your imperfections. It's like turning your frown upside down— look at it from another perspective.

The Backpack:

EXERCISE: BACKPACK BELIEFS Part 1—
Total Time 20-30 minutes

What childhood messages in your backpack no longer serve you? Reflect on "lessons," fears, and protective conclusions you took on and believed to be true. Write them in your Leadership Journal.

EXERCISE: BACKPACK BELIEFS Part 2—
Total Time: 30 minutes

Did you discover an overarching belief in your backpack? How did it serve you as a child? As an adolescent or young adult? *Because at some point it did.* Does it still serve you today? Are you able to step back and realize its original purpose? Have you moved on? Are you able to view the belief through your adult eyes?

If so, what does your adult self say about these beliefs? Do you have a new perspective? Write your findings in your Leadership Journal.

EXERCISE: CORE BELIEFS—
Total Time: 20-30 minutes

CORE beliefs are versions of the childhood messages you worked on in the backpack exercises. Use your responses to see if you can identify an underlying theme or overarching message. Then think about how other decisions in your life were impacted by this. For instance, how you lead today.

Self-Talk:

EXERCISE: SELF-TALK—
Total Time: 15-30 minutes

Journal your stream of self-talk. Although you already know what it sounds like, it is helpful to see it on paper to appreciate the magnitude and tone.

Getting in Your Own Way:

EXERCISE: PULLING BACK THE LAYERS—
Total Time: 15 minutes

How do you get in your own way? What is the overarching theme of *your challenges*? What technique (so far) could you apply to get out of your own way?

The Unknown:

EXERCISE: UNKNOWN—
Total Time: 5 minutes

Take a few deep breaths. Set your timer for 1 minute. Allow your instincts to kick in as you recall seemingly awful instances that turned out okay. Quickly jot them down in your Journal using a word or phrase to help you identify them later. Set your timer for another minute, and silently repeat phrases like "It always works out in the end," "I am courageous," "I have nothing to fear," and "I am excited to experience the unknown."

EXERCISE: NATURE—
Total Time: 5-30 minutes

Go BE in nature. *That's it.* Experience the wonderful non-resistance and easy-going acceptance of nature.

Energy:

EXERCISE: PERSONAL ENERGY—
Total Time: 20 minutes

Journal your personal energy theme. Brainstorm words which describe your ideal energy. Quickly review the list and whittle it down to 3-5 words. Go through your finalists and see how they sit with you. Select the one or two words, or a phrase, which best resonates your personal energetic intention.

Healthiness:

EXERCISE: HEALTHINESS—
Total time: 10 minutes for Journaling, additional 30 minutes if you choose to include confidant feedback.

Evaluate yourself on the Healthiness Scale. Journal your conclusions. It need not be lengthy or complicated. Give yourself an honest score. If you dare, ask a trusted confidant for feedback. Give them permission to be honest, while being kind in their delivery. Then sit back, and listen without judgment or defensiveness. Take notes. *Thank them for their gift of feedback.* Actually, how you react to their feedback will give you additional information as to where you are on the scale.

Limits and Boundaries:

EXERCISE: LIMITS—
Total Time: 30 minutes

Review your initial responses to the sense-of-self exercise in the beginning of the book. Based on those responses, what are your limits? When/where are you strong in your convictions, and when/where do you waver? Is there a pattern? A theme? Journal your thoughts.

Intention vs. Impact:

EXERCISE: INTENTION VS. IMPACT—
Total Time: 15 minutes

Attempt an intention vs. impact conversation using one of the following template conversation starters. Later, Journal the outcome.

1. "What was your intention when X happened, because this is how it impacted me."
2. "This was the impact X had on me, but I'm sure that was not your intention… "
3. "What was your intention when X happened? Oh I thought so. Because this is how it impacted me but I knew that was not what you meant."

ImBalance:

EXERCISE: BALANCE A—
Total Time: 50 minutes

You have a choice. Opt for this bigger general exercise (A), or go in depth in the following two exercises (B) and (C). If you are able to dig in and have awareness, I recommend this one; however, either option will benefit you.

Journaling your thoughts to the questions listed in the paragraph above (*What causes you imbalance? Do you have a default emotion? And how does it get in your way? What indirect messages are you sending when you are out of balance or swirling? Specifically as a leader, how does this pattern erode trust? What communications are you missing (or twisting) because you are not grounded and present?)*

EXERCISE: BALANCE B—
Total Time: 20 minutes

What is your default emotion or pattern of behavior? Write your response in your Leadership Journal.

EXERCISE: BALANCE C—
Total Time: 20 minutes

What is your favorite way to let your default emotion *out?* If you don't have awareness around this, please contemplate what action might best benefit your release. Write your response in your Leadership Journal.

EXERCISE: TREE—
Total Time: 5 minutes

Imagine a deeply rooted tree. Nearby, you see a newly replanted tree with shallow roots. They are about the same size, living in the same weather conditions. There is strong gusty wind (a.k.a. stress, crazy situations, toxic people, etc.). Which one is more likely to weather the storm? *How deep are your roots?* Journal your response.

Leaning In:

EXERCISE: LEANING IN—
Total Time: 45 min.

Please Journal your answers to the following questions.
- Which situations cause you to turn and run away?
- Which emotions are the most easily triggered?
- Can you recall a time when you felt like you were standing in your power? Describe the feeling.

- Describe a time when you've actively leaned in. What was the outcome?
- Describe the feeling when your inner guidance system signals you are connected and whole.

Balance:

EXERCISE: UP and DOWN—
Total Time: 10 minutes

Think of a scenario when you are UP, followed by a scenario when you are DOWN. Now spend a moment in each and feel. Do you sense how light the UP scenario is, versus the heaviness of the DOWN scenario? Spend some time distinguishing the differences. Do you notice yourself sitting up straight vs. slumping over a bit? If you are able to take it a little further, imagine your attitude and performance throughout the day if UP vs. DOWN. Although this only requires thinking, I recommend you jot down the outcome of your two scenarios in your Leadership Journal as a quick point of reference to inspire you positively in the future.

Flow

During coaching sessions, as clients work through their *what's keeping me up at night* professional issues, I see their karate energy: assertiveness, dominance, counterattacking, defensiveness, blocking, kicking, and protection.

My goal is to help them transform their karate energy into *Aikido energy*, a less familiar Asian martial art similarly trained in throws, holds, and locks, with a critical distinction of intention. Aikido means "the way of harmonious spirit," which, in practice, translates into leveraging the other person's energy while never advancing purposely.

If you are curious and want to see a quick visual depiction, jump on the internet and search for a karate demonstration video, and compare it to an Aikido match video. Do you see the difference in energy and intention?

Karate is high spirited and kinetic, combative and aggressive, with clear winners and losers. Most noteworthy is the fragmented choppiness of their movements and the intensity of their focus. My nephews are exceptional athletes and the youngest karate blackbelts in their dojo. Despite their incredible accomplishments, while standing in physical power, their actions are competitive, and therefore binary.

Aikido is a beautiful and graceful, flowing, rhythmic dance. Balance and control are key while sparring, and in maintaining Aikido balance and personal power. Shifting the power balance, both opponents are fully present, connected and flowing and working with each other's energy. It is expansive.

Leaders would do well to take an Aikido stance. Whether experiencing an individual joyful present moment, communicating with another, or resolving a conflict, being in flow elevates you and positively impacts everyone around you, setting the stage for best outcomes.

BALANCING INTO FLOW

Deliberately grounding, removing layers, taking steps forward, and doing my work helped me at a time when I was off kilter. Presence, steadiness, and balance became my new normal. As a result of this shift, as if restoring cosmic congruence, some of my relationships blossomed while others naturally fell away. In the end, it was all good.

During this process, I learned to pull back and just be. This meant less intensity while still in it, which was quite challenging. Less controlling of the outcome while standing more squarely in my power, allowing flow and trusting all would work out for the best gave me peace. In this mindset, *I, you, we* naturally expand and extend grace toward others—viewing things from their perspective, understanding their intention, and holding space for truth. If they too are standing in their power, we enjoy seeing each other eye to eye on equal footing. It is from this place of power and authenticity and wholeness where we join together to "step into our power to light up the world with our beauty," breathing life into Robert's words, allowing for clean and fresh connections, full engagement, partnership, courage, and wholeness.

My personal intention is for my relationships to be balanced and flowing. To be dynamic, connected, and real, with healthy communication and emotional availability, resulting in inspired action.

When we balance into flow, we experience *joy from the inside out*, in the present moment.

YOU IN FLOW

Knowing who you are and speaking your truth requires great fortitude. *Being the real you*, not the *you* others think you should be. Have the courage to risk disappointing me with your truth. Use your words to say *what is*. If we are both healthy and whole, you cannot disappoint me. I see you, because I see myself. I accept you, because I accept myself. I ask you to accept me accepting you, because you see and accept yourself. You— the stronger, healthier, more intuitive, grounded, powerful, authentically, whole version of you—is amazing!

When real, and in genuine relationship with others (remember *kind*, not *nice*), you are at peace, joyful, and in flow, accessing your core goodness. This version of you can't help but lead others to be the best versions of themselves—happy, engaged, open, powerful, productive, accepting, collaborative, and clean. In flow.

The Lesson in Everything

... and the day came
when the risk to remain tight,
in a bud,
became more painful
than the risk it took to blossom.
~Lassie Benton, a.k.a Elizabeth Appell

Uncovering, discovering, and recovering your Whole-Self requires courage. Courage to be vulnerable. Courage to do the work. Courage to blossom.

When you're in the middle of a situation that is heading south, remember you are in *the middle* of the situation. Much like a 2-hour movie, rarely are things going well at 1hr30min. Ride it out and know with every fiber in your being that you will discover a beneficial lesson in the end. A lesson that paves the way for next steps, greatness, and your higher good.

Him

In an earlier chapter I mentioned a conversation I had with my young adult son about leaning in when he gets angsty. This one piece of advice, thankfully, hit home. I see it in his actions. His past behavior preference was to turn away (avoid) when presented with a challenge. Now I see him gathering his bearings (grounding), anticipating moving forward (visualizing), and acting when it feels right (inspired action).

When I see him follow this loose format, I (secretly) enjoy processing with him: "What would have happened if you had not moved forward?" "Where would you be now?" "So, it worked out for the best?" and "Hmmm, what's your takeaway?" or "What did you learn?" I love that he is finding the courage to take risks, move forward, and blossom.

Her

My daughter called me very early one morning because she was filled with anxiety over a text she had received. It was a typical technology misunderstanding. The particulars don't matter as much as her state of mind in the moment. She is a self-admitted *people pleaser*, and was distraught at the idea of holding her ground and saying *no* to this person, again.

While crafting her text response, I referenced the *honor self while respecting others* spectrum to help her strive for balance. There was a critical moment when she wanted to lean on a little white lie to get herself out of the situation—"I have plans that day." While physically nauseated at the idea of disappointing him, it was a great opportunity for her to work through this situation, and to prove something to herself. What a cool opportunity for a bigger lesson. She was worthy of her truth. What a huge dishonor to herself, and a self-betrayal, if she had gotten out of the situation by lying. And the biggest disservice would have been not using the moment to learn and grow. In the end, she sent a beautifully written text that was kind, balanced, and gracious, yet firm. When she hit SEND, I saw her immediate relief. I loved watching her access her inner courage to risk honoring herself, and in the end, blossoming.

WHAT IS THE BAD GOOD FOR?

What is the bad good for? This is one of my favorite phrases, and one, I am sure, my children are tired of hearing. What they might not realize is that I use it on myself frequently as well. When in the middle of the storm, I often go to this phrase to get me out of it, repeating a variation of it like a mantra.

In my past, while working as a recruiter, I was forced to provide negative feedback to many people, "they are moving forward with another candidate" or "you did not get the job." You can only imagine how this tickles the ego, sending the prospective candidate into a negative headspace. Lucky me. However, it did turn out to be *lucky me*. I learned to be balanced in my feedback—honest (and often negative) while being kind, gentle, and real.

One phone conversation with a particular candidate has stayed with me for years. He was adamant the client had made a mistake because he was certain he was the perfect candidate for the job. Referencing his earlier comments of wanting to decrease his travel, I challenged him. The job opportunity actually required *more* travel. "But the pay is so good," was his response, as if the compromise was worth it. I ended every conversation with a version of "I can't wait to see what the bad was good for. I predict you will find something that aligns better with your goals. Please call me when you find that job that fits and you see what the bad was good for." Fortunately, he did call me back six months later, "You were right. I found an awesome job! I travel less. I am there for my family. *And I make more money*. I can't believe it! I am so glad I did not get that other job."

There is a lesson in everything. Be grateful for the moment, whatever the moment is. Look for the lessons. Stand in your power. Access your courage, lean in, learn, flow, and blossom.

A Human Be-ing

It would make more sense if we referred to our species as human *do*-ings versus human *be*-ings. Funny, isn't it? Without explanation, I'm sure you understand the irony. Evaluating yourself and others based on occupation, achievements, and *doing* supports the kind of external power we think we should strive for.

By now you know that this is not the ultimate power. *Has it been right in front of us the whole time?* Have we missed seeing the forest for the trees? Maybe the most powerful thing we can do is be the best human BE-ing possible. Maybe knowing we are enough, and profoundly understanding our worthiness, is the work. Maybe, just maybe, who we are at our core is already powerful, and the goal is to uncover the already-in-us powerful power center.

When you are the best version of you, *the best whole, clean, and fresh human BE-ing version of you,* while stepping into your power, balanced, grounded, and plugged in and operating from your core power, you will certainly transform the world with your magnificent light.

Doing Your Work

Dear Reader,

Do you have it in you to do the work necessary to grow, move forward, be the best you can be, and lead others to new heights? Courage and strength are required to open yourself up to the unknown. *I know you can do this.* You might find cleaning out your backpack to be a bit painful at times—opening up old wounds in an effort to heal. The good news is that you will be free. By releasing and removing the inner baggage from your psyche/backpack with kindness, compassion, and self-forgiveness (for carrying it around for so long), you create space for new awareness. With renewed curiosity and adult context, you reframe your backpack scars and emotions. Doing so will allow you to unleash your incredible power within.

Do you have it in you to unlearn old habits and open yourself to new and healthier habits? Are you ready to expand your awareness and your consciousness? Are you open to new perspectives and new techniques to aid in your growth? Do you have it in you to examine who you are at your core? How will your ego cope? Is your determination strong enough to overcome those self-defeating whispers?

I hope you know you have it in you. *I know you have it in you!* I am excited to meet this incredible, authentic version of you. You've got this. Can you imagine the freedom? Are you excited to be your True Self? As you embark on—or continue—this amazing journey of self-discovery (and remembrance), know that I am there with you in spirit. Remember that *core goodness* each of us has within us? I don't know your particulars—the number of layers you need to remove, the heaviness of your backpack, or how you get in your own way—but I DO know that accessing your core goodness is your holy grail. You will feel peace and lightness, as if donning rose-colored glasses. Propel your SELF to new heights and experience growth extraordinaire. You are way too special and worthy to not do this work.

The key to unlocking this power is inside of you and at your discretion. You get to decide. You have complete control of the process.

I wish you the very best. And the very best, for you, dear reader, is to be the amazing leader I already know you to be. **Be the very best version of YOU, standing in your power, leading authentically from your core, touching and lighting up the world with your beauty.**

Love,
H.

Afterword

The inspiration for this book has been a combination of my own personal development journey and the transformational results I've witnessed within hundreds of clients, in a variety of positions, levels, and industries. Time and time again, similar patterns and themes emerge, indicating a person is out of alignment. Ultimately, it necessitates we begin the *development work* at the foundational layer, resulting in deep introspection, and it feels magical when the transformation is realized.

From the very beginning, my driving intention has been to help leaders, YOU, develop and "do your work," by outlining this first most important phase of the UPwords Inc. coaching process. I hope your thinking, awareness, and perspective has been stimulated.

Prior to my organizational development career, I was in sales for Fortune 500 companies. Despite my sales success, I was better known for my trainer and mentor "magic" within those same companies. I now realize, in addition to my passion for growth and transformation, this was because I applied *sales philosophy* to the training. In sales it was/is important to reach people on an emotional level, inspiring behavioral change, engagement, and sustainable shifts. I did this by making training tangible—bringing learning to life. It allowed trainees to shift in a way that elevated them very quickly. For instance, while in medical device sales and responsible for new hires sent to me in the field, I created a 3D replica of the urinary system by taping fish tank tubing onto an anatomy poster. Although simplistic, it allowed me to insert spit balls into the tubing to represent ureteral stones and strictures, and demonstrated for the trainees how to "operate." This fostered a new level of understanding about how our equipment was used during surgery (long before *learning labs* were a thing), and created necessary awareness instinctively.

After medical device and a number of path-defining moves (recruiting, partnering with an organizational psychologist, and fulfilling a national training contract for a Michigan-based trainer), I formally started my own development firm, UPwords Inc., in 2005. At that time I had the good fortune to work closely with an international leadership program designer/facilitator whose methods were innovative, fun, and effective. *This resonated immediately!* Taking me back to my early medical training days, I quickly merged his creative experiential style with my own unconventional and intuitive style. My programs and development work became richer as a result. Effective, knowledge-based, process-driven, fresh, and fun. *Voila!* As a result, my toolbox is *very full*.

I hope to share more tools with you in the next book (I might have another one in me...), providing more models, metaphors, tools, stories, and examples to help you leverage your Authentic Self in your operational and strategic layers—taking YOU to the next level. *You* the *leader of people*, and *you* the leader of your "self."

Early on, while working with a client who was having a major aha/shift, I had an out-of-body experience. I could literally sense ME on my left side, chiding me. *"Isn't this the best? Should I pinch you? So cool!"* I had never experienced this same sense of deep fulfillment working in sales as I now experience in this phase of my career. I hope you too now understand the magic of this deeply satisfying internal work of expansion.

I wish you well in *plugging in* and BE-coming the best whole version of YOU!

About the Author

Heidi has had the good fortune of many interesting unique twist-and-turn life experiences that have helped shape the woman she is today. As a first-born American to German immigrant parents and eldest of three girls, Heidi's upbringing was *old school*. No sleepovers, no nylons (only tights!), and no boys. The outcome of a strict but tight-knit ethnic family was maturity at a young age, fierce independence, innate leadership, and courage to think/act independently and do the right thing. Always willing to *shake things up* for best results, *she could be a bit of an agitator*. For this, her sisters affectionately nicknamed her "Kenmore." Still accessing her *inner-Kenmore* and born-in-Detroit grittiness, Heidi continues to "inspire" (or push the buttons necessary for) increased awareness, inner growth, and transformational shifts.

Professionally, Heidi grew up in Fortune 500 companies such as Xerox, Boston Scientific Corporation, and EMC, achieving sales performance awards while balancing additional training and development responsibilities. Honing her skills in these and other entrepreneurial business opportunities, including corporate recruiting and organizational development, drove her to achieve her childhood goal of starting her own business, *UPwords Inc.* Since 2005, Heidi has been passionately focused on working with and developing leaders through executive coaching and leadership development. Today, Heidi adds author and public speaker to the list.

Personally, Heidi continues to grow, have fun, and enjoy meaningful relationships with her two children, family, and friends, old and new, as well as push her boundaries (like writing a book!), engage in creative endeavors (creating the back cover art), and experiencing *life* (recently rappelling for the first time!).

If you ever play *Two Truths and a Lie* with Heidi, know: YES, she did jump out of a plane; YES, she did receive a kiss on the cheek by Alex Trebek; YES, she did play the accordion as a child; YES, she loves playing Euchre; and YES, she has a serious all-consuming passion for healthiness, depth, vulnerability, connection, and authenticity.

Bibliography

Angelou, Maya, Poet, https://www.mayaangelou.com

Astonishing Power of Emotions: Let Your Feelings be Your Guide, The 2007 Abraham, Esther, & Jerry Hicks

Beast of Burden, 1978 The Rolling Stones

Brady Bunch, The 1969 ABC

Cake Boss, 2009 TLC

Chopra Center Meditations, 1996 Deepak Chopra

Cuddy, Amy: Your Body Language May Shape Who You Are, 2012 TED Talk

Daring Greatly, 2012 Brené Brown

DiSC Assessment, Everything DiSC® and The Five Behaviors® are registered trademarks of John Wiley & Sons, Inc. and its corporate subsidiaries.

Karate Kid, The 1984 Columbia Pictures/Delphi II Productions

King Kong, 1933 RKO Radio Pictures

Maslow's Hierarchy of Needs, an idea in psychology proposed by American Abraham Maslow in his 1943 paper "A Theory of Human Motivation" in the journal Psychological Review

Mastering Leadership, 2015 Adams & Anderson

Mister Rogers' Neighborhood, 1968 PBS

New Earth: Awakening to Your Life's Purpose, A, 2005 Eckhart Tolle

Odyssey, Peter Kater 2016

Perel, Esther podcast, "Where Should We Begin?"

Pretty Woman, 1990 Touchstone Pictures

Returning, Jennifer Berezan 2013

Stepford Wives, The 1975 Palomar Pictures International

Covey, Stephen R. https://resources.franklincovey.com/mkt-7hv1/circle-of-influence

Tsabary, Dr. Shefali mindvalley podcast, "The Art of Conscious Parenting"

Truth About Leadership, The 2010 Kouzes & Posner

Wizard of Oz, The 1939 Metro-Goldwyn-Mayer

Index

Made in the USA
Middletown, DE
30 December 2021